Korea's Economic Miracle: Fading or Reviving?

Also by Charles Harvie

VIETNAM'S ECONOMIC REFORMS (*with Tran Van Hoa*)

CONTEMPORARY DEVELOPMENTS AND ISSUES IN CHINA'S ECONOMIC TRANSITION (*editor*)

ASIAN FINANCIAL CRISIS (*editor with Tran Van Hoa*)

Also by Hyun-Hoon Lee

FRONTIERS OF RESEARCH IN INTRA-INDUSTRY TRADE (*editor with P. J. Lloyd*)

Korea's Economic Miracle

Fading or Reviving?

Charles Harvie
Associate Professor of Economics
University of Wollongong
Australia

and

Hyun-Hoon Lee
Professor of Economics
Kangwon National University
South Korea

palgrave
macmillan

First published 2003 by
PALGRAVE MACMILLAN
Houndmills, Basingstoke, Hampshire RG21 6XS and
175 Fifth Avenue, New York, N. Y. 10010
Companies and representatives throughout the world

PALGRAVE MACMILLAN is the global academic imprint of the Palgrave Macmillan division of St Martin's Press, LLC and of Palgrave Macmillan Ltd. Macmillan® is a registered trademark in the United States, United Kingdom and other countries. Palgrave is a registered trademark in the European Union and other countries.

ISBN 0–333–92499–1

This book is printed on paper suitable for recycling and made from fully managed and sustained forest sources.

A catalogue record for this book is available from the British Library.

Library of Congress Cataloging-in-Publication Data
Harvie, Charles, 1954–
Korea's economic miracle: fading or reviving?/Charles Harvie, Hyun-Hoon Lee.
p. cm.
Includes bibliographical references and index.
ISBN 0–333–92499–1 (cloth)
1. Korea (South)–Economic conditions–1960– 2. Korea (South)–Economic policy–1960– I. Yi, Hyon-hun, 1959– II. Title.
HC467 .H3675 2002
330.95195'043–dc21 2002022418

10 9 8 7 6 5 4 3 2
12 11 10 09 08 07 06 05 04

Printed and bound in Great Britain by
Antony Rowe Ltd, Chippenham, Wiltshire

To Sonya,
Myung-Hee, Suejin and Joonkyu

Contents

List of Figures

List of Tables

Acknowledgements

This book arose from a seminar on the Korean economy presented by Hyun-Hoon Lee at the University of Wollongong in May 1999. At the time Professor Lee was visiting scholar at the University of Melbourne. The major part of the manuscript was written while both authors were visiting fellows at the Bank of Korea (January to February 2001). We would like to express our sincere gratitude to the Bank of Korea for its generosity in providing office space, computer facilities and access to its excellent library facilities. During that period we had the opportunity to share ideas with many economists at the bank. In particular we would like to thank Dr Junggun Oh and Dr Jeong-Ho Hahm for their helpful and insightful comments. Mr Eunsuk Lee also provided considerable assistance. The manuscript also benefited from helpful comments received at seminars held at the bank in May 2001, at the University of Wollongong in June 2001 and at a symposium at Kangwon National University in October 2001. We would also like to extend our gratitude to our academic colleagues and friends, especially Tran Van Hoa, Yong Kyu Kim and Chung Mo Koo, for their comments and encouragement during the completion of this project.

Charles Harvie is grateful to the International Business Research Institute, Faculty of Commerce, University of Wollongong for financial and other assistance provided during the completion of the manuscript. Hyun Hoon Lee would like to thank Kangwon National University for its financial support, and the University of Melbourne for providing office space and research facilities during his stay there in December 1998 to February 2000. Special thanks go to Peter Lloyd, who offered many useful comments during this period.

We both wish to thank members of our families. Charles Harvie would like to thank Sonya for her encouragement, friendship and support, while Hyun-Hoon Lee would like to thank Myung-Hee Kim for her lifetime companionship and encouragement, and his children Suejin and Joonkyu for reminding him that this book has been written for their generation. Hyun-Hoon Lee would also like to thank his parents (and especially his father, who at the time of writing was in a coma after suffering his second stroke) for their devotion to the education of their children.

Lastly, we thank all the staff associated with Palgrave Macmillan for professionally carrying out all the tasks involved in bringing this book to publication.

CHARLES HARVIE
HYUN-HOON LEE

1
Introduction

1.1 Background

After the devastation of the Korean War and the partitioning of the country, South Korea was one of the poorest countries in the world. Economic recovery during the period 1953–61 was very slow and heavily dependent on US financial assistance. Recovery was based on an import substitution development policy, but by the early 1960s this was acknowledged to have failed and in 1962 emphasis shifted to the development of export-oriented industries. The country's substantial investment in private and public education during the period after the war had provided a well-educated labour force and this formed the backbone of the new industries. The starting point for South Korea's exported industrialisation was, however, inauspicious, with per capita GDP at only US$87 in current prices, much lower than those of most of its regional neighbours.

The country's first five-year plan (1962–66) proved to be a catalyst for the remarkable transformation of the economy, enabling Korea to achieve the status of a newly industrialising country (NIC) in 1970. It continued its rapid growth during the 1970s despite the two oil crises, and by the late 1970s it had even overtaken Malaysia (then the second most advanced ASEAN nation) on a per capita income basis. In the mid 1980s Korea overtook countries such as Mexico, Argentina, Brazil, Portugal, Poland, Yugoslavia and Hungary, and in 1989 it joined the highest-income developing-country group, consisting of Israel, Hong Kong, Singapore and Taiwan. Over the period 1962–89, which was characterised by rapid and sustained economic and trade growth, per capita income increased from $87 to $5199, GDP expanded from $2.3 billion to $220.7 billion, and exports increased from $55 million to $61.4 billion.

In the mid 1980s the economy entered a new phase with the onset of the so-called 'three lows' – low oil prices, a lower US dollar and low interest rates. For the first time in the economic history of Korea domestic savings began consistently to exceed investment, with the savings rate rising to over 30 per cent of GDP and the international balance of payments turning from a chronic deficit into a surplus. As a result Korea was able rapidly to reduce its foreign debt, which had peaked at $46.7 billion in 1985. It was no longer necessary to worry about foreign debt and rely on advanced countries for economic assistance, and by the late 1980s it had realised its goal of economic independence. An economic 'miracle on the River Han' appeared to have been achieved.

Few countries have attained such a high level of development so rapidly. In a single generation this poor nation, which had consisted primarily of subsistence farmers in the 1950s and early 1960s, had become the world's largest producer of home appliances, the second largest producer of semi-conductors, the second largest shipbuilder, the fifth largest car maker, the eleventh largest economy and the twelfth largest trading nation. Rapid economic growth and low unemployment, driven by high savings and investment and export growth, became the norm for the country. In 1996 per capita income exceeded $10 000 and was relatively equally distributed, while the living standards of ordinary Koreans rose dramatically. The country's attainment of OECD membership in December 1996 reflected 35 years of extraordinary growth and marked the economy's coming of age. For many developing countries Korea's economic development model – state-directed capitalism – appeared to offer a viable framework for their own development programmes.

Despite these remarkable achievements, structural weaknesses and the inability of Korea's political and economic organisations to keep pace with the country's material achievements began to undermine the economy from the early 1990s. Reform and liberalisation were urgently required in a number of key areas: the corporate sector; financial markets and the banking sector; the labour market; the small and medium-sized enterprise sector; and trade and investment. At the core of the problem was the close relationship between the government, the banks and the *chaebols* (business conglomerates). In particular the state-guided banks' habit of lending on the basis of political whim rather than proper risk assessment resulted in a severe misallocation of resources and a substantial accumulation by the banks of non-performing loans. Government-backed industrial policy resulted in an overly close relationship between the government and the *chaebols*, which in turn resulted in corruption, the sapping of entrepreneurial endeavour and an unwillingness to open up the economy to foreign trade and investment as the *chaebols* wished to protect their own interests and maintain their dominance over the domestic markets.

This system encouraged excessive and ill-utilised loans being extended to the *chaebols*, with little concern for return and risk. The consequences were overcapacity in many sectors of the economy, dangerously overleveraged *chaebols*, the crowding out of small firms, less innovation and flexibility in the economy, and the accumulation by banks of non-performing loans.

This was exacerbated by the opening up of the capital market in 1993, which led to a rapid increase in capital inflows, overborrowing, particularly in the form of short-term debt, and an overvalued domestic currency (the won). During 1997 the country's financial and corporate fragility was exposed. Unprecedentedly, eight *chaebols* were declared insolvent or sought protection from their creditors, leading to further bad debts for the banks, which then tightened their credit and caused more difficulties and corporate failures. The situation was further exacerbated towards the end of October 1997 by the dramatic decline in the value of the won against the US dollar as investor confidence in the currency and economy waned. The banking and corporate sectors' need to service foreign loans primarily denominated in US dollars, as well as the country's ability to pay back over $100 billion of shortly maturing debt, resulted in a loss of confidence in the country and its institutions and put downward pressure on the currency. By the end of 1997 it was clear that re-establishing confidence in the currency and financial markets should be given top priority, and that major restructuring of the economy was required. The old model of economic development appeared to have run its course, and there was a need to move towards a new, market-oriented economy.

Structural weaknesses in the corporate and banking sectors in particular were pushing the country into a particularly fragile financial situation by the second half of 1997. The danger signs became apparent in early 1997 with the Hanbo Steel debacle, which proved to be the precursor of an unprecedented number of business insolvencies, including eight of the 30 largest *chaebols*. On 2 July 1997 the devaluation of the Thai baht and the contagious effect of this on other regional currencies, including the Malaysian ringgit, the Filipino peso and the Indonesian rupiah, sparked the financial crisis in Korea. The regional financial crisis prompted an unprecedented withdrawal of capital (some $100 billion net of private capital within the space of six months, mainly recalled short-term loans by foreign commercial banks), causing a further downward spiral of regional currencies and stock markets. Korea managed to avoid the brunt of this financial turbulence until October, when Taiwan and Hong Kong succumbed to the crisis. On 21 November the country had to turn to the IMF as the rollover ratio of short-term external borrowing by domestic financial institutions kept falling and the country's usable foreign currency reserves plummeted to $7.3 billion, down sharply from $22.3 billion only a month before. On 3 December Korea and the IMF signed an agreement for a financial aid package totalling $58.3 billion. This was subject to a wide range of conditions, including macroeconomic stabilisation and structural reform. The IMF committed emergency funds of $21 billion, and an additional $14 billion was promised by the World Bank and the Asian Development Bank. As a second line of defence a further $23.3 billion was pledged by the USA, Japan, Australia and other interested countries.

In attempting to isolate the key factors in the Korean crisis we draw an analogy between an economy's financial system and the human circulatory system. In particular we employ the notion of a stroke, which occurs when a blood vessel in the brain is suddenly ruptured or blocked by a blood clot or other debris carried in the bloodstream. This approach can be seen as a type of general systems theory. The 'stroke hypothesis' draws on the most appealing explanations and theories of the financial crisis, and shows how numerous factors intertwined to cause it. The hypothesis also allows a systematic evaluation of the consequences and performance of the IMF's structural reform programme.

The onset of the crisis in late November 1997 focused the attention of the authorities on re-establishing stability in the foreign exchange market and the financial markets more generally. As discussed above, this initially involved turning to the IMF and other international financial organisations and countries for emergency support funds. The limited success of this in calming the financial markets resulted in the government negotiating an extension of the maturity of financial institutions' short-term external debts in January 1998, and issuing foreign-currency-denominated government bonds in April that year. The authorities supplemented these measures with economic stabilisation policies, including a high interest rate policy, and launched wide-ranging structural reforms of the financial, corporate, labour and public sectors. The policy framework and structural reforms eventually had a positive effect on investor confidence, which boosted capital inflows. This was bolstered by a huge current account surplus and led to the stabilisation of the exchange rate from early 1998.

With stability in the foreign exchange market achieved, interest rates were lowered in an attempt to reverse the decline in domestic consumption and investment demand. This was supported by a mildly expansionary fiscal policy. As a result of these moves the economy recovered remarkably in the second half of 1998 and gathered momentum in 1999. This rapid and strong economic recovery facilitated further restructuring of the corporate and financial sectors, which lay at the heart of the structural reforms. However by mid 2000 it was clear that the pace of reform had slowed, due partly to complacency arising from the double-digit output growth achieved in 1999 and partly to the politicisation of economic issues in the run-up to the general election in April 2000. From the second half of 2000 the economy again began to show some instability due to a slowdown in GDP growth and bearish movements on the stock market. This can be attributed to insufficient restructuring of the financial and corporate sectors. The slowdown further exacerbated the weaknesses in these sectors so the government initiated a second round of reforms to try to restore confidence in the economy.

These reforms were aimed at reviving the 'old' economy. However, it is clear that if Korea is to achieve a return to high and sustainable economic growth it will be essential to develop the 'new economy'. The world is experiencing a revolutionary transition away from industrial society and towards a new economic paradigm in which information and knowledge are the principal agents of competitiveness. The driving force behind this new paradigm, which is variously referred to as the 'new economy', the 'digital economy' or the 'information economy', is the rapid advancement of information and communications technology (ICT). The Internet and e-commerce are growing at breathtaking speed and fundamentally altering the way in which people work, consume, communicate and play. Access to ICT-related tools and skills is becoming crucial to economic development worldwide, and huge disparities are emerging between countries in this respect. Hence the answer to the question of whether Korea's economic miracle will fade or revive depends largely on whether it embraces the principles of the new economy. This will require a move away from state direction of the economy and towards resource allocation by the market.

While changing the way in which the economy operates is vital to the future development of the economy, another potentially important development is enhanced economic cooperation between North and South Korea. During 2000 President Kim Dae Jung of South Korea and Chairman Kim Jong Il of North Korea held an inter-Korean summit, marking an historic turning point in inter-Korean relations. The summit produced the South–North Joint Declaration, an agreement aimed at promoting peace, reconciliation and cooperation between the two Koreas. According to the joint statement 'the South and the North have agreed to consolidate mutual trust by promoting balanced development of the national economy through economic cooperation and by stimulating cooperation and exchanges in civic, cultural, sports, public health, environmental and all other fields'.

North Korea, with a population of 22 million, has been effectively isolated from South Korea and the Western world since the end of the Korean War. Depending on how the South responds to the new developments in North Korea, both South and North may be able to stimulate their economies by forming a combined economic territory in a climate of détente.

1.2 Structure of the book

This book consists of four parts. Part I (Chapters 2 and 3) provides further background information on the development of the South Korean economic miracle from 1962–89, and the fading of the miracle with the onset of economic weakness during the period 1990–97. Part II (Chapter 4) focuses on the events that took place immediately before, during and after the financial and economic crisis of 1997–98. Part III (Chapters 5–7) considers three key measures that need to be taken if the country is to return to long-term economic growth: revival of the traditional economy through macroeconomic measures and structural reform, development of the new economy, and the fostering of economic cooperation between North and South Korea. Finally, Part IV (Chapter 8) looks at other measures that need to be taken to promote sustainable growth and improve the quality of life and welfare of the Korean people. There is also a discussion of the future prospects of the Korean economy.

Part I

2
Korea's Economic Miracle, 1962–89

2.1 Introduction

This chapter examines the major factors behind the remarkable transformation of the Korean economy described in Chapter 1. Section 2 provides a brief overview of developments in key macroeconomic variables over the period 1962–89, paying particular attention to economic growth and the growth of exports. Section 3 focuses on Korea's growth patterns, sources of growth, business cycles and related issues. The contribution of trade to structural transformation is also discussed in this section. Section 4 considers Korea's industrial structure and policy during this period, while Section 5 analyses economic planning and policy formulation. Finally, Section 6 presents a summary of the major conclusions to be derived from this chapter.

2.2 Overview of economic performance, 1962–89

2.2.1 Overview

As can be seen from Table 2.1 the Korean economy experienced a remarkable transformation during the period 1960–89, particularly after the introduction of the first five-year plan (1962–66), as exemplified by the attainment of a high and sustained rate of economic growth. An idea of the the magnitude of the transformation can be gained by contrasting the position in 1962 with that in 1989.[1] In the intervening years the economy achieved an average annual real GDP growth rate of 8.5 per cent, per capita income increased from \$87 to \$5199, GDP in current prices increased from \$2.3 billion to \$220.7 billion, the ratio of savings to gross national disposable income (GNDI) increased from 11 per cent to 37.6 per cent, the ratio of investment to GNDI increased from 11.8 per cent to 33.8 per cent, and the unemployment rate fell from 9.8 per cent to 2.6 per cent. In terms of external developments, the trade balance was in deficit by \$335 million in 1962 but had accrued a surplus of \$4.6 billion by 1989, and exports were a negligible \$55 million in 1962 but a sizable \$61.4 billion in 1989.

Table 2.1 Major indicators of Korean economic growth, 1960–89

	GDP per capita (US$)[1]	GDP (US$ billion)	Real GDP growth rate (%)	CPI (%)	Savings rate (%)[2]	Investment rate (%)[3]	Corporate bond yields (%)	Stock price index (1980.1.4 = 100)	Trade balance (US$ million)	Exports (US$ million	Foreign debt (US$ million)
1960	79	2.0	1.2	n.a.	9.0	10.0	n.a.	n.a.	–273	33	–
1961	82	2.1	5.9	n.a.	11.7	12.0	n.a.	n.a.	–242	41	–
1962	87	2.3	2.1	n.a.	11.0	11.8	n.a.	n.a.	–335	55	–
1963	100	2.7	9.1	n.a.	14.4	17.0	n.a.	n.a.	–410	87	157
1964	103	2.9	9.7	n.a.	14.0	13.2	n.a.	n.a.	–245	120	177
1965	105	3.0	5.7	n.a.	13.2	14.1	n.a.	n.a.	–241	175	206
1966	125	3.6	12.2	12.0	16.6	20.4	n.a.	n.a.	–430	250	392
1967	142	4.2	5.9	10.7	15.4	20.9	n.a.	n.a.	–574	335	645
1968	169	5.2	11.3	11.3	18.2	24.9	n.a.	n.a.	–836	486	1 199
1969	210	6.5	13.8	11.6	21.4	27.9	n.a.	n.a.	–992	658	1 800
1970	248	8.0	8.8	16.9	17.8	24.9	n.a.	n.a.	–992	882	2 245
1971	286	9.4	8.6	12.2	16.0	25.1	n.a.	n.a.	–1044	1 133	2 922
1972	316	10.6	4.9	11.9	17.1	21.3	22.9	n.a.	–574	1 676	3 589
1973	396	13.5	12.3	3.5	22.9	25.5	21.8	n.a.	–566	3 284	4 260
1974	542	18.8	7.4	24.8	21.5	32.1	21.0	n.a.	–1938	4 516	5 937
1975	598	21.1	6.5	24.7	19.5	28.9	20.1	89.7	–1671	5 003	8 456
1976	806	28.9	11.2	15.4	25.1	26.8	20.4	184.0	–590	7 814	10 533
1977	1019	37.1	10.0	10.0	28.5	28.7	20.1	137.0	–477	10 046	12 648
1978	1407	52.0	9.0	14.7	30.6	32.8	21.1	144.9	–1780	12 711	14 871
1979	1649	61.9	7.1	18.5	29.9	36.2	26.7	119.0	–4395	14 705	20 287
1980	1632	62.2	–2.1	28.7	24.4	32.2	30.1	106.9	–4384	17 214	27 170
1981	1797	69.6	6.5	21.3	24.3	30.0	24.4	131.4	–3849	20 747	32 433
1982	1892	74.4	7.2	7.1	25.4	29.0	17.3	127.3	–2827	20 934	37 083
1983	2062	82.3	10.7	3.4	29.0	29.3	14.2	121.2	–1849	23 272	40 378
1984	2242	90.6	8.2	2.2	31.0	30.7	14.1	142.5	–1089	26 486	43 053
1985	2289	93.4	6.5	2.3	31.1	30.5	14.2	163.4	–19	26 442	46 729

(continued)

Table 2.1 Major indicators of Korean economic growth, 1960–89 (*continued*)

	GDP per capita (US$)[1]	GDP (US$ billion)	Real GDP growth rate (%)	CPI (%)	Savings rate (%)[2]	Investment rate (%)[3]	Corporate bond yields (%)	Stock price index (1980.1.4 = 100)	Trade balance (US$ million)	Exports (US$ million	Foreign debt (US$ million)
1986	2611	107.6	11.0	2.8	34.9	29.4	12.8	272.6	4 299	34 128	44 500
1987	3248	135.2	11.0	3.1	38.4	30.2	12.6	525.1	7 529	46 560	35 600
1988	4302	180.8	10.5	7.1	40.5	31.2	14.2	907.2	11 283	59 973	32 500
1989	5199	220.7	6.1	5.7	37.6	33.8	15.2	909.7	4 597	61 408	

1. GNP per capita before 1970.
2. Savings/GNDI.
3. Investment/GNDI.

Notes:
GNDI = Gross National Disposable Income.
GDP and GDP per capita are in current prices.
The rate of inflation is based on the Consumer Price Index (CPI).

Sources: Song (1990), pp. 60–1; Bank of Korea (http://www.bok.or.kr); National Statistical Office (http://www.nso.go.kr).

Hence within a single generation the country rid itself of its heavy dependence upon foreign aid and became self-sufficient in terms of funding requirements. The remainder of this section is devoted to analysing the development of these key macroeconomic variables.

2.2.2 Economic growth patterns and characteristics

During the period 1962–89 economic growth slumped only once – in 1980 – due to the sociopolitical unrest that followed the assassination of President Park Chung Hee in 1979. Real GDP growth was –2.1 per cent that year, aggravated by the worst harvest since 1962 and the second global oil price hike. Apart from in 1980 and 1972 the economic growth rate exceeded 5 per cent throughout the period. A number of factors accounted for this rapid growth: the adoption of a sound export strategy; the development of growth-promoting institutions and public policies; the availability of high-quality workers and entrepreneurs; access to, and adoption of, readily available technology as an economic latecomer; the appropriate use of public resources for infrastructural development and education; population control; the capacity of entrepreneurs and policy makers to adjust rapidly and flexibly to external shocks; and the maintenance of a relatively equitable income distribution.

Growth was initiated by the expansion of exports and sustained by the development of export industries, backed up by the allocation of resources by the government to construct key industries and build up social capital. Hence export expansion was effectively led by the government and many export industries, and indeed the economy as a whole during the early stages of development, were subject to extensive government intervention. The basic philosophy of President Park Chung Hee was 'exports first', or 'nation building through export promotion'. Attaining and then exceeding the government's ambitious export targets was regarded as the height of achievement for businessmen and public officials in charge of export promotion. Larger firms were assigned annual export targets by the Ministry of Trade and Industry, and if they reached these targets they received numerous benefits, including preferential credit and loans, administrative support, tax concessions and other benefits. Thus overfulfilment of the export targets – usually determined jointly with the government – became the keystone of exporters' business strategies.

High growth with large fluctuations was one of the most distinctive characteristics of the Korean economy during this period, in contrast with the situation in Japan and Taiwan. In the 1950s economic fluctuations had not been extreme, partly because year-to-year variations in the then largely agricultural economy reflected only variations in crop yields due to such factors as the weather. In some countries agricultural yields fluctuated widely, but in Korea the situation tended to be less extreme because of its more stable climate and extensive irrigation network. With the decrease in the relative importance of agriculture and the rise of manufacturing and service industries the annual fluctuations became larger and more unpredictable. For instance the economic growth rate was 12.2 per cent in 1966, dropped to 5.9 per cent the following year, rose to 11.3 per cent in 1968 and 13.8 per cent in 1969, and then dropped to 8.8 per cent in 1970. Since the scale of the economy remained quite small until well into the 1970s the growth rate depended heavily on the completion of large investment projects, and the economy's outward orientation made it susceptible to fluctuations in oil prices and other external factors. The inexperience of policy makers, especially during the 1960s, also contributed to the variations.

Many Korean industries were developed on the basis of the 'export first' principle and marketed their products overseas rather than domestically, as in the case of colour TVs – the domestic sale of colour TVs was not allowed until 1980 so manufacturers had no choice but to sell their products overseas. The same applied to other high-value items such as record players, portable telephones and mink coats. This method of industrial expansion was in direct contrast with that adopted by Japan (a country with which Korea has often been compared), which was based on the 'domestic market first' principle. Because of the forced nature of industrial growth in Korea the share of manufacturing in GDP was larger than the average in other countries. In addition the shift from agriculture to manufacturing was faster than was typically the case in other developing countries.

As the expansion of industrial capacity tended to be excessive the amount of domestic investment generally exceeded the amount of domestic savings. In addition a considerable proportion of domestic savings was diverted into real estate as a hedge against inflation. Hence the gap between savings and investment had to be filled by foreign borrowing. This was one of the main reasons, along with the need to import oil and other industrial raw materials, why Korea's foreign debt continued to rise until 1985 and the inflow of foreign capital was higher than for other countries at a similar stage of development. Furthermore the debt to equity ratio of large Korean firms, which were being forced to overexpand their production and export capacity, tended to be higher than that of firms in other Asian NICs.

Because of the priority given to the expansion of exports and manufacturing, investment in social capital tended to be neglected and usually lagged far behind investment in productive activities. This was exacerbated by a shortage of investment resources and the relatively high defence expenditure. Industry therefore grew in the face of shortages and bottlenecks in airports, telecommunications, railways and other infrastructure. However in the second half of the 1980s social capital expenditure increased sharply in preparation for the 1988 Olympics.

The expansion of industrial capacity was achieved by expanding existing firms rather than creating new ones. This practice persisted for more than two decades and resulted in the growth of a small number of very large business conglomerates (*chaebols*) at the expense of small firms, as well as a market concentration ratio that was much higher than in Japan and Taiwan. In Japan expansion was based on both large and small firms, while in Taiwan emphasis was placed on the development of small firms. Hence the Korean economy could be described as a large-firm economy, in contrast to the small-firm economy of Taiwan and the bipolar economy of Japan.

Prior to 1985 Korea incurred sizable trade and balance of payments deficits (Table 2.2). To some extent this was due to the country's lack of natural resources, but was principally a consequence of the policy of allowing exporting companies to import the raw materials, parts and machinery required for the large-scale production of export goods. This has been called a negative import substitution policy because exporting firms imported as much as possible and hence the growth rate of imports was

Table 2.2 Balance of payments, 1962–89 ($ millions)

	1962	1965	1970	1975	1980	1985	1989
Trade balance (1)	–335	–241	–922	–1671	–4 384	–19	4 597
Exports	55	175	882	5003	17 214	26 442	61 408
Imports	390	416	1804	6674	21 598	26 461	56 811
Service balance (2)	43	46	119	–442	–1 386	–1 446	210
Receipts	108	114	497	881	5 363	6 664	12 641
Payments	65	68	378	1323	6 749	8 111	12 431
Transfers (net) (3)	236	203	180	227	449	578	247
Current account balance (4) (1 + 2 + 3)	–56	9	–623	–1887	–5 321	–887	5 055
Long-term capital (net) (5)	8	37	449	1178	1 857	1 101	3 362
Basic balance (4 + 5) (6)	–48	46	–174	–709	–3 464	213	1 692
Short-term capital (net) (7)	–7	–23	122	680	1 944	–588	60
Errors and omissions	–2	–2	16	–122	–370	–880	701
Overall balance (6 + 7)	–57	21	–36	–151	–1 890	–1 255	2 453
Gold and foreign exchange reserves	167	138	584	1550	6 571	7 749	15 245
Exchange rate (won/US$)	130	272	317	484	660	890	680

Sources: Bank of Korea, *Economic Statistics Yearbook* (various years); *Economic Indicators of Major Countries* (March 1989); Economic Planning Board, *Major Statistics of Korean Economy* (various years).

very high. From 1986, however, the trade and international balance of payments turned positive.

Korea experienced sharply fluctuating wholesale and consumer prices during the period of rapid economic development, and between the early 1960s and 1981 it had the highest inflation rate among the Asian NICs. This was especially true when the economy was hit by oil price hikes, poor harvests, changes in government and other shocks. The high inflation was mainly due to Korea's aggressive export promotion and growth policy, which necessitated the economy to perform far beyond its capacity and resulted in the forced expansion of investment and output by businesses whose overly ambitious investment plans led to inflationary investment financing.

The adverse consequences of the high inflation were numerous. First, it had a severe impact on income distribution as wealth was redistributed from creditors to debtors. Second, inflation often outstripped the government-set bank interest rates, resulting in negative real interest rates and causing ordinary Koreans to lose faith in the credibility of banks and the government itself. Third, although the available figures indicate that capital flight out of Korea was not a serious problem, many Koreans diverted their savings from financial institutions to real estate. This was one of the main reasons why domestic savings were insufficient to meet the country's investment requirements, as alluded to above.[2] Moreover government intervention in businesses to boost exports became heavy handed, and with real bank interest rates becoming negative firms also hid their money in real estate or generally diverted their savings away from financial institutions. Finally high inflation contributed to the expansion of the unofficial credit market or 'kerb market', which came to play a major role in investment financing.

Price stability was eventually achieved in 1982. Inflation was reduced from over 20 per cent in 1980–81 to 7 per cent in 1982 and less than 3.5 per cent 1983–87, before rising to around 6–7 per cent in 1988–89. The most important contributory factors in this were low energy and raw material prices, the depreciation of the US dollar and low interest rates. In addition the government began to pay more attention to stability, and labour productivity began to outstrip the growth of wages.

Economic growth was accompanied by extensive investment in human resources, facilitated by, and greatly facilitating, rapid modernisation. Public and private expenditure on education regularly exceeded 10 per cent of GDP, the highest rate among all developing countries. The percentage of high school graduates advancing to college or university during the 1980s was the second highest in the world after the USA. This investment in education also led to a high degree of income equality that remained relatively unchanged during the course of development, apart from a slight fall during 1972–80.

Finally, government-driven industrialisation resulted in an excessive concentration of industries and people in the large cities, especially Seoul and its surroundings. The degree of urbanisation in Korea was generally higher than in other countries, and urban problems such as housing shortages, lack of educational facilities and poor public services emerged as serious domestic issues after the 1970s.

2.2.3 Sources of economic growth

The factors that contributed to the growth of the Korean economy can be divided into demand-side factors such as interindustry demand, consumer demand, investment, exports and imports and supply-side factors such as labour, capital, advances in knowledge, improved resource allocation, economies of scale and so on.

Demand-side sources of growth

As can be seen in Table 2.3, consumer demand was the single most important source of manufacturing output growth during the 1970s and 1980s, although its relative importance steadily declined. The table also shows the significance of export growth, which accounted for about 27 per cent of total manufacturing output growth in the 1970s and 33–34 per cent in the 1980s. This was much larger than the contribution made by investment during this period, confirming that economic growth was export-led rather than investment-led. Further evidence of the significance of exports, in this case to overall demand, is shown in Table 2.4. The contribution made by consumer demand continually declined during the period in question while that of investment increased, but the growing significance of export demand is particularly notable.

Supply-side sources of growth

Denison's (1962) method of breaking down the factors that contribute to GNP growth yields interesting results, as follows. The most important

Table 2.3 Demand-side sources of growth in manufacturing output, 1970–87 (per cent)

	1970–75	1975–80	1980–83	1983–87
Consumption	54.8	48.1	45.8	41.7
Investment	15.5	21.1	19.8	21.6
Exports	27.3	27.3	32.9	34.2
Imports	−1.3	1.7	3.7	4.1
Change to input–output coefficient	3.7	1.8	−2.2	−1.6
Total	100.0	100.0	100.0	100.0

Sources: World Bank (1987); Song (1990).

Table 2.4 Changes in demand structure, 1970–89 (per cent)

	1970	1975	1980	1985	1989
Consumption	83.7	82.0	76.6	68.9	64.4
Investment	26.4	27.5	31.2	30.6	33.4
Exports	14.7	30.3	33.7	36.2	34.1
Imports	–24.8	–39.8	–41.5	–35.7	–31.3
Total	100.0	100.0	100.0	100.0	100.0

Source: Bank of Korea, *Economic Statistics Yearbook* (various years).

source of growth between 1963 and 1986 was labour input (Table 2.5), although its relative importance declined in 1973–86 due partly to the shift in 1977 from a labour surplus to a labour shortage. Overall the growth in inputs contributed more to GNP than did increased productivity. A study by Kim and Park (1985) confirms that the rise in productivity contributed relatively little to GNP growth from 1972–82 due to excessive investment in capital-intensive heavy and chemicals industries in the late 1970s. Thereafter, however, the relative importance of productivity increased.

2.2.4 Structural transformation

The rapid economic growth was accompanied by a major transformation of the structure of the economy. In line with the normal pattern of change during the process of development the relative importance of the agricultural sector declined while the non-agricultural sectors – mainly manufacturing and services – rose in importance (see for example Chenery and Syrquin (1975)). The share of agriculture in GDP fell from 39.9 per cent in 1960 to 10.8 per cent in 1987, while the share of the non-agricultural sector rose from 60.1 per cent to 89.2 per cent. During the same period the share of industry in GDP increased from 18.6 per cent to 43.2 per cent.

Table 2.5 Supply-side sources of growth, 1963–86 (per cent)

	1963–73	1973–86
Real GNP growth rate	9.54	7.82
Contribution of inputs	5.41	4.07
Labour	3.24	2.16
Capital	2.17	1.91
Total factor productivity	4.13	3.75
Advances in knowledge	1.36	1.67
Improved resource allocation	0.98	0.62
Economies of scale	1.78	1.46

Source: Song (1990), Table 5.5, p. 68.

In terms of output Korea's industrial structure reflects the country's poor resource endowment, with the mining sector contributing just 2.3 per cent of GDP at its peak in 1960 while the contribution of the manufacturing sector rose from 12.1 per cent in 1960 to 31.6 per cent in 1987 (Table 2.6), much higher than the average 23 per cent reported in advanced economies.

Korea's changing employment structure is shown in Table 2.7. From 1965 the total labour force grew at an annual rate of about 3 per cent compared with about 6 per cent for non-farm labour. In 1980 the share of industrial employment in total employment was 28.7 per cent compared with an average of 23 per cent for middle-income countries at that time. However a relatively large number of Koreans continued to live in rural areas. In 1987 the contribution of agriculture to GDP was 10.8 per cent, and in 1988 its share of employment was 20.6 per cent.

Table 2.6 Structure of production, 1960–87 (percentage of GDP in current prices)

	1960	1965	1970	1975	1980	1987
Agriculture	39.9	41.0	31.1	27.8	14.6	10.8
Industry	18.6	24.1	28.4	33.1	41.4	43.2
Mining	2.3	2.0	1.3	1.5	1.4	0.7
Manufacturing	12.1	17.3	19.1	25.3	29.6	31.6
Construction	3.5	3.6	6.4	4.9	8.2	8.1
Utilities	0.7	1.2	1.6	1.4	2.1	2.8
Services	41.5	34.9	40.5	39.1	44.0	46.0
Total	100.0	100.0	100.0	100.0	100.0	100.0

Note: Sector classification is based on the method suggested in World Bank, *World Development Report* (1987, 1988).

Sources: Bank of Korea, *Economic Statistics Yearbook* (1978, 1989) *New National Accounts* (1986).

Table 2.7 Employment by industry, 1965–88 (per cent)

	1965	1970	1975	1980	1988
Agriculture	58.6	50.4	45.9	34.0	20.6
Industry	13.3	17.3	23.4	28.7	34.6
Mining	1.0	1.2	0.5	0.9	0.8
Manufacturing	9.4	13.2	18.6	21.7	27.7
Construction	2.9	2.9	4.3	6.1	6.1
Services	28.1	32.3	30.7	37.3	44.8
Total	100.0	100.0	100.0	100.0	100.0
Number (million)	8.206	9.745	11.83	13.706	16.87

Source: Bank of Korea, *Economic Statistics Yearbook* (various years).

2.3 Korea's development strategy

From the previous section it is clear that the driving force behind the growth of the economy was the industrial sector, headed by manufacturing. The dramatic rise of this sector is outlined in this section, as is the key contribution made by trade promotion and Korea's growth-oriented development strategy.

2.3.1 Background

During the rule of President Rhee Syngman (1948–60) there were no well-defined economic growth or trade strategies. In fact economic growth was given very low priority as Rhee's main interests were politics and directing the attention of the Korean people to issues such as the unification of the two Koreas. Industrial production was directed at import substitution, made necessary by an unfavourable exchange rate and Korea's heavy reliance on foreign assistance.[3] As most of the domestic industries produced consumer goods such as food and textiles, import substitution took place mainly in those areas. Access to foreign exchange, the securing of government subsidies of various types and the imposition of quantitative restrictions on imports were the key determinants of business success during Rhee's tenure. Securing government-controlled foreign exchange, bank credit and foreign assistance increasingly involved corruption and favouritism, and businessmen who became wealthy were widely suspected of corrupt dealings. When Rhee was ousted by the student revolution of April 1960, public sentiment demanded that such wealth be confiscated and the malefactors punished. Parliamentary government was established and Chang Myon became prime minister. However his tenure would not last long.

In a military coup on 16 May 1961 General Park Chung Hee took power. At that time the economy was in dire straits, most Koreans were poverty stricken and per capita income was a mere $82. Furthermore South Korea lagged behind North Korea in terms of both per capita income and industrial capacity. Therefore the new government was compelled to come up with a suitable development strategy. By that time Korea had virtually completed its import substitution programme for non-durable consumer goods and the intermediate goods used in their manufacture. Extending this to machinery, consumer durables and the necessary inputs was not a viable option because of the smallness of the domestic market and the large capital requirements. Furthermore Korea's natural resource endowment was so poor that a development strategy based on the utilisation of domestic resources was inconceivable. To make matters worse, US assistance, which had financed most of the postwar reconstruction, had peaked in 1957 and was gradually declining. Therefore policy makers had to give serious consideration to alternative sources of foreign currency to address the country's balance of payments difficulties. What Korea did have was a large, cohesive and well-motivated labour force with a high educational level[4] which combined with relatively low wages offered Korea a comparative export advantage in labour-intensive consumer goods whose capital requirement was minimal. This was ideal given the country's shortage of capital. For these reasons the government concluded that the best way forward was industrialisation through trade expansion.

Korea duly switched from import substitution to export expansion in 1962–63 (see for example Ranis 1971, 1989). This involved relaxing import restrictions as increased competition and therefore reduced profits in the market would encourage consumer goods manufacturers to turn their attention to overseas markets.

The urgent need to catch up with and outperform North Korea and to escape from poverty necessitated the fastest possible growth, even growth at any cost, and this formed the basis of the enforced expansion of exports and investment during the Park era. The Park government was in a position to deal as it wished with the businessmen accused of corruption during the Rhee period, but it chose a compromise arrangement whereby it would exempt the suspects from legal action if they paid off their obligations and devoted themselves fully to nation building through industrialisation. By this means Park both enlisted the support of and held control over businessmen during the rapid expansion of trade and industrial growth from 1961 until his death in 1979.

In theory the export targets were mutually agreed between the government and individual firms, but in fact the targets were more akin to compulsory orders and firms that failed to meet them without a plausible excuse ran the risk of heavy sanctions from the government. During the 1960s, therefore, the primary controller of export promotion was the government. When the first five-year economic plan (1962–66) was implemented the total value of Korean exports amounted to a mere $55 million, however this was to change radically.

Because the success of firms during this period was measured by their export figures they tended to increase production as much as possible. This resulted in a high debt–equity ratio and distorted firms' internal decision making. Large firms were in a better position than small ones to increase their export capacity because the government-controlled banks preferred to lend to large firms. The latter were probably also better able than small firms to handle the complicated red tape procedures, which involved many government departments.

2.3.2 Growth strategy

Korea's sustained growth from the early 1960s was due largely to strict adherence to its outward-oriented industrial growth strategy. While many developing countries at the time were focusing on the mobilisation of domestic resources, rather than promoting foreign trade,[5] only a few countries, including Korea, appeared to recognise the advantages of an outward orientation. Resource-poor countries such as Korea could only grow by developing their manufacturing sector. Population size also had an important bearing on the pattern and course of growth, especially in the case of products such as cars and televisions, and industries such as iron, steel and petrochemicals, which required large-scale investment and economies of scale to be efficient. As a relatively large country, Korea was in a better position than smaller countries such as Taiwan, Hong Kong and Singapore to take advantage of economies of scale. But even so the domestic market was not large enough to sustain the relevant industries. Only external markets could do this.

Before 1960 exports growth contributed less than 10 per cent to GDP growth. This rose to 25 per cent in the early 1970s and slightly over 33 per cent in the late 1970s. It is estimated that 33 per cent of total manufacturing employment was directly or indirectly related to export production in 1966, rising to about 45 per cent in 1980. Song (1990) estimates that the proportion of manufacturing employment accounted for by export production was 27.8 per cent in 1968, 29.6 per cent in 1970, 44.7 per cent in 1980 and 52.5 per cent in 1985.

The linkages between export promotion and economic growth fall into three categories: static efficiency gains, dynamic efficiency gains and improved economic policy instruments. In terms of static efficiency gains, the shift from import substitution to export promotion helped to correct the substantial resource allocation distortions that are typically associated with import substitution. Dynamic efficiency gains were reaped from the pressure on firms to compete in the world market, economies of scale, improvements in technology and skill development among employees and entrepreneurs. Such dynamic gains tend to be long lasting but are extremely difficult to measure. With regard to improved economic policy instruments, combined with the incentive system the following were particularly important to Korea's trade and industrial development.

Credit allocation

To comply with the government's export expansion programme cash-poor manufacturing firms had to take out bank loans to finance their expansion. The government encouraged them to borrow, and because the official interest rates were kept at or close to zero businesses tended to borrow as much as they could, often more than they actually needed. The excess funds were frequently used for land speculation.

This heavy borrowing from banks owned or controlled by the government in effect put businesses under tight government control and resulted in the control of bank credit being made a key policy instrument. The very low interest rates meant a continuing demand for bank credit and a consequent need for credit allocation, with the government exercising control over the amount borrowed, interest rates and renewal terms. A similar situation prevailed in the allocation of foreign credit, putting the government in an excellent position to wield strong discretionary control over firms.

Taxes

The second important policy instrument was taxation. Firms were made exempt from indirect taxes on income from exports, and 50 per cent of export earnings were made exempt from corporate and personal income tax during 1961–71. Equally or more important was the use of tax investigations to enforce government directives. Because of the many informal credit transactions and land speculation, dual accounting was common among firms that borrowed heavily from banks, and the threat of a tax investigation put them in a very vulnerable position.

Administrative support

Administrative support for business was also an effective policy instrument. Until the early 1970s the laws and regulations governing trade and industry were largely leftovers from the Japanese colonial period. The regulations enacted during that time were mainly aimed at controlling – not promoting – business activities, especially by the indigenous population. Thus the red tape involved in arranging exports was virtually insurmountable.

A monthly export promotion conference, established in December 1962, was one of the most important administrative support mechanisms because it was always attended by President Park. The meeting served as a forum for revising and extending various sorts of administrative support, and was attended by all important public officials and private experts concerned with trade. It also served as an excellent forum for the exchange of information among policy makers, businessmen and economic experts. The attendees included the president's chief economic secretary, the minister of the Economic Planning Board, the minister of Trade and Industry, the director of the Korea Trade Promotion Agency and the chairman of the Korea Traders Association. The president himself checked the progress of exports and the performance of exporting firms. Almost every month the president presented successful businessmen with medals and citations. The ability to tell one's problems directly to the president and cut through all the red tape was very important.

Industrial zones and wage controls

Finding a suitable site upon which to build a plant for export production was of prime importance to manufacturing firms. To support them in this the government developed export industrial estates in Seoul, Masan (near

Pusan) and Kumi (the home town of President Park, near Taegu) during the 1960s and 1970s. In 1969 the government enacted the Regional Industrial Development Law and developed at least one industrial estate in every provincial capital. Export firms were able to purchase industrial sites at greatly discounted prices, and the cost of electricity, water, transportation, communications and other services was kept under government control.

The government also took action to control the wages of workers at exporting firms and restricted union activities, which enabled firms to maintain their international competitiveness and freed them from union unrest.

Exchange rate adjustment and import privileges

Upon adoption of its export-oriented strategy in the early 1960s the government normalised the highly overvalued exchange rate and abandoned the complicated multitier exchange rate system in favour of a single rate. This reform and the monetary and fiscal policies introduced during 1964–67 greatly facilitated the growth and ensured the international competitiveness of Korea's export industries.

Rationalisation of imports

Because Korean manufacturers relied heavily on imported raw materials and machinery the government set up a system of export-linked import privileges that allowed exporting firms freely to import the raw materials, capital goods and parts required for the production of exports, up to the amount of export earnings.

Table 2.8 summarises the various policy tools used by the government in the conduct of its export-oriented industrialisation strategy. It used both incentive systems and command procedures, some of which were discretionary and some non-discretionary. Direct intervention was generally highly selective, short term and rather effective, especially during the early years of the Park administration. However with the growth of firms and the accumulation of experience by government and business community alike a different policy strategy was needed. Under the fifth five-year plan (1982–86), for example, the government came to rely more on free market mechanisms and non-discretionary measures and used incentives rather than command procedures.

2.3.3 General trading companies

To speed up export expansion the legal framework needed to establish general trading companies (GTCs) was introduced in 1975 by the Ministry of Trade and Industry. Trading companies were designated as GTCs if they

Table 2.8 Export expansion measures

	Incentives	Command procedures
Non-discretionary	• Special tax measures • Financial subsidies and export credit • Exchange rate • Cost of borrowing, including interest rate subsidies • Tariff reductions	• Administrative support, including new laws and acts • Price controls on electricity and water for industrial use • Control of unions and wages of industrial workers • Development of industrial estates • Provision of infrastructural facilities • Tax inspections (automatic audits) • Deferment of trade and capital liberalisation measures • Export–import link (permitting the use of export earnings for imports)
Discretionary	• Credit rationing, including foreign loans (amount, interest rate, loan period, time of renewal, etc.) • Decisions concerning subsidies.	• Government persuasion and 'window' guidance of various types • Upward adjustment of controlled prices • Allocation of export targets • Tax inspections (selective audits) • Coordination of investment in plant and equipment. • Encouragement of mergers to promote economies of scale and efficiency

Source: Song (1990), p. 99.

could meet the following requirements: minimum paid-in capital of $2.1 million, annual exports of $50 million, 10 overseas branch offices, public stock offerings and other qualifications. On the basis of these requirements Samsung, Daewoo, Hanil, Kukje and Ssangyong were designated as GTCs in 1975. Three years later the number of GTCs had risen to 13 with the inclusion of Bando, Hyundai, Hyosung, Koryo, Kumho, Samwha, Sunkyong and Yulsan. However by 1985 companies had lost their GTC status due to bankruptcy or poor performance. In their first year of operation 13.6 per cent of exports were handled by the 10 largest GTCs, but by 1983 their share had increased to 51.3 per cent.

The government put continuous pressure on GTCs to increase their exports by regularly raising the minimum export value requirement, which rose from $50 million in 1975 to $301 million in 1979 – the latter amounting to 2 per cent of Korea's total exports. Two GTCs, Yulsan and Samwha, lost their accreditation when their exports fell short of the required minimum. On the plus side the government provided GTCs with various benefits, including cash subsidies tied to export volumes. Because the total value of these benefits exceeded the marginal cost of expanding their exports the GTCs had a clear incentive to increase production as much as possible, making the GTC system and the accompanying incentive system powerful engines in the process of export expansion. Although the Korean GTCs were successfully modelled on the Japanese GTCs they lagged behind their Japanese counterparts in terms of size, intelligence gathering networks, global marketing strength, ability to raise capital and organisational capability.

2.3.4 Consequences of the incentive and disincentive systems

The monetary incentives in particular and the market system in general proved very successful in mobilising the Korean people behind the banner of rapid economic growth. This was backed up by moral persuasion – because of their long tradition of Confucianism, Koreans, like other East Asians, respond strongly to calls for loyalty to family, firm and country, so Park's maxim 'Loyalty to the country through exports' was very effective in enlisting the support of entrepreneurs and the people generally.

Firms were expected to maximise exports rather than profits, and those which failed to meet the government's expectations were under constant threat of tax investigations and other punitive measures. On the other hand firms that efficiently used their government-backed loans to expand their exports were favoured with additional support, including loans at negligible interest rates to start new lines of business. Indeed government support was the major reason for the success of Korean firms with little business expertise.

2.4 Industrial structure and policy

2.4.1 Changing export structure

As can be seen from Tables 2.9 and 2.10 there were several pronounced shifts in the composition of exports over the period 1962–89.

In the early 1960s exports were dominated by primary commodities such as silk, tungsten, fish and fish products, but as industrialisation proceeded, manufactured goods took the dominant position. The proportion of primary commodities (food and live animals, crude materials, mineral fuels, animal and vegetable oils and fats) in the export total was 84.3 per cent in 1960, but this had fallen to 17 per cent by 1975 and 5.9 per cent by 1989. During the 1960s the major manufactured exports were labour-intensive goods such as plywood, wigs and clothing, all of which could be manufactured with relatively simple technology. In the 1970s the balance shifted to textiles, ships and steel plate, which required somewhat more complex

Table 2.9 Korea's top ten exports, 1962–89 (in rank order)

1962	Silk, tungsten, fish and fish products, animal oil and fat, plywood, miscellaneous products, textiles, machinery, clothing, chemical products.
1974	Clothing, electronic products, ships, textiles, sweaters, plywood, footwear, steel plate, cotton goods, synthetic resin products.
1984	Textiles and garments, ships, electronic products, steel products, footwear, synthetic resin products, metal products, petroleum products, electrical products, tyres.
1986	Textiles and garments, electronic products, steel products, footwear, ships, cars, fish and fish products, general machinery, electrical products, synthetic resin products.
1989	Electronic products, textiles and garments, steel products, footwear, cars, chemical products, ships, fish and fish products, general machinery, plastic products.

Table 2.10 Exports by SITC group, 1960–89 (per cent)

	1960	1965	1975	1985	1989
0. Food and live animals	30.4	16.1	11.9	3.8	3.5
1. Beverages and tobacco	1.4	0.5	1.3	0.4	0.2
2. Crude materials, inedible	49.7	21.2	3.0	1.0	1.4
3. Mineral fuels	3.6	1.1	2.1	1.6	1.0
4. Animal and vegetable oils and fats	0.6	–	–	–	–
5. Chemicals	1.3	0.2	1.5	3.1	3.2
6. Manufactured goods	12.4	37.9	29.1	23.3	22.0
7. Machinery and transport equipment	0.3	3.1	13.8	37.6	37.8
8. Miscellaneous manufactures	0.3	19.7	37.1	27.6	30.4
9. Other	–	0.2	0.2	0.1	0.2
Total export value ($ million)	22	175	5081	30 283	62 377

Sources: Bank of Korea, *Economic Statistics Yearbook* (1962, 1968, 1978, 1988, 1991).

technology, and by the early 1980s export commodities had become even more capital intensive. The late 1980s represented a turning point as manufactured exports shifted decisively to skill-intensive goods such as computers, semiconductors, colour television sets and cars.

As discussed earlier, Korea lacked the natural and technological resources required for industrialisation so their share in imports were very high. By 1989 machinery and transport equipment amounted to over a third of total imports, as shown in Table 2.11.

2.4.2 Changing industrial structure

In line with the move away from labour-intensive and towards capital- and technology-intensive exports the number of capital-intensive industries grew, and after 1980 the proportion of heavy and chemical industries

Table 2.11 Import structure by SITC group, 1960–89 (per cent)

	1960	1965	1975	1985	1989
0. Food and live animals	9.6	13.7	13.0	4.5	5.0
1. Beverages and tobacco	–	–	0.2	0.2	0.3
2. Crude materials, inedible	19.9	23.7	15.4	12.4	14.0
3. Mineral fuels	7.1	6.7	19.0	23.6	12.0
4. Animal and vegetable oils and fats	0.8	0.8	0.7	0.5	0.3
5. Chemicals	23.1	22.3	10.9	9.0	11.0
6. Manufactured goods	14.3	15.4	11.9	11.4	15.0
7. Machinery and transport equipment	12.2	15.8	26.2	34.2	34.0
8. Miscellaneous manufactures	1.8	1.6	2.6	4.0	5.8
9. Other	11.2	–	0.1	0.3	0.3
Total import value ($ million)	329	463	7274	31 136	61 465

Sources: Bank of Korea, *Economic Statistics Yearbook* (1962, 1968, 1978, 1988, 1991).

exceeded that of light industries. One interesting point about Korea's manufacturing structure is that due to the premature and large-scale expansion of heavy industry, which usually takes place late in the development cycle, the proportion of middle industries was relatively small. According to Chenery and Taylor (1968), 'early industries' such as food and textiles are closely associated with the satisfaction of basic needs, and their share in GDP generally stops growing once per capita income reaches about $600 (in 1983 prices). 'Middle industries' such as wood products, rubber products and chemicals continue to expand until per capita income reaches the $1200–1500 level. 'Late industries' such as machinery, metal products, printing and publishing begin to grow in importance only after per capita income reaches $900. According to this schema, Korea jumped straight from the early industrial stage to the late industrial stage as a result of the government's policies in the 1970s. By the late 1980s it was starting to resemble a mature advanced economy and was still undergoing rapid industrial, financial and social transformation.

2.4.3 Number and size of firms, concentration and market power

Number and size of firms

Although the industrial structure underwent rapid change the number of manufacturing firms did not change much until the early 1980s. This was partly because of the government's policy of encouraging existing firms to increase their production capacity, particularly in the 1970s when it concentrated on fostering the heavy and chemical industries. As a consequence the number of firms with 5–49 employees decreased from 21 013 in 1966 to 19 844 in 1976. Although the total number of manufacturing establishments increased by just under one tenth between 1966 and 1976, the average employee level rose from 25 to 69. After 1981, however, the number of firms started to increase rapidly (Table 2.12).

When the heavy and chemical industries expanded in the 1970s the gap between large and small firms increased and this subsequently became an important economic and political issue. There was a growing need for small subcontracting firms to supply components and services to large firms. Furthermore an increasing number of young Koreans wished to establish their own businesses, but bureaucratic regulations made this almost impossible. However the promotion of small manufacturing firms emerged as a major policy issue in the mid-term revision of the fifth five year plan. In the revised document, covering the period 1984–86, a separate section was devoted to the matter. This resulted in the enactment in 1986 of a special law to support the creation of small firms, and thereafter the number of manufacturing establishments increased rapidly. The number of establishments with more than five employees increased from 24 957 in 1976 to 44 037 in 1985, according to the census of manufacturing. However in 1986 the Establishment Census of the National Bureau of Statistics put the number much higher at 76 042. It can be seen from Table 2.12 that firms with more than 300 employees contributed more to total employment than did smaller firms in the 1970s, particularly in comparison with the 1980s and 1960s.

Concentration and market power

The government's policy of promoting rapid growth firms and rewarding them with preferential access to credit and other incentives, as well as its promotion of heavy and chemical industries in the 1970s, served to

Table 2.12 Number of manufacturing establishments, employees and value added by firm size, 1966–85

	Number (and percentage) of establishments			**Number (and percentage) of employees thousands**			**Value added (billion won and percentage)**		
	1966	**1976**	**1985**	**1966**	**1976**	**1985**	**1966**	**1976**	**1985**
5–49	21 013	19 844	35 676	223.7	276.5	570.1	38.8	323.6	3137.9
	(92.5)	(79.5)	(81.0)	(39.5)	(16.1)	(23.4)	(24.9)	(7.9)	(11.7)
50–99	874	2094	4273	59.5	147.5	300.3	13.4	262.8	2198.9
	(3.8)	(8.4)	(9.7)	(10.5)	(8.6)	(12.3)	(8.6)	(6.5)	(8.2)
100–299	593	1990	3001	92.3	332.6	497.2	26	635.8	4722.4
	(2.6)	(8.0)	(6.8)	(16.3)	(19.4)	(20.4)	(16.6)	15.6	(17.7)
Over 300	238	1029	1087	191.2	960.6	1070.4	78	2852.9	16 677.4
	(1.1)	(4.1)	(2.5)	(33.7)	(55.9)	(43.9)	(49.9)	(70.0)	(62.4)
Total	22 718	24 957	44 037	566.7	1717.3	2438	156.2	4075.1	26 36.6

Sources: Economic Planning Board; *Mining and Manufacturing Census* (1966, 1976, 1985).

increase industrial concentration. This was encouraged by government officials, who preferred there to be a small number of large firms rather than a large number of small firms because this eased the administration of credit and taxation. According to the World Bank, aggregate concentration, measured by the sales value of the largest 100 firms in the Korean manufacturing sector, was 40.6 per cent in 1970, 44.9 per cent in 1977 and 46.8 per cent in 1982. Korea therefore had an extremely high aggregate concentration by the standards of industrialised non-communist nations, particularly when adjusted for the size of the economy.

One of the most important aspects of industrial concentration was the market power exercised by the business conglomerates, the *chaebols*, or the Korean counterparts of the Japanese *zaibatsu*. In 1987 there were 32 *chaebols* but by 1989 the number had increased to 40 as the total assets of the companies belonging to an additional eight groups had come to exceed 400 billion won (about $500 million), which was the official dividing line between *chaebol* and non-*chaebol* enterprises. The 40 *chaebols* consisted of 672 industrial companies and encompassed nearly the full complement of large private corporations. *Chaebol*-affiliated firms grew faster than non-*chaebol* firms, as indicated by their continuously increasing share of total sales from 1977 (Table 2.13). The 30 largest *chaebols* controlled 270 firms and contributed about 10 per cent of Korea's GNP in 1985 (Table 2.14).

Table 2.13 Change in the *chaebols'* share of manufacturing sales and employment, 1977–85

	Sales			Employment		
	1977	1980	1985	1977	1980	1985
Top 5 *chaebol*	15.7	16.9	23.0	9.1	9.1	9.7
Top 10	21.2	23.8	30.2	12.5	12.8	11.7
Top 20	29.3	31.4	36.4	17.4	17.9	15.5
Top 30	34.1	36.0	40.2	20.5	22.4	17.6

Sources: Lee and Lee (1985); Korea Development Institute.

Table 2.14 The *chaebols'* share of manufacturing capacity and GNP, 1985

	Manufacturing value added	Sector fixed capital	Share of GNP	No. of subsidiaries
Top 5 *chaebols*	18.7	20.4	5.5	94
Top 10	24.2	27.9	7.1	147
Top 20	29.5	34.4	8.6	218
Top 30	33.1	39.6	9.7	270

Sources: Lee (1987), Bank of Korea, *Economic Statistics Yearbook* (1987).

There were a number of arguments for and against the expansion of *chaebols* in Korea. One criticism, especially by non-economists, was that the *chaebols* were apt to engage in predatory or exclusionary activities and were exploiting small industries. Another was the danger that they would exert too much control over the economy and the government. On the positive side the *chaebols* enabled Korea to compete with Japan and other advanced countries. The markets of the *chaebols* were primarily global and therefore their market concentration had to be judged on this basis and not simply in connection with the domestic market. Furthermore they imported foreign technology and provided training for both workers and entrepreneurs; they were mobilisers and repositories of managerial and entrepreneurial talent; and they were more efficient than small firms.

The development of the *chaebols* was rooted in the country's need to escape grinding poverty, to overtake and outperform North Korea, to import foreign technology and to overcome its lack of natural resources – all in a short period of time. They obtained special favours from the government that small firms did not, so their growth was artificially high. However the promotion of a competitive market environment became increasingly essential to Korea's free enterprise market economy and this had important implications for the further development of *chaebols*.

2.4.4 Korean industrial policy: a comparison with Japan

A key element of Korean industrial policy, especially during 1962–79, was government – business cooperation, in which the government clearly took the lead and business followed. In this the main government figure was the president himself, supported by the Economic Planning Board and the Ministry of Trade and Industry. In the case of Japan, large privately owned banks were important partners in the government – business cooperative effort, but in Korea the banks were small and government run, and as such played only a subordinate, largely implementing role in the process.

The objectives of the Korean and Japanese industrialisation policies differed in that Japan's goal was to catch up with the advanced countries while Korea's was to increases its export manufacturing capacity as much as possible and to catch up with North Korea's lead in industrialisation. Industrial policy in Japan did not focus on promoting selected infant industries, rather it sought to promote the entire modern manufacturing sector. Korea's policy was also broadly directed, but since virtually all industries were at the infant stage it tended to promote those which offered the most promise at any given stage.

Import substitution in Japan was closely linked to export promotion, but in Korea export promotion was accompanied by the importation of inputs. As discussed earlier, firms were allowed to import the raw materials, parts and machinery required for export production, up to the value of their export earnings. This was the main reason why imports increased rapidly with the rise in exports, and why the trade deficit grew sharply between 1962 and 1985. Import substitution, as such, was not considered an explicit policy objective after the adoption of the export-oriented growth strategy.

Japan's huge domestic market (over 100 million people) facilitated export promotion in that any firm that could compete successfully with other firms in the domestic market was well positioned to do the same with foreign firms in overseas markets. In Korea, however, many firms entered the global market from the start because domestic demand was very small, especially in the case of heavy industrial goods. After they had succeeded overseas they began to cater to the pent-up domestic demand that had been preserved for them by tariff and other barriers against non-essential consumer imports. Examples included colour televisions and high-quality garments.

The relationship between export expansion and domestic demand was very strong in Japan and this facilitated high economic growth. Because a large proportion of the parts and machinery required for the production of export commodities could be produced domestically by Japanese firms there were considerable interindustry linkages among Japanese industries. But in Korea there were few interindustry linkages. Finally, the high growth in Japan was not merely export led, to a large extent it was also investment led. In Korea, where the domestic market was relatively small, the investment aspect was weaker.[6]

2.5 Economic planning and policy formulation

The developments discussed in this chapter occurred in the context of a series of economic plans prepared by the government in conjunction with other interested parties. This section looks at the planning framework within which the economic growth and industrialisation of the economy took place. It outlines the major plans, their objectives, policies and outcomes. It also considers the measures adopted by the government to ensure compliance by the business sector, and then contrasts this with the planning framework adopted by Japan during its period of rapid growth.

2.5.1 Economic planning

Formal economic planning started with the first five-year economic development plan (1962–66). Plans had been drafted earlier but these had not been implemented because of the toppling of the Rhee Syngman government in 1960 and the shelving of a new five-year plan by Park Chung Hee's military government in 1961. The 1962–66 plan was carried through to completion. By the end of the 1980s, Korea had completed five five-year planning cycles, and was about to enter into the sixth five year Plan (1987–91).

The objectives of the successive plans, as shown in Table 2.15, changed over time with income growth, shifts in the economic structure and changes in economic issues and priorities. These changing objectives can be examined in relation to four major governmental functions: creating economic and legal frameworks, ensuring stability, promoting efficiency and promoting equity.

First five-year plan (1962–66)

The first plan, which was prepared in a hurry when the military government seized power in 1961, is considered to have been the worst of the six plans. It was no more than a list of the costs and projected outputs of future development projects, plus policy proposals to achieve the maximum growth of exports, income and employment.

The main objectives of the first plan were to alleviate poverty and build the necessary foundation for self-sustaining growth. To this end it was necessary to establish economic and legal frameworks, which is perhaps the most important task for poor countries starting out on the road to economic development.

The legal framework determined the scope of property rights, regulations on business activities and the nature of contracts. The fiscal and financial policies largely involved reform of the tax, budgetary and monetary systems, the financial markets and the foreign exchange system. Trade policy was aimed at expanding exports as much and as quickly as possible by providing export manufacturers with cheap loans, tax benefits, compensation schemes and various types of administrative support.

The rapid expansion of both exports and output was accompanied by a rapid increase in prices so inflation became very severe towards the end of the first plan, exceeding 30 per cent in 1964. As a consequence the government needed to take emergency measures to stabilise prices.

Second five-year plan (1966–71)

The second plan was aimed mainly at promoting the efficient allocation of resources through agricultural, industrial, trade and social infrastructure policies.

Towards the end of the previous plan the government had introduced various policy measures to stabilise prices and facilitate sound economic growth. These included a September 1965 financial reform to ensure positive and realistic interest rates, a March 1965 exchange rate reform that normalised the highly overvalued exchange rates, a 1964 trade reform to allow the importation of parts and machinery used in the production of export goods, and a 1965 fiscal reform to stabilise government expenditure. All these were included and extended in the second plan. They resulted in the rapid growth of exports and GDP, stable prices and higher domestic savings. But as investment requirements greatly exceeded domestic savings

Table 2.15 Overview of Korea's Five Year Plans

Plan	Period	Growth rate	Objectives	Major policy objectives
First FYP	1962–66	7.1* 7.9**	1. Breaking the vicious circle of poverty 2. Establishing the foundations for self sustaining economic development	1 Securing energy supply sources 2 Correcting structural imbalances 3. Expanding basic industries and infrastructure 4. Effective mobilisation of idle resources 5. Improving the balance of payments position 6. Promoting technology
Second FYP	1967–71	7* 9.7**	1. Modernisation of industrial structure 2. Promotion of self sustaining economic development	1. Self sufficiency in food, development of fisheries and forestry 2 Laying the foundation for industrialisation 3. Improving the balance of payments position 4. Employment creation, family planning and population control 5. Raising farm household income 6. Improving technology and productivity
Third FYP	1972–76	8.6* 10.2**	1. Harmonising growth, stability, and equity 2. Realising a self reliant economy 3. Comprehensive national land development and balanced regional development	1. Self sufficiency in staple food 2 Improving the living environment in rural areas 3. Promotion of heavy and chemical industries 4. Improving science, technology and human resources 5. Development of national land resources and efficient spatial distribution of industries 6. Improving the living environment and national welfare

Table 2.15 Overview of Korea's Five Year Plans (*continued*)

Plan	Period	Growth rate	Objectives	Major policy objectives
Fourth FYP	1977–81	9.2* 5.7**	1. Achievement of a self-sustaining economy 2 Promoting equity through social development 3. Promoting technology and improving efficiency	1. Self sufficiency in investment capital 2. Achieving balance of payments equilibrium 3. Industrial restucturing and promoting international competitiveness 4. Employment expansion and manpower development 5. Improving the living environment 6. Expanding investment for science and technology 7. Improving economic management and institutions
Fifth FYP	1982–86	7.5* 8.7**	1. Establishing the foundations for price stability and a self sustaining economy 2. Technology improvement 3. Improving the quality of life 4. Restructuring government's economic functions	1. Eradicating inflation oriented economic behaviour 2 Increasing competitiveness in heavy industries 3. Improving agricultural policy 4. Overcoming energy constraints 5. Improving financial institutions 6. Readjusting government functions and rationalising fiscal management 7. Solidifying the competitive system and promoting an open door policy 8. Manpower development and the promotion of science and technology

Table 2.15 An overview of Korea's Five Year Plans (*continued*)

Plan	Period	Growth rate	Objectives	Major policy objectives
				9. Establishing new labour relations 10. Expanding social development
Sixth FYP	1987–91	7.3*	1. Establishing a socio-economic system promoting creative potential and initiative 2. Industrial restructuring and improvement of technology. 3. Improving national welfare through balanced regional development and income distribution	1. Expanding employment opportunities 2. Solidifying the foundation for price stability 3. Realising balance of payments surplus and reducing foreign debt 4. Industrial restructuring and technology improvement 5. Balanced regional and rural development 6. Improving national welfare through improved social equity 7. Promoting the market economic system and readjusting government functions

Notes:
1. Prepared from the successive five year plans formulated by the Economic Planning Board.
2. Goals and major policy issues of the Fifth Five Year Plan (1982–86) are those of the Revised Five Year Plan (1984–86).
3. See Economic Planning Board, 1961, 1966, 1971, 1976, 1981, and 1986.

* Planned growth rate
** Actual growth rate

Source: Song (1990) Table 8.1, pp. 130–3.

there was a need to increase domestic savings (and thereby reduce foreign borrowing) even further. Another negative factor was that the rapid growth of the economy had resulted in a growing disparity between income classes, between export and domestic industries, between firms of different sizes, and between regions.

Third five-year plan (1972–76)

The third plan emphasised the promotion of heavy and chemical industries (HCIs), so 1972 marked the start of Korea's HCI drive. Accordingly the provision of loans, special depreciation allowances, low tax rates, improved public services and administrative support to HCIs constituted the core of economic policies during the third plan period. A great effort was made to raise domestic savings to finance the HCI drive, but again savings fell far short of investment requirements. As a consequence foreign borrowing increased enormously and the management of foreign borrowing and debt emerged as a major issue.

As industrial growth had caused the gap between the urban industrial and the rural agricultural sectors to increase substantially since the early 1960s the promotion of equity was an important policy issue in the third plan. A farm price support policy had been implemented in 1969 and was one of the major causes of government budget deficits, but it had failed to eliminate the rural – urban disparity. Hence more systematic measures were necessary and in 1971 the government introduced the New Village Movement (NVM) to improve the income and living conditions of rural people. The NVM, together with the HCI drive, represented a serious nationwide effort to increase the income and equity of the Korean people throughout the 1970s.

The first oil crisis of 1973 had a profound effect on Korea. The economy became highly unstable and inflation exceeded 20 per cent. Thus the control of supply-side inflation emerged as a new issue to be addressed, along with the control of existing inflation, which was largely due to demand-side factors.

Fourth five-year plan (1977–81)

Income distribution was given even greater priority in the fourth plan and the government's focus shifted from the quantitative aspects of economic growth to the qualitative aspects of life. The fourth plan placed great emphasis on social development and was even officially named the Five-Year Socio-Economic Development Plan.

In addition, because of the high inflation caused by the first oil price shock and demand-side factors, stability was given relatively high priority in the fourth plan. One related measure was to fix money supply growth at a constant rate of 20 per cent per annum in order to stabilise the money supply, prices and the overall economy. Another was the adoption of value added tax.

The major changes in trade policy during the fourth plan period included the expansion of 'policy imports' (imports related to exports), the maintenance of competitive exchange rates, and an increase in export subsidies, tax benefits and foreign loans to export firms. Indirect support in the form of manpower training and R&D was also increased, as were administrative support and the number of industrial estates and free export zones.

The general trading company system, introduced in 1975, was further expanded to boost trade in the world markets

Fifth five-year plan (1982–86)

In the early 1980s the economy was characterised by relatively slow growth, rapidly growing foreign debt and high inflation, so the need to speed up export-led growth became ever greater. Related trade policies included extensive promotion of export goods and market diversification, reform of the export support systems, lowering the tariff rates on imported goods used in manufacturing, and increasing loans to producers of durable export goods such as machinery and ships.

Foreign debt management was also given high priority. The goals of the debt-management policy were to reduce the debt service ratio from 13.2 per cent to 11.1 per cent during the period of the plan, and consequently to boost the still flagging domestic savings rate.

Fiscal policy consisted largely of reducing fiscal expenditure, expanding depreciation allowances and R&D-related tax benefits to export firms, and tax reforms aimed at improving income distribution. Monetary policy involved upwardly adjusting the annual money supply growth rate to 22 per cent and switching from direct to indirect controls. Emphasis was also placed on the development of financial markets.

After 1986 Korea experienced large trade surpluses and a strong economic performance. There were two reasons for this: the favourable external conditions known as the three lows – low oil and natural gas prices, the low value of the dollar, and low international interest rates – which gave a great boost to the Korean economy, especially through exports; and the sweeping economic reforms carried out by the government in the early 1980s to achieve price stability and improve efficiency through competition. Tight monetary and fiscal policies brought inflation, measured in wholesale prices, down from 39 per cent in 1980 to –1.5 per cent in 1986. At the same time the fiscal deficit was reduced from 4.7 per cent of GNP to 0.1 per cent. Other measures included the privatisation of government-owned banks and public enterprises, reducing or removing various administrative controls, and the enactment of the Fair Trade and Anti monopoly Law in 1981. Imports and foreign investment were also liberalised to introduce foreign competition. It was thought that this would promote efficiency at home, which in turn would translate into greater external competitiveness. The government also liberalised foreign investment through a 'negative list' system in which industries not on the list were made open to foreign investment. By the late 1980s, 97.5 per cent of all manufacturing industries were open to foreign investment.

Industrial policy was also restructured. As the international competitiveness of Korean firms improved the government switched from supporting specific industries with preferential loans and interest rates to a more general policy of providing technical assistance, information and man-power training. It also dropped its policy of giving preferential treatment only to larger firms and adopted a more balanced policy that was designed to promote SMEs as well.

Sixth five-year plan (1987–91)

In the late 1980s, stability emerged once again as one of the most important policy objectives. Both policy makers and the Korean people saw economic stability, especially in the face of growing labour–management friction, as a key policy goal.

The broad goal of the sixth plan was to enhance the efficiency and strengthen the international competitiveness of the economy in general by reforming the free enterprise system. This involved the drastic reduction of various government regulations that were constraining the growth of large enterprises, the extensive liberalisation of finance, imports and currency exchange, the gradual reduction of various fiscal subsidies, the privatisation of public enterprises, a shift from direct to indirect monetary controls, a reduction of foreign borrowing and improved exchange rate management.

During the period discussed in this section the relative importance of the public and private sectors changed substantially. During the early planning periods the public sector had played the dominant role as the market system was not well developed, but as the urban industrial sector expanded and the market system was modernised the part played by the private sector expanded greatly relative to that of the government. Enhancing free market competition and promoting creative potential and an innovative spirit were major goals of the sixth plan.

2.5.2 Planning implementation and compliance

One of the most important characteristics of the government's method of plan implementation was its extensive use of both incentive and disincentive measures, as alluded to earlier. Particularly during the period of highly centralised and growth-oriented development under President Park, the government made extensive use of its discretionary authority to manipulate subsidies, tax differentials and loans, and to terminate infrastructural services. Whenever incentive procedures were not proving effective the government was quick to employ disincentive mechanisms or command procedures to secure compliance by private firms. These disincentives usually took the following forms.

1 Tax audits

Systematic and detailed investigation of tax returns by the Office of Tax Administration were used to discipline firms that failed to comply with the government's economic policies. Such audits were usually very time consuming and sometimes lasted as long as six months. Korean firms came to see these investigations as akin to lethal punishment, and many were in fact driven into bankruptcy by protracted audits and investigations.

2 Suspension of bank credit or the recall of loans

The debt–equity ratio of most Korean firms was very high (usually exceeding three to one) as a result of massive borrowing, typically at artificially low rates, to finance expansion. This high degree of indebtedness meant that firms were dependent on bank credit even for their operating funds, and hence for their very survival. Consequently if the government cut off the supply of credit to a firm or recalled its loans, collapse was inevitable.

3 Disconnection of infrastructural services

Without basic infrastructural services such as electricity, water and telephones most firms would not be able to function. The Park government withdrew such services to punish firms that did not comply with its economic policies, so firms soon learned that in order to survive and prosper they had to comply with the government's directives. For this to work, effective communication and close consultation between firms and policy makers was essential.

As the economy became increasingly complex, however, non-discretionary rather than discretionary measures were adopted, and were judged by Korean businessmen to be a more desirable approach to policy implementation. This important change in economic management in the early 1980s represented a major shift towards a purely market-directed system and a readjustment of government functions.

2.5.3 Contrasts with Japan

Japan's economic development policies were governed more by a set of economic objectives than by discretionary measures such as those used in Korea under President Park. As Kosai and Ogino (1984) point out, the major objectives governing Japan's economic policies during its period of high economic growth (1955–70) were maintaining a stable exchange rate of 360 yen to the dollar, ensuring a balanced budget, keeping the tax burden below 20 per cent of the national income, and using monetary measures to keep the balance of payments at the target level. Because of these objectives there was far less scope for Japanese policy makers to use discretionary mechanisms than was the case in Korea. In both countries, however, excellent cooperation between government and private firms contributed greatly to the success of economic policies.

Not all government economic policies were chosen wisely, however. In the case of Korea the overexpansion of heavy industries and shipbuilding in the late 1970s was a direct result of excessive government direction. In addition the decision to delay development of the Korean car industry on the assumption that the country did not have a comparative advantage was, in hindsight, probably wrong. The success of the Japanese car industry was due more to increasingly fierce competition among domestic car manufacturers than to successful government promotion.

Other differences between Korea and Japan concern the economic roles played by small companies and households. In Japan small firms made a major contribution to the growth of the economy, and household savings were the main source of investment capital. In Korea, in contrast, the government relied chiefly on large companies to expand exports and household savings were insufficient to meet the country's investment requirements.

2.6 Summary

Korea's economic performance during the period 1962–89 can rightly be described as an economic miracle. From being a poverty stricken, inward looking and economically backward country in 1960, by 1989 it had transformed itself into a globally competitive economy. In 1989 its GDP per capita was 65 times higher, its GDP 110 times higher and its export level 1860 times higher than they had been in 1960. Furthermore its domestic savings stood at 37.6 per cent of GNDI compared with just 9 per cent in 1960. The catalyst for this remarkable transformation was the government's economic growth and industrialisation development strategy, which was based on export expansion. Strong government direction and policy makers' considerable foresight ensured successful implementation of this strategy.

The strong focus on large rather than small enterprises until 1979 resulted in considerable market concentration and the development of *chaebols*, which were key players in the success of the export-oriented development plan. In the 1980s, with the economy beginning to resemble that of a developed country the government relaxed its tight control and left more to market forces. The development of a more competitive and liberalised economy had become paramount, as had the development of SMEs.

By the late 1980s Korea had accumulated a trade surplus and was becoming financially self-sufficient as the level of foreign debt fell. The future of the Korean economy at that time appeared to depend on how the country managed its transition to maturity. In this regard a number of issues were especially important: managing trade in the global context, conducting institutional reform, balancing equity and efficiency, fostering the development of the market economy and coping with capital market opening.

The following chapter analyses Korea's performance in the 1990s and the fading of its bright prospects.

3
The Fading Miracle, 1990–97

3.1 Introduction

This chapter proceeds as follows. Section 2 conducts a brief overview of Korea's macroeconomic performance during the 1990s. International trade, investment, debt and exchange rate developments are discussed in detail in Section 3, while the development of structural weaknesses in the economy is investigated in Section 4. Section 5 reviews other deficiencies in the economy during this period and policy weaknesses are discussed in Section 6. Section 7 compares the achievements of the Korean economy with that of the other so-called Tiger economies (Hong Kong, Singapore and Taiwan), the newly industrialising economies of South-East Asia (Malaysia, Thailand and Indonesia) and the developing economies of China and the Philippines. In doing so it identifies the early warning signs for the region in terms of slowing exports and GDP growth. Finally, Section 8 presents a summary of the major conclusions of this chapter.

3.2 Korea's macroeconomic performance during the 1990s

From the early 1960s Korea became one of the fastest growing economies in Asia, with an average annual rate of economic growth of 9 per cent. In the period 1990–97 the average real GDP growth rate was 7.3 per cent (Tables 3.1 and 3.13). In 1990–91 the 9 per cent growth rate was driven by a strong rise in investment[1] and consumption expenditure. The subsequent decline in 1992–93 was primarily due to a significant slowdown in these variables with the introduction of a stabilisation policy to reduce inflationary pressure. Growth increased again in 1994 following the implementation of an expansionary economic plan under the new government led by Kim Young Sam, the opening of domestic markets to increased foreign competition, the liberalisation of foreign capital inflows, a strong export performance (assisted by the high yen, which gave Korean exporters competitive advantage over Japanese exporters), a boom in construction and

Table 3.1 Macroeconomic indicators, 1990–97

	1990	1991	1992	1993	1994	1995	1996	1997
Nominal GDP ($ billion)	252.5	295.1	314.7	345.7	402.4	489.4	520.0	476.6
Per capita GDP ($)	5890	6816	7193	7822	9014	10853	11417	10363
GDP real growth rate (%)	9.0	9.2	5.4	5.5	8.3	8.9	6.8	5.0
Real growth in demand components (%)								
Private consumption	10.7	9.5	6.6	5.7	7.6	8.3	6.8	3.1
Government consumption	7.2	8.5	7.6	3.0	4.2	1.0	7.8	5.7
Gross fixed capital formation	25.9	12.6	–0.8	5.2	11.8	11.7	7.1	–3.5
Total domestic demand	13.1	11.3	3.4	4.3	10.2	8.3	8.2	–2.8
Exports of goods and services	4.2	11.8	11.0	11.3	16.5	24.0	13.0	23.6
Imports of goods and services	14.3	19.2	5.1	6.7	21.7	22.0	14.8	3.8
Industrial production (% growth)	9.0	9.5	5.9	4.3	10.9	11.9	7.7	6.8
Real growth in sectoral output (%)								
Manufacturing	9.2	9.5	5.3	5.4	10.8	11.3	6.8	6.6
Construction	25.5	15.1	–0.4	8.3	4.6	8.8	6.9	1.4
Agriculture, forestry and fishing	–5.9	2.9	9.6	–4.5	0.2	6.6	3.3	4.6
Services	9.3	10.3	7.0	7.2	10.3	9.6	7.8	5.4
Unemployment (%)	2.4	2.3	2.4	2.8	2.4	2.0	2.0	2.6
Productivity (GDP/employment)	6.3	6.0	3.1	4.1	5.4	6.0	5.1	4.1
Unit labour costs (compensation/GDP)	12.3	13.6	6.9	4.0	4.2	6.6	5.9	1.9
Investment rate (% of GNDI)	37.6	39.8	37.3	35.4	36.5	37.3	38.1	34.4
Savings rate (% of GNDI)	37.5	37.3	36.4	36.2	35.5	35.5	33.8	33.4
CPI (%)	8.5	9.3	6.3	4.8	6.2	4.5	4.9	4.5
Government fiscal balance (% of GDP)	–0.7	–1.6	–0.5	0.6	0.3	0.3	0.5	0.3
Interest rate (%)								
Corporate bond yields	16.5	18.9	16.2	12.6	12.9	13.7	11.8	13.4
Stock market price index	696	611	678	866	1027	883	651	376

Sources: Bank of Korea; Korea Development Institute.

domestic infrastructural investment, and a steady increase in private consumption. Growth peaked in 1995 and the economy began to slow in 1996 due to a rapid decline in both consumption and investment expenditure and particularly weak export growth. The primary source of growth over the entire period was the manufacturing sector, although its contribution declined in 1996 and 1997. The service sector also made a significant contribution to economic growth during the period in question.

The main causes of the downturn after 1995 were as follows. First, there was a slump in export earning from semiconductors, metals and petrochemicals when Korea was hit by its worst terms of trade conditions since the oil shock of 1979. The spot price of industry standard 16M DRAM chips[2] fell from $54 to $8 during the course of 1996 and stayed at about that level in 1997. Consequently the share of semiconductor exports in total Korean exports fell from a record 21 per cent in 1995 to 18.9 per cent in 1996, despite a rise in the volume exported.

Second, the weakening of the yen in 1996 significantly eroded the price competitiveness of Korean products in world markets where they were competing against similarly priced but better quality Japanese products. Korean exporters were forced to reduce their prices, resulting in reduced corporate profits and adversely affecting the trade and current account balances (Table 3.2).

Third, the equipment and infrastructural investment boom of 1994 and 1995 came to an end. This resulted in excess capacity, which was exacerbated by an unanticipated reduction in global demand. The completion of several large-scale projects during 1994 and 1995 partly accounted for the lower growth of equipment investment and building construction in 1996. There was also a global oversupply of Korea's major exports, such as steel, cars and petrochemicals, which suppressed prices after 1996. So while Korea's export volumes increased substantially in 1997, company incomes fell dramatically. This had major financial repercussions on a number of the country's over-leveraged *chaebols*.

Finally, Korean businesses were increasingly suffering from high wages, high interest rates and high land prices, which were causing Korea to become the highest-cost country among the Asian Tigers. In addition, relatively poor efficiency, particularly in sectors such as banking, and excessively strict government regulations were creating an increasingly difficult and less competitive business environment. This not only deterred prospective foreign investors but also prompted some Korean companies to move to off-shore production locations.

Macroeconomic conditions continued to deteriorate in the early part of 1997, when the country experienced its worst labour unrest in history. For a number of weeks workers across the nation went on strike to protest against the introduction of a new law that made lay-offs easier and restricted union activities. The work stoppages caused an estimated $3.15 billion in lost

Table 3.2 Trade, balance of payments and exchange rate, 1990–1997 ($ billion)

	1990	1991	1992	1993	1994	1995	1996	1997
Merchandise exports (fob)	63.7	70.5	76.2	82.1	95.0	124.6	130.0	138.6
Merchandise imports (fob)	66.1	77.3	78.0	79.8	97.8	129.1	144.9	141.8
Trade balance	–2.5	–6.8	–1.8	2.3	–2.9	–4.4	–15.0	–3.2
Invisibles balance	0.5	–1.5	–2.2	–1.3	–1.0	–4.1	–8.1	–5.0
Current account balance	–2.0	–8.3	–3.9	1.0	–3.9	–8.5	–23.0	–8.2
(% of GDP)	–0.8	–2.8	–1.3	0.3	–1.0	–1.9	–4.7	–1.8
Exports	65.0	71.9	76.6	82.2	96.0	125.1	129.7	136.2
(% change from previous year)	4.2	10.5	6.6	7.3	16.8	30.3	3.7	5.0
Imports (cif)	69.8	81.5	81.8	83.8	102.3	135.1	150.3	144.6
(% change from previous year)	13.5	16.8	0.4	2.4	22.1	32.1	11.3	–3.8
Gross external debt	31.9	39.3	42.6	43.9	56.9	78.4	104.7	120.8
Net external debt	4.9	12.5	11.0	7.9	10.3	17.1	34.7	55.7
Foreign-exchange reserves	14.5	13.3	16.6	19.7	25.0	31.9	33.2	19.7
Gold and foreign exchange reserves	14.8	13.7	17.2	20.3	25.7	32.7	33.2	20.4
Total debt (% of GDP)	12.6	13.3	13.5	12.7	14.1	16.0	20.1	25.3
Short-term debt (% of total debt)	30.9	28.2	27.1	25.8	43.6	54.2	57.5	39.3
Short-term debt/foreign exchange reserves (%)	74.5	84.2	71.7	61.9	126.4	146.1	200.6	273.1
Exchange rate: (won/$) (year end)	716.4	760.8	788.4	808.1	788.7	774.7	884.2	1695.0
Real exchange rate (1990 = 100) (year end)	100	99	94	93	91	88	88	157

Note: External liabilities calculated to IBRD standards.
Sources: IMF; Bank of Korea; Korean Development Institute.

output. Soon after this came the Hanbo debacle – on 23 January the country's second largest steel company collapsed under the weight of its $5.9 billion debt, and took with it its entire parent group, then the fourteenth largest *chaebol*, amid allegations of corruption against *chaebol* owners and government officials. A swift liquidity injection of 6 trillion won ($7 billion) by the Bank of Korea prevented a possible chain reaction of bankruptcies. This further undermined the country's already shaky financial system and many banks became loan shy. In addition the extra liquidity in the system deepened inflationary concerns, and achievement of the government's CPI target of 4.5 per cent for 1997 appeared unlikely.

These developments contributed to the generally gloomy economic outlook during the first months of 1997, but prospects looked decidedly worse by late October 1997 as there was doubt about Korea's ability to service its foreign debt[3], 60 per cent of which had a short-term maturity of 12 months or less. At that point the currency contagion afflicting East Asia finally hit the Korean currency and stock markets. All this, in conjunction with the implementation of reforms under the conditions of the IMF rescue programme, contributed to GDP growth slowing to 5 per cent in 1997.

Despite the fluctuations in GDP the unemployment rate remained low during the early and mid 1990s: just 2 per cent in 1995–96 and rising a mere 0.6 percentage points in 1997.[4] Considering that the natural rate of unemployment in Korea was in the region of 2.3–2.5 per cent, the actual unemployment rate was remarkably low.[5]

Productivity appeared to vary according to the stage of the business cycle, improving during upturns and declining during down turns. Likewise unit labour costs reflected fluctuations in the growth cycle, rising noticeably during the high-growth periods of 1990–91 and 1994–95 but slowing during the downturns in 1992–93 and 1996–97.

A major and growing strength of the Korean economy, particularly from the mid 1980s and even more so during the 1990s, was the country's high level of savings. As Table 3.1 shows, the savings rate remained at around 33.4–37.5 per cent of GNDI during the 1990s, enabling the country to maintain its very high investment rate of around 34.4–39.8 per cent of GNDI. However questions could be asked about the efficient use of these funds.

Consumer price inflation (CPI) generally followed a downward trend during the 1990s (Table 3.1), apart from a slight rise in 1994. Price stability was the government's primary focus during 1996, and stable agricultural prices, increased competition from imports and subdued consumption led to lower price increases in 1996, particularly in the second half of the year.

The government's fiscal position was also strong throughout the 1990s. The modest deficits in 1990–92 turned into modest surpluses in 1993–97, which reflected the prudent monetary and fiscal policies pursued by the authorities during this period. In 1996, for example, Korea's general government outlays and government gross debt were the lowest of all the

OECD countries (see OECD, 1998, p. 43). Its financial balance was in surplus and its net debt was actually negative.[6]

Corporate bond yields ranged from 11.8–18.9 per cent during the 1990s, while fluctuating nominal interest rates, in conjunction with generally declining inflation rates, contributed to quite volatile real interest rates, particularly in the latter half of the decade. This caused major problems for the heavily leveraged *chaebols*, and imposed a further burden on less favoured SMEs during periods when real interest rates were rising. The deterioration of the financial markets from late October 1997 and compliance with the terms of the IMF rescue package resulted in interest rates rising to over 25 per cent, creating even more problems for the heavily leveraged corporate sector.

The domestic stock markets also experienced a roller-coaster ride during this decade. The stock market price index remained relatively stable in 1990–92, increased dramatically in 1993–94 and then slid steadily downhill, culminating in the crash of 1997. The latter and subsequent developments will be discussed further in Chapter 4.

3.3 External developments

For Korea, as for the other Tiger Economies, international trade was the key to success. By the mid 1990s Korea had emerged as a major trading nation. It was the world's twelfth largest exporter by value (129.7 billion in 1996), enjoyed a 2.4 per cent share of world exports, and was the world's eleventh largest importing nation by value ($150.3 billion, equivalent to 2.8 per cent of world imports). This section briefly reviews the international trade and investment developments that took place during the 1990s.

3.3.1 International trade flows

During the 1990s export growth rates remained high, with the exception of the general slowdown in 1996 and 1997. However this was accompanied by equally rapid import growth (Table 3.2) and as a consequence the country ran persistent trade and current account deficits in all years but 1993. After 1995 there was a considerable deterioration in the current account deficit, which rose from $8.5 billion (1.9 per cent of GDP) to a blow-out $23 billion (4.7 per cent of GDP) in 1996.

The country's emphasis on heavy industry at the expense of light industry, and manufacturing at the expense of services, is most clearly demonstrated by its over-dependence on exports such as cars, ships, steel, petrochemicals and semiconductors.[7] This made the country particularly susceptible to changes in the global prices of these goods. As shown in Table 3.3, in 1990 machinery, transport equipment, manufactured goods and chemicals represented 93.4 per cent of total exports, and their contribution remained around 90 per cent in 1996–97.[8] During 1995–96 the global decline in the demand for and price of DRAM semiconductors, the fall in the price of steel, rising labour costs, declining per capita productivity and the weakening of the Japanese yen combined to reduce the growth of export value and competitiveness and contributed heavily to the current account deficit and the slowdown of GDP growth. The impact on the Korean economy of the fall in the spot price of standard 16M DRAM chips from $54 to $8 in 1996 has been placed on a par with the effects of the oil price shocks in 1973 and 1979. Many Korean firms were hit hard. For instance Samsung's profits on semiconductors fell from $3 billion in 1995 to a mere $190 million in 1996 – a drop of 93 per cent. It is estimated that 90 per cent of the increase in the current account deficit in 1996 was attributable to this drop in export prices. While export values improved modestly in 1997, the slowdown in the economy resulted in a fall in imports and a significant reduction of the current account deficit (to $8.2 billion, or 1.8 per cent of GDP).

Imports, with the exception of 1992, 1993 and 1997 also grew rapidly during the 1990s, but most notably in the period 1994–96 (Table 3.2). In 1995 the value of imports amounted to $135.1 billion, fuelled by an increased demand for capital goods (32.5 per cent), industrial materials (32.6 per cent) and consumer goods (27.8 per cent). Substantial imports of machinery and equipment were apparent throughout the 1990s and represented an increasing proportion of total imports. These were essential to the expansion and upgrading of production facilities, but they considerably worsened the country's trade balance. The reduction of tariff barriers between 1988 and 1996 (Table 3.4) also contributed to this surge in

Table 3.3 Exports and imports by commodity group, 1990–97 (percentage of total exports and imports)

	1990	1991	1992	1993	1994	1995	1996	1997
Major exports:								
Machinery and transport equipment	37.7	36.6	41.6	44.9	49.0	52.5	52.1	50.0
Manufactured goods	52.4	46.0	46.5	42.5	38.0	32.7	30.2	30.2
Chemicals	3.3	3.7	4.4	6.0	6.6	7.1	7.0	7.8
Mineral fuels	1.1	1.1	2.1	2.3	1.8	1.9	3.0	3.9
Major imports:								
Machinery and transport equipment	32.7	32.8	33.3	33.9	36.5	36.6	36.3	33.7
Manufactured goods	21.5	20.7	22.6	21.7	23.5	23.7	21.9	21.3
Mineral fuels	12.4	15.9	15.6	18.0	15.1	14.1	16.1	18.9
Raw materials	14.2	12.2	10.9	10.6	9.2	8.7	8.1	7.5
Chemicals	11.6	10.3	10.0	9.8	9.5	9.7	8.8	9.1

Sources: Korean Customs Service; Korean International Trade Association.

Table 3.4 International tariff barriers, 1988 and 1996 (average tariffs, %)

	1988	1996
Australia	15.6	5.0
Canada	3.7	1.6
Chile	19.9	11.0
China	39.5	23.0
European Union	5.7	3.6
Hong Kong	0.0	0.0
Indonesia	18.1	13.1
Japan	4.3	4.0
Korea	19.2	7.9
Malaysia	13.6	9.0
Mexico	10.5	9.8
New Zealand	14.9	5.7
Philippines	27.9	15.6
Singapore	0.3	0.0
Taiwan	12.6	8.6
Thailand	31.2	17.0
USA	4.2	3.4

Sources: Manila Action Plan for APEC; EU sources.

imports. Economic reforms, as well as further reductions in tariff barriers, were seen as vital to the international competitiveness of domestic companies and the integration of Korea into the global economy.

Developments in Korea's import structure therefore reflected its restructuring efforts. As its production capability shifted to higher value added items, imported items followed suit, causing a rising trade deficit with developed countries. In 1995 this deficit stood at $29.1 billion compared with a trade surplus of $19.2 billion with developing countries. Import growth fell from 32.1 per cent in 1995 to 11.3 per cent in 1996 in response to weaker investment and slower export growth. However imports of consumer goods rose by 22 per cent, in part due to the removal of import barriers, increasing affluence and a decline in loyalty to domestic products. With the onset of the financial crisis in 1997 import growth plummeted to –3.8 per cent.[9]

3.3.2 Direction of trade flows

Korea's major trading partners during the 1990s are shown in Table 3.5. The USA, Japan and the EU together accounted for about a half of Korea's total trade in 1996 and about 46 per cent in 1997. Despite the dominance of these three economic superpowers there was a clear move away from the mature markets of the USA and Japan where Korean products faced severe competition, and towards emerging markets such as China, Eastern Europe, South-East Asia and South America. In 1996 developing countries

Table 3.5 Major trading partners, 1990–97 (percentage of total trade)

	1990	1991	1992	1993	1994	1995	1996	1997
USA	29.5	26.9	24.4	21.7	21.2	21.0	19.6	18.4
Japan	22.6	23.1	21.8	19.0	19.6	19.1	16.8	15.2
EU	12.8	12.8	11.3	11.8	12.0	13.2	13.0	12.7
China	1.7	2.1	2.9	4.0	5.9	6.4	7.1	8.9
Hong Kong	3.2	3.3	3.6	4.4	4.4	4.4	4.3	4.5
Australia	2.6	2.6	2.6	2.7	2.5	2.5	2.9	2.9
Saudi Arabia	1.5	1.8	2.8	2.8	2.4	2.5	2.8	2.9

Source: National Statistical Office.

emerged as Korea's largest export destination, accounting for 50.9 per cent ($62.6 billion) of total exports (Table 3.6).

Another key feature of Korea's trade was the large deficits it had with the USA, the EU and Japan and the large surpluses it had with developing countries. For example its total trade with the ASEAN countries reached $32.3 billion in 1996, with exports of $20.2 billion and imports of $12.1 billion, making the ASEAN countries Korea's fourth largest trading partner after the USA, Japan and the EU. The ASEAN region was also a major destination for Korean investment and technological expertise, which drove exports of machinery and electronic components. It was also an important destination for Korea's construction orders, which totalled $4 billion in 1996. Hence this market had assumed huge importance and consequently the financial and economic crisis in the ASEAN countries during 1997 and 1998 was of particular concern to Korea.

Table 3.6 Export destinations, 1995–98 (percentage of total)

	1995	1996	1997	1998
Industrial countries	48.6	42.7	44.1	48.1
Australia	1.3	1.4	1.6	2.1
Canada	1.4	0.9	1.1	1.2
EU	12.2	10.8	12.4	13.8
Japan	13.6	12.3	10.9	9.3
USA	19.3	16.7	16.1	17.4
Developing countries	46.4	50.9	55.7	51.8
Africa	1.2	1.1	2.4	2.4
Asia	35.1	37.8	39.1	34.0
Of which China	7.3	8.8	10.0	9.0
Europe	2.2	3.1	4.6	4.2
Middle East	3.1	3.4	3.6	4.7
Western hemisphere	4.7	5.5	6.1	6.5
Other	5.0	6.4	0.1	0.1

Sources: IMF (1999d); Bank of Korea.

Table 3.7 Imports by country of origin, 1995–98 (percentage of total)

	1995	1996	1997	1998
Industrial countries	67.4	65.3	61.4	61.3
EU	13.4	14.1	13.1	11.7
Japan	24.1	20.9	19.3	18.1
USA	22.5	22.1	20.8	21.9
Developing countries	29.4	31.4	38.5	38.7
Africa	1.5	1.3	1.7	1.8
Asia	16.0	16.7	19.0	20.2
Europe	1.5	1.3	1.7	1.8
Middle East	8.6	9.7	11.8	12.1
Western Hemisphere	2.4	2.5	2.8	2.3
Other	3.2	3.3	0.0	0.0

Source: IMF (1999d); Bank of Korea.

Imports also showed a move towards developing countries (Table 3.7), although overall imports were still dominated by the USA, Japan and the EU. This was because Korea's efforts to enhance its global competitiveness and move into higher value added production required the importation of technologically advanced equipment and machinery that could only be obtained from these economies.

3.3.3 International investment

The extent of foreign direct investment (FDI) in Korea and Korean investment overseas is shown in Tables 3.8 and 3.9. As can be seen from Table 3.8, the extent of FDI in Korea was very low in the early 1990s, certainly in comparison with elsewhere in the region. This reflects the general perception by overseas investors that Korea was not an attractive country in which to invest. There were several reasons for this, including high wages, expensive finance, abuse of intellectual property rights, the requirement that profits be reinvested, and excessive government regulation. Such problems required urgent attention by the authorities, given the important role that FDI could play in upgrading the technology used in the country. However Korea was less than receptive to FDI and preferred to rely on domestic savings, foreign borrowing by the financial sector and state-directed loans to industry. This policy meant that it missed out on the transfer of technology, management expertise and marketing know-how that FDI could bring.

From the mid 1990s, however, FDI emerged as a central pillar of economic policy. In an effort to restructure industry by means of high technology transfers from advanced countries, the government set out to attract foreign investors and encourage Korean corporations to enter into strategic alliances with foreign companies. Towards this end, in late 1994 it reduced corporate tax on firms with foreign investors, relaxed the regulations on foreign ownership of land and simplified the approval procedure. A particular effort was made to attract Japanese investment in the manufacture of car parts, electric/electronic parts and machinery as Japanese manufacturers were relocating their production bases to overseas countries in order to counteract the increased production costs arising from the strength of the yen. The government's efforts soon bore fruit and FDI began to flow in. In 1995 FDI accounted for 578 projects/transactions valued at $1.9 billion, an increase from $1.3 billion in 1994 and almost double the flow in 1993. In 1996 it reached $3.2 billion, in 1997 $7 billion and in 1998 $8.9 billion (Table 3.8).

As Table 3.8 shows, FDI in Korea was predominantly from developed economies, with the USA, Japan and Europe contributing 79 per cent of the total FDI inflow in 1995, 68 per cent in 1996, 84 per cent in 1997 and 73 per cent in 1998. By sector, investment in chemicals, foodstuffs and electronics remained strong until 1996, but in 1997 hotels and tourism rose to dominance. However the pattern remained variable.

With the onset of the financial crisis in November 1997[10] the government recognised that foreign investment would be essential to Korea's restructuring and recovery programme. The immediate objectives would be to put Korean companies onto a sound financial footing and to undertake

Table 3.8 Foreign direct investment in Korea, 1993–98 ($ billion)

	1993	1994	1995	1996	1997	1998
By source country:						
USA	341	311	645	876	3189	2975
Japan	286	428	418	255	266	504
Europe	307	407	475	1058	2409	2968
Other	110	170	403	1014	1107	2405
Total	1044	1316	1941	3203	6971	8852
By industry:						
Chemicals		107	174	389	235	755
Foodstuffs		18	15	253	851	719
Pharmaceuticals		38	65	32	44	134
Metal		7	7	13	14	7
Machinery		49	102	159	166	587
Electronics		63	228	436	291	1377
Financial services		294	378	250	265	506
Hotels and tourism		293	216	228	2596	303
Construction		7	11	32	64	5
Other		440	745	1411	2445	4459
Total		1316	1941	3203	6971	8852

Source: Ministry of Finance and Economy.

economic restructuring. Other factors in the attraction of FDI were the transfer of technology and know-how, and access to foreign supply chains. To this end foreign investment was further liberalised[11] and in May 1998 Korea boasted a 98 per cent liberalisation rate, which meant that of the 1600 industrial sectors classified by the government only 31 were closed to FDI. Just a few years previously the figure had been around 85 per cent. The excluded industries were those with national security or cultural considerations (for example coastal fisheries, the media) and those for which FDI was subject to international negotiations (for example communications and shipping).

The FDI application procedure was simplified and the law amended so that foreigners would be treated the same as nationals in respect of the purchase of land and real estate. The government also continued to offer incentives to foreign companies in high technology industries and those in designated export zones. These include company and income tax exemptions and low land rent. In addition local governments were allowed to establish free investment zones in order to attract FDI. Change also occurred at the social level, with the historical resistance to foreign investors crumbling in the face of rising unemployment.

As a consequence of the easing of the regulatory regime, the cumulative stock of outward investment by Korean companies had risen to $10.2 billion by the end of 1995, with North America accounting for 14.2 per cent of the total. However, in terms of recent Korean investment overseas an increasingly clearer pattern has emerged. As can be seen from Table 3.9, in 1995 investment moved away from traditionally favoured destinations such as the USA to Asian countries, and China in particular. The overall share of investment in Asia other than China (primarily South-East Asia) remained remarkably stable during the 1990s at around 28–29 per cent of total investment overseas, while China emerged as a major recipient, with investment rising from only $16 million in 1990 (or 1.7 per cent of total

Table 3.9 Outward foreign investment, 1990–97 ($ million)

	1990	1991	1992	1993	1994	1995	1996	1997
Asia (excl. China)	275	384	380	237	518	884	869	943
China	16	42	141	264	632	824	836	633
Middle East	40	59	75	86	38	32	26	69
North America	438	459	391	390	567	545	1552	736
Latin America	67	42	37	44	49	120	256	258
Europe	64	89	143	175	357	585	590	349
Africa	27	18	29	31	114	42	12	109
Oceania	32	23	24	35	25	39	72	129
Total	959	1115	1219	1262	2300	3070	4214	3227

Source: Export–Import Bank of Korea.

investment) to $824 million in 1995 (28.6 per cent of total investment). However in 1997 there was a reversal of this trend and investment in China fell to $633 or 19.6 per cent of the total.

The overall increases in overseas investment reflected the growing concern among labour-intensive manufacturers, particularly, SMEs producing textiles, footwear and fabricated metals, about their loss of competitiveness due to rising domestic wages. To counteract this many companies relocated some of their manufacturing and assembly facilities in lower-cost countries such as China, Vietnam, Indonesia and, more recently, North Korea. China was particularly seen as a desirable country for investment because of its proximity to Korea, its cheap labour and its huge market potential. Asia, including China, received about 50 per cent of total overseas investment in 1997 compared with only 30 per cent in 1990. Conversely investment in North America fell from 45.7 per cent of total investment in 1990 to 23 per cent in 1997.

From 10 October 1995 all Korean companies were required to fund at least 20 per cent of overseas projects costing $100 million or more from domestic lenders or from their own capital or cash reserves. This policy was designed to put a check on Korea's increasing foreign debt and to allay the government's concern that many companies were overextending themselves.

3.3.4 External debt

As Table 3.2 shows, Korea's gross foreign debt increased steadily during the 1990s, with the most significant increase taking place from 1994 onwards.[12] Gross foreign debt had increased to $105 billion by the end of 1996, almost double that in 1994 and equivalent to 20.1 per cent of GDP, compared with around 12.6 per cent of GDP at the end of 1990. The increase was due mostly to a significant deterioration of the trade deficit and increased borrowing from overseas to meet facility investment needs. By the end of 1997 gross foreign debt stood at $120.8 billion, equivalent to 25.3 per cent of GDP. Net foreign debt also increased steadily during the 1990s. The government was concerned not only with the build-up of this debt, but also with its increasingly short-term nature and the country's ability to repay it. Short-term debt as a proportion of total debt stood at 57.5 per cent by the end of 1996, up from around 30 per cent in the early 1990s.

The sharp rise in foreign debt, particularly short-term debt, was due to four factors. First, in 1993 the government permitted enterprises to borrow from abroad – either directly or through Korean banks – to finance imports of capital goods.[13] This only applied to loans with a maturity of less than one year – restrictions on long-term foreign loans were maintained.[14] Consequently there was a dramatic rise in short-term foreign borrowing to finance the industrial investment boom. In contrast to some South-East Asian countries, however, the increased debt did not lead to a speculative bubble in asset prices in Korea. Land prices, which had risen at a rapid pace in the second half of the 1980s and early 1990s, remained fairly stable prior to the crisis. Second, overseas borrowing was facilitated by an increase in the number of financial institutions dealing in foreign currency following the licensing of 24 merchant banks between 1994 and 1996.[15] Third, overseas borrowing was encouraged by the widespread perception that the won was undervalued during much of the 1990s. Finally, the implicit government backing of financial institutions encouraged high levels of borrowing by Korean banks and lending by their foreign creditors.

It was not just the rise in short-term debt that left Korea vulnerable to a financial crisis, but also the lack of sound risk management at banks, which were inexperienced in the field of overseas borrowing. In particular, the new merchant banks took on high levels of liquidity and exchange rate risk.[16] Moreover there was a lack of prudential supervision; basic regulations, such as capital adequacy ratios for merchant banks, did not exist.

Concern about the accumulation of short-term debt was compounded by the rapid deterioration of the country's foreign exchange reserves. This was of particular concern from 1994 onwards as short-term debt increasingly exceeded the foreign exchange reserves (Table 3.2). Although the latter accumulated rapidly during the 1990s to reach $33.2 billion by the end of 1996, short-term debt simultaneously rose to $93.3 billion. Worse still was the steep decline in foreign exchange reserves to $19.7 at the end of 1997. This was largely due to the Bank of Korea's aggressive intervention in the foreign currency market in an attempt to stabilise the value of the won in the face of a sizable deterioration in the current account position. By mid December 1997 the foreign reserves had fallen to the disastrously low level of $7 billion. It was therefore not surprising that investors began to lose confidence in the currency and the government had to turn to the IMF for financial assistance.

3.3.5 Exchange rate

The won continually depreciated against the US dollar in nominal terms during the early part of the 1990s, as can be seen in Table 3.2. With the weakening of the dollar against the Japanese yen, this implied a gain in competitiveness for Korean products relative to those of Japan. However in 1994–95 the won began to appreciate against the dollar, and with the dollar strengthening against all major international currencies this resulted in a loss of international competitiveness for Korea. Furthermore the strengthening of the won against the yen had major implications for Korea's competitiveness vis-à-vis Japan in Asian markets, as manifested in reduced export demand for goods such as steel, chemicals, consumer electronic products, petroleum products and plastics. This was offset to some extent by the benefits that flowed to the more technologically advanced Korean industries that were substantial importers of sophisticated Japanese capital goods and technology.

In 1996 the won depreciated sharply (by about 14 per cent) against the dollar. While this improved the price competitiveness of Korean exports it increased the repayment burden of foreign debt and the cost of imported raw materials. The key reasons for the depreciation were the strengthening of the US dollar, the increase in Korea's current account deficit and the fall in foreign capital inflows. More significantly for Korea's exports, the won–yen exchange rate showed no signs of improvement, with the depreciation of the won against the yen being offset by a sharp drop in the value of the yen against the dollar. With the onset of the financial crisis in 1997 there was a dramatic decline of some 91.7 per cent in the nominal value of the won relative to the dollar.

This brief overview of macroeconomic conditions in Korea prior to the onset of the crisis has highlighted some of the long-standing strengths that provided the basis of the country's high economic growth over some 35 years: strong export growth, moderate inflation, high levels of saving and investment, small external deficits and prudent fiscal policy, as exemplified by government financial surpluses. However it has also revealed a number of developments that led to the currency crisis: a drastic slowdown in export growth, particularly in 1996; a significant deterioration of the current account deficit, which became unsustainable in the medium to long term; overinvestment in the domestic economy, particularly in 1994 and 1995, which resulted in overcapacity and growing dependence on dollar-denominated foreign capital flows; and heavy reliance on short-term capital flows.

The following section looks in detail at structural weaknesses that are not made apparent by reviewing macroeconomic data alone.

3.4 Structural weaknesses

Korea's macroeconomic trends until October 1997 obscured the dichotomy between a benign real economy on the one hand, and weak profitability, an excessively indebted corporate sector and a poorly supervised and shaky financial system on the other. In the past, high GDP growth had masked many of Korea's financial problems, and perhaps lulled regulators and investors into a false sense of security. It gradually became clear, however, that certain structural weaknesses were making Korea increasingly vulnerable to financial turbulence. First, the corporate sector was characterised by low profitability and high debt, reflecting the tendency of the *chaebols* to diversify into capital-intensive industries. Second, Korea's already poorly functioning financial system was further weakened by a string of major corporate bankruptcies in 1997. Third, its short-term foreign debt was high relative to its international reserves, a consequence of its decision to liberalise short-term borrowing rather than FDI. This section explores each of these factors and their interrelatedness.

3.4.1 The chaebol–government–banking relationship

Many of the problems in Korea's industrial and financial sectors, particularly from the late 1980s, were due to the close relationship between the government, the banking sector and the *chaebols*.[17] While the government's industrialisation policy had produced rapid economic growth, by the 1990s the increasing complexity of the economy and developments in the global economy meant that Korea's institutional system had become outmoded.[18] This system contributed to a number of difficulties: inefficiency in resource allocation, excessively overleveraged and financially fragile enterprises, and emphasis on growth without due consideration of profits and risks. Furthermore the overly close relations between the government and the corporate sector resulted in institutionalised corruption[19] and complacency; the preferential treatment of the *chaebols* and their resulting dominance of the economy hindered entrepreneurialism and caused imbalances in the economy by constraining the growth of SMEs; the protection of domestic markets led to a general lack of competition; and the insufficient integration of the *chaebols* into the global economy caused a loss of international competitiveness

Capital, production and exports were heavily skewed towards the *chaebols*, which had a myriad of cross-guarantees on borrowing, plus limited transparency and accountability. The 'too big to fail' mentality of the *chaebols* resulted in excessive risk taking, overinvestment and insufficient attention to credit and exchange rate risks. The natural outcome of this was overindebtedness, overcapacity and poor earning power. In addition excessive government control of the banking system meant that banks paid more attention to government interventions than to profit-making business. This in turn resulted in misguided bank loans to non-viable or insolvent borrowers. In short, active government involvement in the market not only resulted in corruption but also caused inefficiency in the general economic sector and weakened the competitiveness of enterprises and banks. While some of these problems proved not to be significant in the context of Korea's growing economy, they left the country vulnerable to shocks in the increasingly globalised financial market. During the period of economic downturn in 1996 and 1997 they combined to produce severe difficulties for the economy.

3.4.2 The corporate sector

Korea's corporate sector was excessively indebted, a legacy of Korea's ambitious strategy of achieving rapid growth on a global scale by diversifying into capital-intensive industries in order to leap-frog up the value-added chain into higher technology products. Although this approach was successful in the 1970s and 1980s when domestic firms were relatively small, and when achieving economies of scale and establishing extensive distribution channels were essential to increased productivity and shareholder value, by the late 1980s the global competitive environment had changed radically and the strategy of debt-financed growth became increasingly risky in the face of falling profitability. It also proved ill-suited to the keenly competitive environment of the 1990s. Part of the dependence on debt also reflected supply-side factors, notably Korea's traditional aversion to FDI, its underdeveloped equity market and the tax advantages of debt financing. The corporate sector was characterised by agency problems, moral hazard problems and a poor governance system.

By the end of 1997 the average corporate debt to equity ratio was around 400 per cent, equivalent to 167 per cent of GDP. For the 30 largest *chaebols* the ratio was even higher at 519 per cent, about 100 per cent higher than in the previous five years. This contrasted sharply with 154 per cent in the USA and 193 per cent in Japan, and raised serious questions about corporate governance and viability (Table 3.10). Such debts imposed onerous debt service costs on corporate cash flows. These costs amounted to about 17 per cent of total business costs in 1997, more than three times the level in the USA and Japan. Interest expenses in the manufacturing sector rose from 5.5 per cent of sales in 1995 to 6.8 per cent in 1997. This aggravated the already low profitability of Korean companies.[20] Worse still, by 1996 there had been a rapid build-up of short-term domestic and foreign debt to finance the *chaebols'* investment boom. Some two thirds of corporate debt was short term, about a quarter of which was foreign debt, leaving cash-starved firms exposed to tighter short-term credit lines, declines in the won and the global financial markets, and interest rate rises. This increased reliance on short-term borrowing probably reflected attempts to reduce interest costs by borrowing at shorter maturities.

Other salient features of the corporate sector included low profit margins[21] and poor shareholder returns (which averaged 6.2 per cent in 1990–96, barely one half the growth of nominal GDP and a third of that achieved in the USA), despite the unprecedented economic growth since 1963; very low stockholder equity, which dropped by a third during the course of 1997; and high and rising debt service as a proportion of corporate cash flow, particularly in 1996 and 1997. Indeed financial costs stood at 15–17 per cent of total business costs in 1996–97, three times higher than in the USA, Japan and Taiwan. Heavy debt service was a quintessential feature of fragile firms, and combined with rigid lay-off laws, weak cash flows and cross-debt guarantees this was a recipe for serial bankruptcy and high systemic risk. Although 1995 brought a peak in profitability, reflecting the rapid growth of the electronics sector, the rise in interest costs exposed fragile firms to the terms of trade shock that started in 1996. Primarily because of an 80 per cent fall in the price of semiconductors,

Table 3.10 Performance and debt–equity ratios[1] of the top 30 *chaebols*

Rank[2]	Group	Total assets[3] (trillion won)	Total sales[3] (trillion won)	Net profit[3] (trillion won)	Profit/assets[3] (%)	Debt–equity ratio, 1996[3] (%)	Debt–equity ratio, 1997 (%)	Debt–equity ratio, 1998[4] (%)
1	Hyundai	531.8	680.1	1.8	0.3	439.1	578.7	508.1
2	Samsung	508.6	601.1	1.8	0.4	268.2	370.9	321.4
3	LG	370.7	466.7	3.6	1.0	346.5	505.8	481.7
4	Daewoo	342.1	382.5	3.6	1.1	337.3	472.0	406.9
5	Sunkyong	227.3	266.1	2.9	1.3	385.0	468.0	378.6
6	Ssangyong	158.1	194.5	–1.0	–0.6	409.0	399.7	395.5
7	Kia	141.6	121.0	–1.3	–0.9	523.6	–	–
8	Hanjin	139.0	87.0	–1.9	–1.4	556.9	907.8	632.5
9	Hanwha	109.7	96.9	–1.8	–1.6	778.2	1214.7	1108.0
10	Lotte	77.5	71.9	0.5	0.6	191.2	216.5	203.5
11	Kumho	74.0	44.4	–0.2	–0.3	477.9	944.1	1120.9
12	Halla[5]	66.3	52.9	0.2	0.3	2067.6	–	–
13	Doosan	64.0	40.5	–1.1	–1.7	692.3	590.3	610.9
14	Dongah	62.9	38.9	0.4	0.6	355.0	359.9	502.3
15	Daelim	57.9	48.3	0.1	0.2	380.1	513.6	472.2
16	Hansol	47.9	25.5	–0.1	–0.2	343.2	399.9	532.7
17	Hyosung	41.2	54.8	0.4	1.0	373.2	465.1	463.5
18	Jinro[5]	39.4	14.8	–1.6	–4.1	8598.7	–	–
19	Kolon	38.0	41.3	0.2	0.5	316.5	433.5	412.7
20	Dongguk Jaekank	37.0	30.7	0.9	2.4	210.4	323.8	261.9
21	Kohap[6]	36.5	25.2	0.3	0.8	589.5	472.1	–
22	Haitai[6]	34.0	27.2	0.4	1.2	658.3	1501.3	–
23	New Core	28.0	18.3	0.2	0.7	1224.0	1784.1	–
24	Anam Industrial	26.4	19.8	0.1	0.4	478.1	1498.5	1713.7
25	Hanil	26.3	13.0	–1.2	–4.6	563.2	–	–

(continued)

Table 3.10 Performance and debt–equity ratios[1] of the top 30 *chaebols* (*continued*)

Rank[2]	Group	Total assets[3] (trillion won)	Total sales[3] (trillion won)	Net profit[3] (trillion won)	Profit/assets[3] (%)	Debt–equity ratio, 1996[3] (%)	Debt–equity ratio, 1997 (%)	Debt–equity ratio, 1998[4] (%)
26	Sammi	25.2	14.9	–2.5	–9.9	3245.0	–	–
27	Sinho Jaeji[6]	21.3	12.2	–0.1	–0.5	489.5	676.8	–
28	Bongil	20.3	8.7	–0.9	–4.4	920.5	–	–
29	Dongguk Muyok	16.2	10.7	–0.2	–1.2	587.9	–	–
30	Hansin Kongyong	13.3	10.6	0	0	648.8	–	–
Total[7]						386.5	519.0	458.2

Notes:
1. Non-financial companies only.
2. Based on total assets.
3. As at the end of December 1996.
4. As at the end of June 1998.
5. Negative equity in 1997 and did not qualify for the list in 1998.
6. Negative equity in 1998.
7. Total Figure taken from NAM *et al.* (1999).

Sources: NAM *et al.* (1999); OECD (1999a), p. 124.

overall export prices in dollar terms fell by 13 per cent in 1996 (equivalent to 4 per cent of the national income) and a further 16 per cent in 1997. At the same time export volume fell and overcapacity emerged in key export sectors following the investment boom in semiconductors, cars, steel and petrochemicals. With firms unable to lay off redundant workers and reduce labour costs, net income dropped to 0.5 per cent of manufacturing sales in 1996.

Despite a modest recovery in profit margins a critical point was reached around mid 1997, when faced with slumping operating income due to slower growth, the decline in the terms of trade and rising financial costs the corporate sector's net income turned negative and corporate cash flow was caught in a savage squeeze. This, in conjunction with the depreciation of the won later in the year, triggered a 50 per cent jump in the number of insolvencies in 1997 and a sharp increase in the rate of default. Among those affected were eight of the 30 largest *chaebols*, including major groups such as Hanbo, Jinro, Sammi, Halla and, most importantly, the Kia group, which was the country's seventh largest chaebol.[22] Together they accounted for about 4 per cent of the assets of non-farm, non-financial businesses. Financial market confidence was particularly shaken in January 1997 by the first insolvency, that of Hanbo Steel (part of the fourteenth largest *chaebol*). The scale of the ensuing bribes for loans scandal was stunning, even for a Korean public long hardened to 'cosy' arrangements; and foreign investors' confidence appeared to be irrevocably shaken. At that point some foreign banks began to reduce their exposure to Korea, first by cutting back their credit lines. This fragile situation calmed in spring 1997, in part because Korean banks, in the face of strong pressure to keep 'solvent' firms afloat, entered into a voluntary 'standstill agreement' to avoid driving firms into receivership.[23] But this respite proved short lived. Obviously these developments in the corporate sector had major implications for the third partner in Korea Inc. – the banks.

3.4.3 The financial system

The surge in corporate insolvencies had a devastating effect on the second critical area of structural weakness – Korea's financial system. The corporate problems, although severe, might have been contained if the financial system had been adequately capitalised and well supervised. However the opposite was true, and this further weakened foreign confidence. While Korea's manufacturing sector had become almost comparable to those of the world's leading industrialised countries, its financial sector was quite unsophisticated. The banks had been privatised in the early 1980s but they lacked dynamism because the government had continued to exert a high degree of control over their management. They also lacked experience as profit-seeking entities and failed to adhere to stringent prudential standards, and as a consequence strong governance practices failed to emerge.

During the 1990s Korea's banking sector was characterised by poor and declining profitability, as measured by the return on assets and equity, steadily deteriorating capital adequacy ratios and tight interest margins (Table 3.11), partly reflecting competition by new entrants after 1991.[24] The banks' poor profitability reflected increased competition from non-bank financial institutions, which were permitted to enter into direct competition with the banks in the 1980s and 1990s and were subject to relatively lax restrictions compared with those imposed on the banks. In addition the banks' limited control over costs combined with regulations on product innovation depressed their profitability even further.[25]

Official figures suggest a steady decline in non-performing loans as a proportion of total loans during the 1990s, reaching a low of 4.1 per cent of total credit in 1996 before increasing to 6 per cent in 1997. While this ratio was not especially high by past standards, the increase was troubling in light of the financial turbulence in the other South-East Asian countries, which were also characterised by weak financial systems and poor corpo-

Table 3.11 Banking profitability, 1990–98

	Average 1990–93	1994	1995	1996	1997	1998
Return on assets (%)						
Nationwide banks	0.51	0.40	0.28	0.23	–0.90	–2.99
Regional banks	0.84	0.53	0.56	0.47	–1.17	–5.83
All banks	0.56	0.42	0.32	0.26	–0.93	–3.15
Return on equity (%)						
Five major banks	6.10	6.00	3.40	1.20	–31.60	na
Nationwide banks	6.30	6.17	3.91	3.49	–14.09	–48.63
Regional banks	6.70	5.73	5.63	5.41	–14.77	–84.40
All banks	6.40	6.09	4.19	3.80	–14.18	–52.53
Net interest margin (basis points)						
Five major banks	2.37	1.87	2.70	na	na	na
Nationwide banks	2.31	1.21	2.40	2.98	2.03	0.94
Regional banks	4.37	4.30	3.76	3.99	2.32	0.95
All banks	2.72	1.74	2.68	3.18	2.07	0.94
Non performing loans at commercial banks						
In billion won	9394	11 390	12 484	11 874	22 652	22 225
As percentage of total loans	7.3	5.8	5.2	4.1	6.0	7.4
Capital adequacy ratios of banks (%)						
Five major banks	8.87	10.46	9.21	8.86	4.46	na
Nationwide banks	9.39	10.19	8.97	8.97	6.66	8.22
Regional banks	13.95	13.11	11.44	10.15	9.80	8.31
All banks	10.00	10.62	9.33	9.14	7.04	8.23
Employees (1990 = 100)	104.80	106.10	125.60	126.40	138.70	92.40

Source: Financial Supervisory Service.

rate governance practices. There was also concern about transparency: the deterioration of the banks' health was not fully reflected in the reported statistics because of loose loan classification standards and accounting rules, there was only partial recognition of stock revaluation losses and the loan-loss provisions were inadequate.[26]

The chronically poor quality of the banks' loan portfolios was exacerbated by the squeeze on corporate profits between mid 1996 and 1997.[27] Non-performing loans were already on the rise, especially among banks with a legacy of government-directed loans and imprudent dealings with large troubled firms and/or cyclically depressed sectors (for example Korea First Bank and Seoul Bank).[28] Aggravating the situation even further was the instruction by the Korean authorities for commercial banks to intervene in the stock markets. This required the banks to sell shares and ease the prices down when the market was overheated, and to purchase shares and hold them in order to stimulate the market when it was overly bearish. As the Korean Composite Stock Index had dropped continuously since mid 1995 the banks suffered huge losses, exacerbating the difficulties they were already facing. This was compounded by the deteriorating performance of the corporate sector. By late 1996 the banks had begun to report large losses on share investments and on loans to the *chaebols*. The government of President Kim Young Sam, however, did not demand a thorough clean-up, which would have required closing several major banks and forcing some of Korea's biggest companies into bankruptcy. But the string of *chaebol* bankruptcies in 1997 compounded the banks' difficulties and forced them to carry a very heavy bad debt burden.

Furthermore, regulations and institutional factors combined to encourage the channelling of international borrowing through the financial system for on-lending to corporations. Large amounts of foreign currency credit were taken on, directly or indirectly, by Korean financial institutions to provide finance for enterprises at home and abroad, and many firms took on increasing amounts of short-term foreign currency debt, of which little was hedged. Between 1993 and 1996 the foreign exposure of both Korean banks and enterprises nearly doubled, reaching almost $100 billion in 1997.

There were numerous weak points elsewhere in the financial sector. Non-bank financial institutions also had considerable exposure to the *chaebols* and faced significant market risks. Merchant banks,[29] securities companies and investment trust companies had significant dealings with the currency, bond and equity markets. In markets where margins were often under pressure, these institutions sought to maintain profitability by accepting increased risk. Many of them used leveraged positions, but most lacked the ability to manage and price market risk. Furthermore the supervisory authorities were relatively unconcerned about the adequacy of their risk management systems.

The financial system did not become weak overnight. Rather it was the result of a combination of factors that occurred before the corporate and financial crisis of 1997, the most important of which were as follows.

Poor supervision and regulation

The problems faced by the financial system reflected the weakness of the supervisory and regulatory framework and the legacy of government-directed lending practices, which had led to excessive leveraging in the corporate sector and delayed necessary restructuring efforts. Strict regulatory and supervisory policies were important for minimising moral hazard, including corruption, fraud and excessive risk taking in the banking system, but in Korea and other East Asian economies there was little prudential supervision of the banking system early in the process of financial liberalisation,[30] especially in the case of non-bank financial institutions and particularly merchant banks.

Heavy government intervention

Preferential loans mandated by the government to key sectors, often refinanced by the central bank at relatively favourable interest rates, resulted in the banks having little incentive to assess and price their credit risk properly. This was inconsistent with sound banking practice and caused the banks to accumulate huge debts from uncreditworthy and heavily leveraged *chaebol* firms.

Poor accounting standards and transparency

Poor accounting standards and limited information-disclosure requirements made risk assessment of creditors very difficult. Added to this use of fictitious names and the maintenance of multiple accounts greatly diminished the reliability of reported information. The regulators did not require banks to declare loans as 'non-performing' until the interest had gone unpaid for six months, and even then they had to set aside only 15 per cent of loans to cover the losses. Tougher standards were phased in during 1998, but until then the actual financial position of the banks was likely to be worse than their financial reports suggested. Information difficulties were compounded by the fact that before the crisis financial data had been regarded as a state secret. For example on 10 December 1997 the authorities admitted that the country's short term-debt exceeded $100 billion, nearly double the figure it had given the IMF a few weeks earlier when the negotiations for a rescue plan had begun.

Underdeveloped capital markets

Recent banking experiences highlight the problems that can arise if banks are the sole source of financial intermediation,[31] for example their breakdown causes a sharp weakening of economic growth. The existence of a wide range of non-bank institutions and capital market institutions more generally, including viable debt and equity markets, is important to safeguard economic activity when banks fail. However the financial markets in Korea and other economies in East Asia were small and underdeveloped. For instance bonds were not an important source of finance for businesses or an investment outlet for households.

The previous factors also contributed to financial system vulnerability arising from a loss of confidence by international investors, as well as contributing to a slower growth of the economy and increased difficulties for non financial corporations that in turn further deteriorated banks' loan portfolios. Too little attention was paid to prudent analysis and containment of risks. At the end of 1996, according to unofficial estimates, banks' non-performing loans, net of reserves, were equivalent to almost 70 per cent of their equity, and the true quality of their assets may have been far worse than this figure suggests. The unprecedented number of *chaebol* bankruptcies in 1997 severely weakened the banking system and non-performing loans rose sharply. By October 1997, according to unofficial estimates, over 20 per cent of bank loans in Korea were impaired. At the same time a steep decline in stock prices cut the value of the banks' equity and further reduced their net worth.

While the Korean banking system lacked dynamism, showed poor profitability and was plainly vulnerable to deteriorating credit conditions, it did not appear to be on the brink of insolvency or at least on the basis of official figures. Furthermore it had one or two positive features. First, the government's policy of preventing ownership concentration meant that there were few ownership linkages and conflicts of interest between banking and industry. Second, the banks had little direct involvement in the real estate sector, a major element in most banking crises since the 1980s, although they had considerable indirect involvement in that a large amount of lending was collateralised by real estate.

3.5 Other deficiencies

3.5.1 Labour market rigidities and the education system

A key ingredient of Korea's prolonged economic growth and development was the diligence of its people, who worked long hours and had a high savings rate. They were also well educated due to the strong Confucian emphasis on education. Despite this the rapid rise in wages, continuing labour market rigidities and the lack of creativity among the labour force weakened the international competitiveness of Korean firms. With the advent of democracy in 1987 and the subsequent liberalisation of trade unions,[32] nominal wages increased by 15 per cent per annum until 1996 while productivity rose by just 11 per cent per annum. Tight labour market conditions and strong trade union power prevented reform of the labour market, which remained full of rigidities. There was an excessive degree of job protection, which prevented lay-offs and encouraged overmanning; plus a lack of flexibility over working hours and few limits on strike action (Fitch ICBA, 1999).

Even more importantly the education system was not providing the creative, entrepreneurial and highly skilled workers needed for the new Korea. Instead it retained the repetitive, learning by rote system that had been so successful when the economy had been at a less developed stage.

3.5.2 Total factor productivity slowdown

Kim and Hong (1997) suggest that the growth of the Korean economy over the period 1963–95 was based on roughly equal contributions from input growth and improvements in factor productivity. According to them, in 1985–95 inputs of capital and labour generated 4.75 per cent of growth while improvements in total factor productivity (TFP), due primarily to improved resource allocation, economies of scale and advances in knowledge, contributed a further 4 per cent, giving a total growth of National Income of 8.8 per cent. Kim and Hong also suggest that the contribution by TFP will remain significant, since an improved corporate governance framework and a better managed banking system will eventually enhance the gains from improved resource allocation and economies of scale. This contrasts with a study by the World Bank (1999), which suggests that growth was primarily driven by factor accumulation (increased inputs of labour and capital) and that TFP growth contributed only 1.8 per cent per annum – one fourth of total growth, while Kim (1999) presents evidence that the rate of TFP growth decelerated in most industries (Table 3.12).

As Table 3.12 shows, TFP deteriorated significantly during the 1990s in comparison with the 1980s in all sectors but transport and communications, and agriculture, forestry and fishing. The most disturbing deterioration was in the manufacturing sector. This suggests that considerable improvements in resource allocation, economies of scale and advances in knowledge were urgently required if Korea was to compete effectively in global markets.

Investment efficiency also deteriorated in the 1990s relative to the 1980s. The investment boom of the 1990s served to increase capacity but had a detrimental effect on overall efficiency.

Table 3.12 Total factor productivity growth, 1980–96 (per cent)

	1980–89	1990–96
Average annual change in total factor productivity:		
Total industry	2.90	1.34
Agriculture, forestry and fishing	2.88	9.74
Mining and quarrying	4.23	3.99
Manufacturing	9.33	1.26
Electricity, gas and water	5.22	0.61
Construction	0.89	–0.31
Transportation and communications	2.04	4.85
Finance, insurance and business services.	0.82	–2.74
Investment efficiency[1]		
Total industry	0.41	0.29
Agriculture, forestry and fishing	0.58	0.12
Mining and quarrying	–0.04	–1.41
Manufacturing	0.63	0.36
Electricity, gas and water	0.47	0.30
Construction	2.77	2.50
Transportation and communications	0.93	0.92
Finance, insurance and business services	0.38	0.48

Note: [1] change in output divided by change in capital stock.
Source: Kim (1999).

3.5.3 Unfriendly global economic environment

Korea's rapid growth was in part due to favourable international circumstances until the late 1980s. Firstly, under the terms of GATT the developed countries further opened their domestic markets, enabling Korea to pursue its export-oriented growth strategy, while as a less developed country it was allowed to keep its domestic market effectively closed until the end of the 1980s. Secondly, the USA provided Korea, now part of the Western capitalist world, with a considerable amount of economic assistance during the Cold War era and also became the largest market for Korean exports.

From the late 1980s, however, Korean companies faced increasingly strong competition from companies in the new Newly Industrialised Economies (NNIEs) of south-east Asia. In addition Korea and the USA began to conflict over trade, supposedly because of Korea's relatively heavy protectionism and state intervention in the market. A more compelling reason is that Korea's strategic importance had lessened dramatically since the Soviet Union had fallen apart, and even though the USA continued to station troops in Korea it became less tolerant of Korea's industrial policy. Between 1990 and 1996, 36 per cent of Korea's trade conflicts with other countries, were with the USA. From 1991 the pattern of Korea–US trade reversed and Korea had a continuous trade deficit with the USA, except in 1993 when it recorded a $0.2 billion surplus. This was yet another sign of the weakening of Korea's competitiveness.

3.5.4 Developments in the advanced economies

While the financial problems experienced by Korea and other East Asian countries were mostly home-grown, developments in advanced economies and the global financial markets contributed significantly to the imbalances that eventually led to the financial crisis of 1997. The World Bank (1999b) estimated that the net flow of long-term debt, FDI and equity to the Asia-Pacific region was about $25 billion in 1990 but had soared to more than $110 billion by 1996. A major factor in this was the global stock market boom of the 1990s. As this boom progressed, investors in many industrial countries realised that the rates of return on the securities of many companies in the developed world were lower than could be expected from companies in emerging economies, especially in East Asia. The resulting sharp increase in capital flows into East Asia contributed to a property and stock market boom in the economies concerned, as well as overinvestment in productive assets, largely by investors from the USA, Western Europe and Japan. The rising value of the yen also prompted a substantial increase in direct investment from Japan.

With hindsight it is clear that more investment funds flowed into East Asia than could be profitably employed at moderate risk (see Greenspan, 1998), and that this encouraged imprudent and unprofitable investment by domestic banks. At the same time intense pressure was put on Korea to liberalise its financial market. It made the fundamental mistake of liberalising short-term capital flows, thereby enabling an excessive build-up of short-term debt to foreign banks that were eager to lend.

3.5.5 Rapid opening of the domestic market

In 1989 Korea announced that it would no longer restrict trade for the sake of its balance of payments (as covered in GATT Article XVIIIB) and would adhere to Article XI. This involved import liberalisation, the pace of which was speeded up with the conclusion of the Uruguay Round and the founding of the World Trade Organisation (WTO). Furthermore when President Kim Young Sam came to power in 1993 he proclaimed that Korea would join the OECD during his term of office, which would require even greater liberalisation of the domestic market. As a result, by 1996 the number of restrictions and the average tariff rates on manufactured goods were comparable to those of most industrialised countries.

The financial market underwent even faster liberalisation. During the early 1990s nearly all restrictions on the inflow and outflow of mobile capital were removed.[33] However little attention was paid to the consequent need for new regulations and inexperienced private domestic banks and corporations were able to take out large foreign-currency-denominated loans from foreign lenders, making the economy vulnerable to the instabilities of the international financial markets.

3.5.6 Like a nut in a nutcracker

From the early 1980s China strongly pursued its new 'reform and open-door policy'. This proved very successful and between 1980 and 1996 real GDP grew by more than 10 per cent per annum. Between 1990 and 1996 manufactured exports grew by more than 20 per cent per annum in US dollar terms, and Chinese firms began to compete directly with Korean firms in textiles, clothing and electronics. Added to this the rapid growth of South-East Asian economies such as Indonesia, Malaysia, Thailand and the Philippines meant even harsher competition for Korea.

In order to compete without reducing wages Korea had to change its industrial structure and become more high-tech oriented. Following the textbook example of Japan it duly invested substantial amounts of capital in economically strategic industries such as electronics, cars and biochemicals. As a consequence Korean companies found themselves competing directly against Japanese companies on the one hand and against their counterparts in China and other newly industrialised countries on the other. That is, as Booz Allen & Hamilton (1997) put it just before the financial crisis, Korea was being squeezed like 'a nut in a nut cracker'. The pressure tightened in January 1994 when China devalued the yuan by 50 per cent and when the Japanese yen progressively depreciated against the US dollar. Then in 1996 semiconductor prices plummeted by a massive 80 per cent. This represented a severe terms-of-trade shock for Korea as the semiconductor industry accounted for 20 per cent of its total exports by value.

3.6 Policy mistakes

Among the policy mistakes made by the government during the 1990s, three are particularly noteworthy: its exchange rate policy, inappropriate and inadequate financial market supervision, and its failure to respond appropriately to the *chaebols'* repeated defaults and to speculative attacks in early 1997.

3.6.1 The strong won policy

From the late 1980s the international competitiveness of Korean industry continued to falter as economic fundamentals and international circumstances deteriorated. Instead of allowing the won to depreciate, thereby alleviating the country's current account deficit, the government adopted a strong won policy. The strong won was maintained through the so-called market-average foreign exchange rate system, which was adopted in 1990. The exchange rate was allowed to move within a narrow daily fluctuation band (Figure 3.1). Radelet and Sachs (1998b) estimate that the won appreciated by about 12 per cent in real terms between 1990 and 1997.

Why did the government insist on a strong won? The following are possible answers. First, to achieve its single-digit inflation target the government insisted on nominal exchange rate stability. That is, inflation control was the overriding priority of macroeconomic policy and the exchange rate was an anchor for it. Second, the government considered that a strong won would push firms to increase their productivity and hence their international competitiveness. Third, it wanted to keep the exchange rate stable as this would help domestic corporations and financial institutions by lowering the domestic currency costs of servicing foreign debts denominated in foreign currency. Fourth, when the targeted $10 000 per capita income level was achieved in 1995 the government did not want it to slide because of a depreciation of the domestic currency.

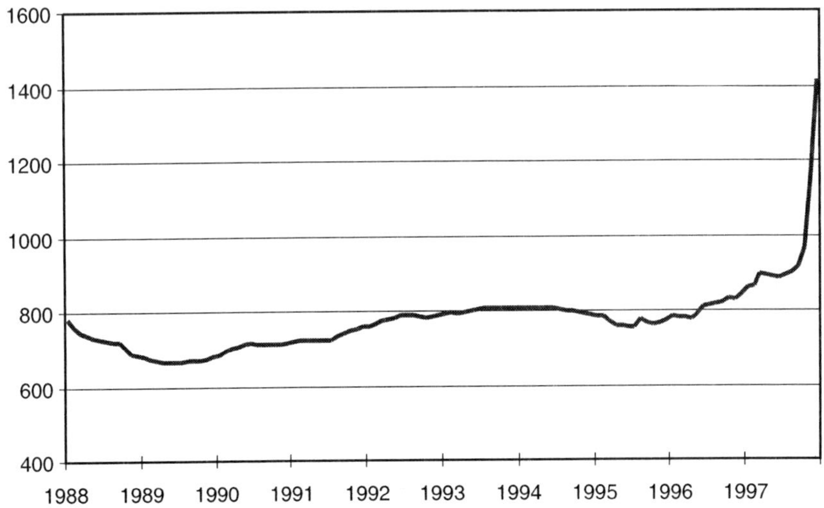

Source: Bank of Korea.

Figure 3.1 Nominal exchange rate, January 1988 to December 1997 (won/dollar)

3.6.2 Inappropriate and inadequate supervision of the financial sector

As noted earlier the financial market underwent very rapid liberalisation and deregulation during the early 1990s.[34] This gave domestic financial institutions easy access to foreign capital to finance domestic investment. Two major deficiencies were evident in the process. First, financial liberalisation was carried out mostly on short-term rather than long-term capital inflows. For instance net foreign portfolio investment, which was just $0.1 billion in 1990, rose dramatically to $3.1 billion in 1991, $5.8 billion in 1992 and $10.0 billion in 1993. This upward trend continued until 1997. However net direct investment continuously produced negative values, indicating that FDI in Korea was lower than Korea's direct investment overseas (Figure 3.2).

Second, liberalisation was not accompanied by appropriate supervision and prudential regulation. In particular merchant banks, which rose in number from six in 1993 to 30 in 1996, were not subject to supervision. Believing that the government would not allow financial institutions to fail, Korean banks borrowed unhedged, short-term foreign capital at low rates (denominated in US dollars) and made long-term loans at higher rates in the expectation that they would be able continually to renew their short-term borrowing. This led to a serious mismatch between the maturity of borrowing and lending and made Korea very vulnerable to instabilities in the international financial markets. Short-term loans accounted for 63 per cent of total debt on the eve of the financial crisis.

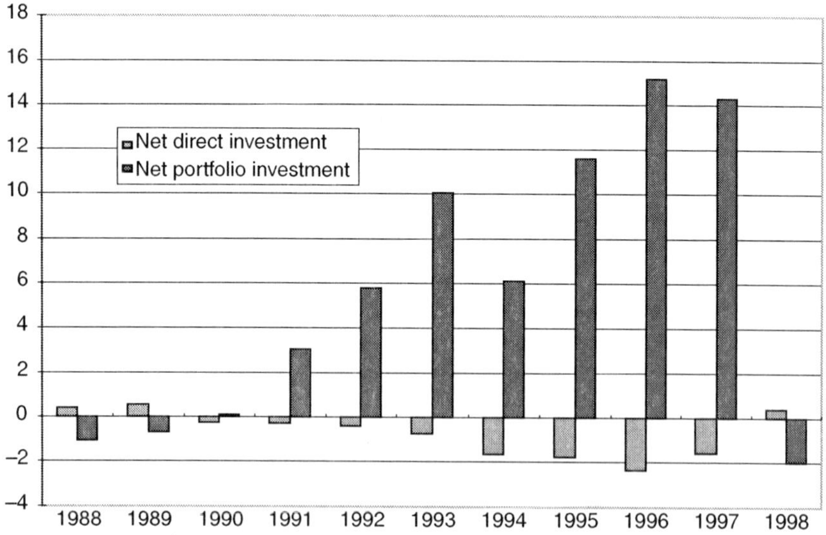

Source: Bank of Korea.

Figure 3.2 Investment flows, direct and portfolio (net), 1988–98 ($ billion)

3.6.3 Naive policy responses to the early warning signs

A series of policy mistakes were made in response to signs of an impending crisis in early 1997. First, the government failed to deal swiftly with corporate insolvencies, which had a devastating effect on the financial system. It preferred instead to leave troubled firms to be dealt with by market mechanisms, but then took measures that were contrary to market principles, such as introducing the Bankruptcy Prevention Accord and providing state subsidies to the hopelessly ailing *chaebols*. In particular the government's decision to convert Kia Motors – the insolvent, seventh largest *chaebol* Table 3.10) – into a public enterprise heightened the confusion and distrust among foreign investors.

The government's second mistake was its exchange rate policy. After the collapse of the Thai baht in July 1997 the contagion spread to Indonesia, Malaysia and even Singapore and Hong Kong. Despite speculative attacks on the won in October and November the government maintained its narrow daily fluctuation band. As a consequence Korea's foreign exchange reserves fell far below the level of outstanding short-term foreign debts. If the band had been widened and the exchange rate had been allowed to float freely, the won would have depreciated gradually and this would have helped limit the extent of the crisis.

Third, the government waited until the foreign currency reserves plummeted to $7.3 billion and the country was facing a debt moratorium before turning to the IMF for help. As the banks were finding it difficult to roll over their short-term foreign liabilities the Bank of Korea shifted foreign exchange reserves to the banks' offshore branches and announced that it would guarantee foreign borrowing by the banks. However this helped foreign creditors to escape from Korea and the country soon found itself on the brink of insolvency as its useable reserves were almost gone.

Why did the Korean administration, once considered shrewd and efficient, make such disastrous policy mistakes? The foremost reason was that the government was in total disarray because of the lame duck nature of Kim Young Sam's presidency in the run-up to the presidential election in December 1997. Furthermore, when the crisis was escalating a disruptive struggle broke out between the Ministry of Finance and Economy and the central bank over their roles in the financial market.

3.7 Korea and the East Asian economic miracle

Korea's remarkable economic growth occurred in tandem with similar developments in a number of other East Asian economies. As Table 3.13 shows the four Tiger Economies of Singapore, Hong Kong, Taiwan and South Korea attained growth rates in excess of 9 per cent during the 1970s and well above 7 per cent during the 1980s. Korea's relative performance amongst this group of countries was impressive and it also compared very favourably with that of the newly industrialising economies of South-East Asia. However there was a general slowdown of economic growth across the region after 1996 (Table 3.13) following a slump in export growth (Table 3.14).

The World Bank (1993) has identified a number of reasons for the region's remarkable success: relatively inexpensive labour combined with high human capital and a strong work ethic; high domestic savings, which stimulated domestic investment and capital stock accumulation; the establishment and maintenance of macroeconomic stability; the implementation of agricultural reforms; the adoption of export-led growth and the attraction of foreign investment and technology; and increased labour productivity arising from technological innovation. Some economists, however, led by Paul Krugman (1995), predicted that Asia's rapid expansion could not be sustained because it was based primarily on 'perspiration rather than inspiration' and that the region displayed little growth of total factor productivity (a measure of overall economic efficiency in terms of capital and labour) needed to sustain growth. When resource inputs reached saturation level, Asia's miracle would start to fade. The slowdown in output and export growth in the region was therefore structural and inevitable.

On the other hand, more optimistic economists gave little weight to the suggestion that something was structurally wrong with the miracle economies. Instead they argued that the slowdown was cyclical and that sooner or later the Asian miracle would restart, albeit at a slower rate of growth.[35] A number of explanations were advanced for the cyclical slowdown in economic growth and export growth after 1995. First, demand from North America and Europe was weak as industrial production had slowed in 1995 and early 1996, and historically Asian exports tended to move in line with trends in developed economies. Second, an appreciation of the US dollar, to which many Asian currencies were effectively tied, had depressed exports. The weakness of the dollar in 1994–95 had helped to boost exports, but in 1996 the situation had been reversed when the dollar had risen by 50 per cent against the yen from a low in April 1995, eroding the competitiveness of many East Asian exports *vis-à-vis* Japanese products. This was particularly detrimental to Korea, whose product demand was highly price sensitive. Third, as discussed previously there had been a slump in the world semiconductor market, with memory chip prices falling by around 80 per cent in 1996. This had had a particularly severe impact on Korea as electronic components accounted for a sizeable proportion of its exports. In addition the steel and petrochemical industries were plagued by global overcapacity. Finally, regional demand and hence intra-Asian trade, which accounted for an increasing share of East Asian countries' total trade, was being curtailed by the tight monetary policies being applied in

Table 3.13 Per capita GDP and real growth rates, East Asia, 1970–97

	Per capita GNP, PPP[1] 1997 (US$)	GDP growth rates (%)									
		1970–79	1980–89	1990	1991	1992	1993	1994	1995	1996	1997
Singapore	29 000	9.4	7.2	9.0	7.3	6.2	10.4	10.5	8.7	7.8	6.8
Hong Kong	24 540	9.2	7.5	3.4	5.1	6.3	6.1	5.4	3.9	4.5	5.3
Taiwan	15 370[2]	10.2	8.1	5.4	7.6	6.8	6.3	6.5	6.0	5.7	6.7
South Korea	13 500	9.3	8.0	9.0	9.2	5.4	5.5	8.3	8.9	6.8	5.0
Malaysia	10 920	8.0	5.7	9.7	8.6	7.8	8.3	9.3	9.4	8.6	7.7
Thailand	6 590	7.3	7.2	11.2	8.6	8.1	8.7	8.6	8.8	5.5	–0.4
Indonesia	3 450	7.8	5.7	7.2	7.0	6.5	6.5	7.5	8.2	7.8	4.9
China	3 570	7.5	9.3	3.8	9.2	14.2	13.5	12.7	10.5	9.5	8.8
Philippines	3 670	6.1	1.8	3.0	–0.6	0.3	2.1	4.4	4.7	5.8	5.2
Industrial countries	22 770[3]	3.4	2.6	2.4	1.4	1.7	0.9	2.9	2.3	2.8	2.9

Notes:
1. Purchasing power parity.
2. Per capita GDP, 1996.
3. High-income economies.

Sources: IMF (1999a); IMF (1999b); World Bank (1999b).

Table 3.14 Export growth rates, East Asia, 1990–98 (per cent)

	1990	1991	1992	1993	1994	1995	1996	1997	1998
Singapore	18.1	11.9	7.6	16.6	30.8	22.1	5.7	0.0	–12.1
Hong Kong	12.3	20.0	21.2	13.2	11.9	14.8	4.0	4.0	–7.5
Taiwan	1.6	13.4	6.9	4.0	9.6	20.2	3.7	4.8	–8.9
South Korea	4.2	10.5	6.6	7.3	16.8	30.3	3.7	5.0	–2.8
Malaysia	17.4	16.8	18.5	15.7	24.7	26.0	5.8	0.5	–6.9
Thailand	14.9	23.2	14.2	13.3	23.1	24.7	–1.3	3.3	–5.4
Indonesia	15.9	13.5	16.6	8.4	8.8	13.4	9.7	7.3	–8.6
China	18.2	15.8	18.1	7.1	33.1	22.9	1.6	21.0	0.4
Philippines	4.0	8.7	11.2	13.7	20.0	31.6	16.7	22.9	10.7
Industrial countries	15.3	2.0	5.8	–2.2	12.5	19.0	2.6	2.2	0.4

Source: IMF (1999a).

the overheating economies of China, Malaysia and Thailand, resulting in a reduction of import demand.

The idea that Asia's export slowdown was caused largely by cyclical factors rather than loss of competitiveness was also supported by other evidence. First, imports fell as sharply as exports, with the rate of export growth falling from 30 per cent in 1995 to 4 per cent in 1996 and import growth falling from 32 per cent to 11 per cent. If competitiveness had been the problem imports would have accelerated. Second, the export growth of other developing countries, such as those in Latin America, also slowed in 1996. Consequently East Asia's share of US and Japanese imports hardly changed in volume terms.

Even if the pessimists' view had been exaggerated and the main causes of the slowdown had been cyclical, the slowdown revealed and provided early warning of several structural problems that needed to be overcome if East Asia was to reactivate and sustain its economic growth. The problems and the policies required varied from country to country. In the case of Korea, its heavy concentration on a few export industries, such as electronics and petrochemicals, was problematic. There was also a clear need for the country to be opened up to more competition, for the power enjoyed by the indebted industrial *chaebols* to be reduced, and for labour and capital market rigidities to be relaxed and weaknesses resolved. In contrast to Korea, Hong Kong, Singapore and Taiwan had more flexible labour markets, less government intervention and small, nimble firms. Taiwan was pushing ahead with deregulation more swiftly than Korea, and its more flexible industrial policy appeared to be better suited to the rapidly changing business conditions.

3.8 Summary and conclusions

The seeds of the financial crisis that hit Korea in late 1997 were planted earlier in the decade. The benign macroeconomic environment of the 1990s – characterised by high GDP and export growth until 1996, low inflation, fiscal surpluses in general, high savings and investment, low unemployment and, until 1996, modest trade and current account balances – hid growing financial weaknesses in the corporate and financial sectors and an unprecedented accumulation of short-term debt. The latter increasingly exposed the country to financial turbulence in the global and regional markets. However this provoked little concern in an environment of rapidly growing exports and output. With the deterioration of the country's terms of trade and the resulting slowdown in export values in 1996 and 1997, however, the highly overleveraged corporate sector came under intense profitability and cash flow pressures. In 1997 a number of *chaebols* became insolvent or had to seek protection from creditors. The already shaky financial sector, weakened by imprudent and excessive lending to the *chaebols*, experienced a sharp rise in non-performing loans. No government action was taken to tackle this problem head-on. By October 1997 strong pressure on the currency was being applied by international investors as concern about Korea's excessive short-term foreign debt came into play. The ability of the country to meet its short-term interest and debt repayments became questionable as the usable foreign exchange reserves were diminishing alarmingly.

Part II

4
Financial Crisis and the IMF Bailout

> Anyone who claims to fully understand the economic disaster that has overtaken Asia proves, by that certainty, that he doesn't know what he is talking about. (Krugman, 1998b)

4.1 Introduction

As discussed in Chapter 3, Korea's financial situation had become extremely fragile by the second half of 1997, but later developments plunged it into a financial abyss. The crisis started with an unprecedented number of business insolvencies (including eight of the 30 largest *chaebols*), and the devaluation of the Thai baht, the effect of which quickly spread to other regional currencies. During the second half of 1997 the region was afflicted by an unprecedented withdrawal of private capital, which contributed to the further downward spiral of regional currencies and stock markets. Korea managed to avoid the brunt of this until Taiwan and Hong Kong succumbed to the crisis in October.

After the crisis there was an outpouring of literature on its causes and consequences.[1] While no overall consensus was reached the major contributions can be broken down into two broad groupings.[2] The first considered that structural weaknesses and policy distortions were the major causes of the crisis, a position taken by the IMF, although it was acknowledged that investor panic played an important role (for example Corsetti *et al.*, 1998a, 1998b). There was also an emphasis on the role of moral hazard and its contribution to imprudent banking and corporate failure, arising from overinvestment due to the widespread belief among debtors and creditors that they would be bailed out if their investments went bad (see Krugman, 1998a).[3]

The other major grouping, which includes Radelet and Sachs (1998a, 1998b), Feldstein (1998) and Stiglitz (1999), concluded that the primary source of the crisis was the sudden shift in market expectations and confidence. While it was recognised that structural and policy weaknesses were also at work, these could not explain the depth of the ensuing crisis. According to these authors, foreign lenders and institutional investors were so alarmed by the Thai crisis in July 1997 that they abruptly pulled out their investments from other countries in the region, thus causing the crisis to spread. Their withdrawal was prompted by the belief that these countries suffered from similar structural problems to those which had prompted the speculative attack on the Thai baht.

Blaming the crisis on only one factor, however, is much too simplistic. In the case of Korea, blaming it solely on the economic system is not satisfactory, particularly given that the economy had been crisis-free for many years under the same circumstances. Similarly, attributing it exclusively to irrational (or rational) speculative attacks and contagion is insufficient, since the effects varied widely across the East Asian countries. The truth is likely to contain elements of both these explanations. As Hill (1998, p. 10) points out, any 'explanation has to (1) be coherent yet reasonably eclectic, recognising that no one single explanation is likely to provide all the answers; (2) distinguish between, and chart the interaction among, precipitating "triggers" and core "vulnerability" factors; (3) develop an integrated framework, which allows for significant country differences; (4) emphasise the economic and political inter-connections; and (5) draw on the past "crises and panic" literature, while recognising that to a significant extent we are in uncharted territory'.

This chapter proceeds as follows. Section 2 reviews the developments that immediately preceded the crisis and identifies its key triggers. Section 3 develops a systematic and comprehensive analytical framework in the form of a 'stroke hypothesis'. Section 4 critically evaluates the IMF's structural reform programme and Section 5 reviews the developments that took place in the aftermath of the crisis. Finally, Section 6 summarises the major conclusions of this chapter.

4.2 Financial crisis

Among the crisis afflicted East Asian countries, Korea suffered one of the most painful, and certainly the most unexpected, period of financial turbulence. Between October and December 1997 this new OECD member was reduced from being the world's eleventh largest economy to an economy surviving on overnight loans from the international money markets. Assistance from the IMF was sought in November 1997, after which the country engaged in the long and painful process of restructuring and reforming its economy.

Even as late as October 1997 no one, including the IMF and the international credit agencies, could have predicted that the Korean economy would suffer such severe financial distress. The won fell by more than 50 per cent against the US dollar between 19 November 1997, when Korea decided to accept an IMF rescue plan, and 24 December 1997, when the G-7 countries pledged additional finance to avert debt default by Korea. During the same period the stock price index (KOSPI) plummeted by 30 per cent and the short-term interest rate shot up to 40 per cent per annum.

What was it that made foreign investors to so drastically change their minds about the prospects of the Korean economy? It is often suggested that they had become increasingly dismayed by and concerned about the structural weaknesses in the economy (see for example Park and Song, 2000), which seemed to make Korea a highly risky place for portfolio investment and bank lending. It is true that they had long known and complained about the lack of transparency in corporate management in Korea, questioned the reliability of the balance sheets and income statements of large corporations and banks, and warned about the risks involved in cross-ownership and cross-debt guarantees between the affiliates of the chaebols. However these problems had not been considered serious enough to warrant sudden withdrawal from Korea before the South-East Asian currency crisis erupted. In fact, even well into November 1997, according to a survey by the Korea Development Institute, many foreign investors were optimistic about the future of the economy. Yet two weeks later they withdrew their investments, regardless of whether those investments were good or bad.

The crisis for the region as a whole started in early July 1997 with Thailand's surprise decision to float its currency. This was followed a few weeks later in Korea by Kia Motors' request for a debt work-out programme with its major creditors (involving some $8 billion) to avoid bankruptcy, which drew investors' attention to financial sector problems in Korea. Soon after, major international credit ratings agencies, which had failed to foresee the Thai situation, began to reassess countries with similar characteristics. Paradoxically neither Standard and Poor nor Moody significantly changed their sovereign debt ratings for Korea (A1 and AA respectively) until after the introduction of the IMF rescue package, as its sound macroeconomic fundamentals (low inflation, high national savings, budget surplus, falling current account deficit and relatively low levels of external debt) appeared to differentiate it from the afflicted ASEAN countries.[4]

One month after the Thai baht came under speculative attack, foreign investors began to withdraw their funds from the Korean stock market and out of the country. By the fourth week of September the stock price index had fallen by more than 100 points. Throughout this turbulent period the lack of reliable information on the state of Korean banks' non-performing loans, the official foreign exchange reserves and foreign debt added to investors' uncertainty, and wildly exaggerated press estimates served to heighten market volatility. During October, foreign portfolio investors again moved out of the stock market in droves and Korean banks found it increasingly difficult to secure new loans or roll-over their existing short-term loans.

The total amount of short-term foreign liabilities at domestic financial institutions stood at $78 billion during the first nine months of the year, but within two months the figure fell by $15 billion because of foreign banks' refusal to renew short-term loans and trade-related credit facilities (Table 4.1). Consequently the Korean financial institutions were forced to turn to the Bank of Korea for liquidity. In November alone the Bank of Korea lost $15 billion of its usable reserves, and by the end of the month these reserves had fallen to $7.3 billion (Table 4.2).

The catalyst for the collapse of the won was probably the Hong Kong financial market panic of 24 October 1997. This had a severe affect on investor confidence and from that point onwards the Korean authorities

Table 4.1 Korea's total external liabilities, 1995–97 (end of period, $ billion)

			1997			
	1995[1]	1996	June	Sept.	Nov.	Dec.
Long-term liabilities (A)[2]	33.1	57.5	60.7	66.6	72.9	86.0
A/C (%)	42.2	36.5	37.1	39.0	45.0	55.7
Financial institutions		41.5	43.4	47.6	53.2	50.3
Domestic financial institutions		38.3	39.7	43.8	49.4	46.3
Domestic branches		24.5	27.9	31.3	31.0	29.9
Offshore		8.5	9.6	9.6	9.6	9.2
Foreign branches		5.3	2.2	2.9	8.8	7.3
Foreign financial institutions		3.2	3.7	3.8	3.8	4.0
Domestic firms		13.6	15.1	16.9	17.6	17.6
Public sector		2.4	2.2	2.1	2.0	1.8
Short term liabilities (B)	45.3	100.0	102.8	104.0	88.9	68.4
B/C (%)	57.8	63.5	62.9	61.0	55.0	44.3
Financial institutions		78.0	77.7	78.3	63.1	43.8
Domestic financial institutions		65.2	63.5	62.0	45.9	28.9
Domestic branches		26.2	28.5	23.6	18.7	11.7
Offshore		12.7	13.0	13.1	11.3	8.7
Foreign branches		26.4	22.0	25.3	16.0	8.5
Foreign financial institutions		12.8	14.2	16.3	17.2	14.9
Domestic firms		22.0	25.1	25.8	25.8	24.7
Total liabilities (C)	78.4	157.5	163.5	170.6	161.8	154.4

Notes:
1. The figures for 1995 are for external debts, as defined by the World Bank.
2. Long-term liabilities are those with a maturity of more than one year, while short-term liabilities mature in less than one year.

Source: Ministry of Finance and Economy.

Table 4.2 Bank of Korea, foreign reserves, 1996–98 (end of period, $ billion)

		1997						Jan.
	1996	March	June	Sept.	Oct.	Nov.	Dec.	1998
Official foreign reserves (A)	33.2	29.2	33.3	30.4	30.5	24.4	20.4	23.5
Deposits at overseas branches (B)	3.8	8.0	8.0	8.0	8.0	16.9	11.3	11.0
Other (C)	–	–	–	–	0.2	0.2	0.2	0.2
Useable reserves (A–B–C)	29.4	21.2	25.3	22.4	22.3	7.3	8.9	12.3

Notes: Official foreign reserve holdings are based on the IMF definition. Deposits at overseas branches are deposits by the Bank of Korea at overseas branches of Korean commercial banks.

Source: Bank of Korea.

were faced with capital flight. On 17 November 1997 the government abandoned its effort to support the won, and two days later it announced an emergency programme to stem the crisis. Even though the programme included concrete initiatives to clean up the bad loan problem,[5] measures to restructure the financial system and the widening of the won's daily trading range to 10 per cent it was too little too late. Unable to control the situation, on 21 November 1997 the government was obliged to seek emergency support from the IMF to avoid a debt moratorium.

4.2.1 The ingredients of the crisis

Contagion effects from South-East Asia

Developments in the East Asian financial markets after the crisis arose in Thailand in July 1997 suggest that the contagion spread first to the neighbouring ASEAN[6] economies and then to the NIE4.[7] Of the four more advanced economies, Singapore was the first to experience serious fallout from the crisis, followed by Taiwan. The crisis then reached Hong Kong, whose stock market plunged in the third week of October 1997. This brought about the dive in the Korean market and the outflow of foreign equity investment in subsequent weeks.

Empirical evidence by Park and Song (2000) suggests that the crisis in the ASEAN 4[8] was not as contagious to Hong Kong and Korea as it might have been in different circumstances. However there is clear evidence that Taiwan's financial turbulence spread to Hong Kong and Korea through the foreign exchange market. Park and Song concluded that Taiwan was at the centre of the East Asian contagion process because it was only after Taiwan had come under speculative attack that Hong Kong experienced and then Korea succumbed to a similar attack.

There is evidence to suggest that the stock markets of Taiwan, Hong Kong and Singapore were closely linked to each other, and that the crisis spread through the stock market (ibid.). With the onset of the crisis, the stock market collapse in the ASEAN 4 spilt over into the markets of all of the NIEs, including Korea. Unexpectedly, Park and Song found that the stock market plunge in Taiwan, Hong Kong and Singapore did not cause the Korean market to sink to the degree that might have been expected. This was probably due to the fact that a foreign investor sell-off in the Korean stock markets was unlikely to precipitate a financial crisis because their holdings at that time accounted for less than 15 per cent of total market capitalisation. However when Taiwan became the target of a speculative attack following the crisis in the ASEAN 4, foreign banks with a large exposure to Korea began to recall their short- and medium-term loans, reduce the availability of trade credit facilities and cut off lines of credit. This provoked a liquidity crisis in Korea's banking sector, which led to the draining of foreign exchange reserves and eventually to the collapse of the foreign exchange market. This was consistent with the argument that the crisis in Korea was precipitated by foreign banks refusing to roll over short-term loans and drastically curtail interbank lending, rather than by foreign equity investors.

This chain of events leading up to the crisis in November 1997 shows that Korea was adversely affected by the South-East Asian crisis, and in particular that the stock market crash of Taiwan and Hong Kong sparked off the exodus of institutional investors from Korea. Given the country's relatively strong economic fundamentals, one could speculate that Korea might not have come under speculative attack had measures been taken earlier to contain the situation in South-East Asia.

Why was Taiwan so important in spreading the crisis to Hong Kong and Korea? Park and Song (Ibid.) refer to a channel of contagion based on economic similarities. Taiwan, Hong Kong and Korea were fast growing economies that shared an export-oriented development strategy and increasingly relied on the markets of ASEAN for their export earnings. When foreign investors, particularly international banks and institutional investors, including hedge fund managers, saw that such a stable country as Taiwan was vulnerable to the crisis they must have concluded that Hong Kong and Korea would not be immune, and therefore started to attack the foreign exchange markets of these countries. Hong Kong was able to withstand the attack because of its sizeable foreign exchange reserves, but Korea was not.

Investors may also have been concerned about the possibility of competitive devaluations in East Asia. Most of the East Asian countries were locked into competition for market share both within the region and in the USA and Europe. If Taiwan's exchange rate depreciated vis-à-vis the US dollar it was likely that Korea would also need to adjust its exchange rate so as not to lose relative export competitiveness. This would certainly have deepened the crisis and hastened the departure of foreign investors.

A number of recent studies on contagion show that macroeconomic similarities and strong trade and financial linkages between countries cause crises to spread from one country to others. Before the Asian crisis broke out the East Asian NIEs shared few macroeconomic similarities with the ASEAN 4 and were not linked to them through capital account transactions. Although their exports to the region were growing the trade linkage between them was not strong enough to serve as a major channel of contagion. This leads to the conclusion that financial panic and herd behaviour were important causes of the spread of the Thai crisis to the NIE 4. The financial market fallout effect on the NIE 4 could have been contained if foreign institutional investors had been less frightened about the vulnerability of Taiwan to crisis and the equal assailability of Hong Kong and Korea.

Capital flight

Another key ingredient of the financial crisis was the extent of footloose capital. Following the liberalisation of capital controls, on average Korea received an inflow of about $20 billion a year between 1995 and 1996, mostly in the form of portfolio and short-term capital. The sharp shift in international sentiment following the Thai financial crisis brought about a swing on the capital account equivalent to some $40 billion at annual rates. Salient features after July 1997 included:

- Large-scale, short-term capital outflows (including errors and omissions), notwithstanding a temporary period of calm prior to the events in Hong Kong in October. Thereafter short-term capital flight of almost $100 billion at annual rates brought an end to the authorities' futile attempt to shore up the won.
- Portfolio investment added to the financial panic. After the severe Hong Kong stock market correction foreigners became very large sellers of Korean financial assets while domestic residents became large purchasers of foreign assets.
- FDI inflows remained remarkably stable throughout the crisis, albeit somewhat scaled back, while investment outflows were sharply cut in line with the corporate liquidity problems.

The way in which the different elements of the capital account reacted to the crisis is also revealing. The principal elements of capital outflow, in descending order, were foreign banks calling in their loans or cutting off their credit lines, followed by large shifts in portfolio investment, leads and lags (that is, shifts in the timing of international payments), and calls on the Bank of Korea to cover the open foreign exchange positions of the banking system. In sum, Korea's failure in the mid 1990s to liberalise long-term flows relative to portfolio investment and short-term capital flows, owing to the country's hostility to FDI, was a major reason for the severity and speed of the financial crisis.[9]

Policy naivety

A third ingredient was the implementation of naive policies in the throes of the crisis. Monetary policy lacked credibility and consistency since it did not focus on a single overarching objective, such as low inflation or a fixed exchange rate. Although money growth was well sustained during 1997, it masked significant shifts and distortions in the allocation of credit. Bank loans to the 30 largest *chaebols* actually increased by 43 per cent over the year, and indeed some 40 per cent of the growth in bank credit during the second half of 1997 may have been emergency loans to distressed firms at below market rates.[10] Such non-market lending practices continued into 1998,[11] resulting in an acute liquidity shortage for some healthy SMEs.

On 25 August 1997 the government announced the possibility of guaranteeing, if necessary, the foreign liabilities of Korean financial institutions to facilitate their overseas borrowing needs, even though some of these institutions may have been close to insolvency. Despite this announcement, both domestic and foreign financial institutions refused to increase their exposure to the shaky merchant banks. More importantly, the decision to underwrite the foreign liabilities of the banks meant that the Bank of Korea intended to act as lender of last resort in US dollars.

This high-risk strategy was compounded by the decision to prop up the won. Between August and the end of November the Bank of Korea lost at least $8–10 billion in foreign reserves through exchange market intervention, even though the won was theoretically floating within a predetermined band.[12] In short, during the latter part of 1997 monetary policy was being run in a fixed exchange rate mode. With the benefit of hindsight the quick adoption of a freely floating exchange rate, even as late as July, might have staved off some of the worst excesses of the crisis, although a severe financial crisis and loss of international confidence would still have been inevitable. While it is impossible to say whether the attack on the won would have been tempered, the Bank of Korea would at least have been able to act as lender of last resort in the domestic currency.

A final action that added fuel to the flames was an ill-judged decision to bail out Kia Motors in late October, after repeated public statements by the government that it would not do so. But by that time foreign banks had already sharply reduced their credit lines[13] and investors were exiting Korea in large numbers.

4.3 Financial crisis framework – a stroke analogy

The financial system of an economy consists of the central bank, commercial banks and numerous kinds of financial intermediary. The main functions of the financial system are to generate finance and deliver it to the real sector, and to provide a channel to link those who want to save with those who want to invest. If the financial system does not work properly it directly affects the real sector. If there is too much money, for example, the real sector experiences inflation. If there is too little money, recession in the real sector is a natural consequence.

The human circulatory system consists of the heart, arteries, veins and capillaries, whose function is to deliver blood throughout the body, and to act as a medium for the exchange of oxygen and carbon dioxide. Just as in the financial system, a defect in the circulatory system can cause systemic malfunction. A financial crisis, which normally starts with a liquidity crunch, is very similar to a human stroke, which happens when a blood vessel in the brain ruptures, or an artery leading to the brain is blocked by a blood clot, air bubble or some other abnormal particle. A financial crisis can result in the paralysis of the real sector, while a stroke can limit physiological processes such as movement and speech.

Therefore an understanding of the nature of a stroke can aid understanding of the nature of a financial crisis.[14] To most people, strokes appear to strike healthy people who have been living their lives quite normally. However this is not actually the case. Figure 4.1 illustrates how strokes normally occur. As can be seen, the chance of having a stroke depends on a person's physical constitution, how well that person responds to the warning signs of a stroke, and the quality of the person's environmental surroundings and lifestyle.

Smoking, heavy alcohol intake, lack of exercise and high fat consumption contribute to high blood pressure, a high cholesterol level and obesity, which speed up the hardening of the arteries. When people's physical constitution becomes weak the risk of having a stroke increases. Therefore if they have high blood pressure and so on it is very important for them to change their lifestyle by stopping smoking, limiting the amount of alcohol intake, taking regular exercise and eating less fat. If they fail to attend properly to these requirements they become constitutionally predisposed to a stroke. Hostile environmental factors such as family apathy about their condition, competitive personal relationships and a heavy work burden add to the likelihood of having a stroke.

Strokes are normally preceded by warning signs: the sudden loss or blurring of vision in one eye, dizziness, fainting or tingling in a limb. Failure to take appropriate action after a warning sign significantly increases the risk of a stroke. Finally, exogenous shocks such as sudden stress, worry, heavy exercise or exposure to cold weather can trigger a stroke, with serious damage to the body.

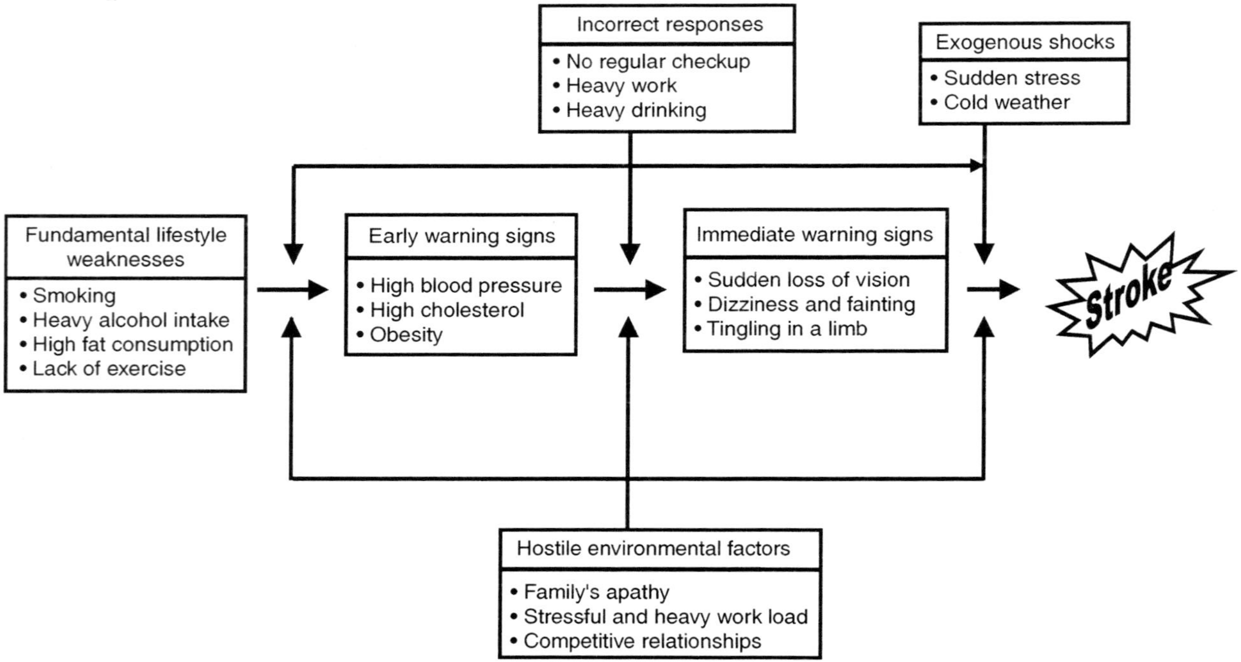

Figure 4.1 The stroke framework

Korea's financial crisis followed a very similar process. To most observers it appeared to erupt suddenly in an apparently healthy and strong economy when panicked foreign investors turned their backs on the country and region. In retrospect, however, there were several early warning signs. As discussed in Chapter 3, fundamental weaknesses, policy mistakes, unfriendly international circumstances and exogenous shocks all played a critical role in the crisis.

The stroke framework is applied to the Korean financial crisis in Figure 4.2. As can be seen, four factors systematically intertwined to cause the crisis. First, from the late 1980s three fundamental weaknesses accumulated and combined to undermine the international competitiveness of Korean exports. Second, the international environment, which had been friendly to Korea's export-oriented growth strategy, rapidly became hostile. This also weakened Korea's international competitiveness and made the economy even more vulnerable to sudden changes in the world economy. Third, the government (and foreign investors) overlooked the signs of weakening competitiveness and the possibility of financial crisis, and instead aggravated the situation by making a series of policy mistakes. Finally, sudden exogenous shocks in early 1997 and the regional crisis in mid 1997 triggered the crisis in Korea.

4.3.1 Exogenous shocks: the trigger

Strokes are usually triggered by an exogenous shock such as severe stress or sudden exposure to cold weather. The Korean financial crisis was triggered by a drastic increase in corporate insolvencies and the financial crisis in South-East Asia which acted as stress and sudden cold weather to which the Korean economy was exposed.

The series of corporate bankruptcies began in January 1997 with Hanbo Steel, the fourteenth largest *chaebol*. By the time Korea turned to the IMF for assistance in November, seven of the top 30 *chaebols*, including Kia Motors, the seventh largest, faced insolvency.[15] This resulted in a surge of non-performing loans in the financial sector, including the commercial and merchant banks. At the end of September non-performing loans amounted to 32 trillion won (7 per cent of GDP), about double the level at the end of 1996.[16]

The financial crisis in South-East Asia acted as a trigger in two ways. First, drastic devaluation of the currencies of the crisis countries further undermined Korea's international competitiveness, which in turn put intense downward pressure on the Korean currency. Second, the trouble in South-East Asia prompted foreign investors to re-evaluate the risk of their investments in Korea, and they soon found out that Korea had experienced a surge in non-performing loans. When the Hong Kong Hang Seng Index recorded a big downturn on 23 October 1997, foreign investors withdrew their investments and en masse cut back their short-term loans

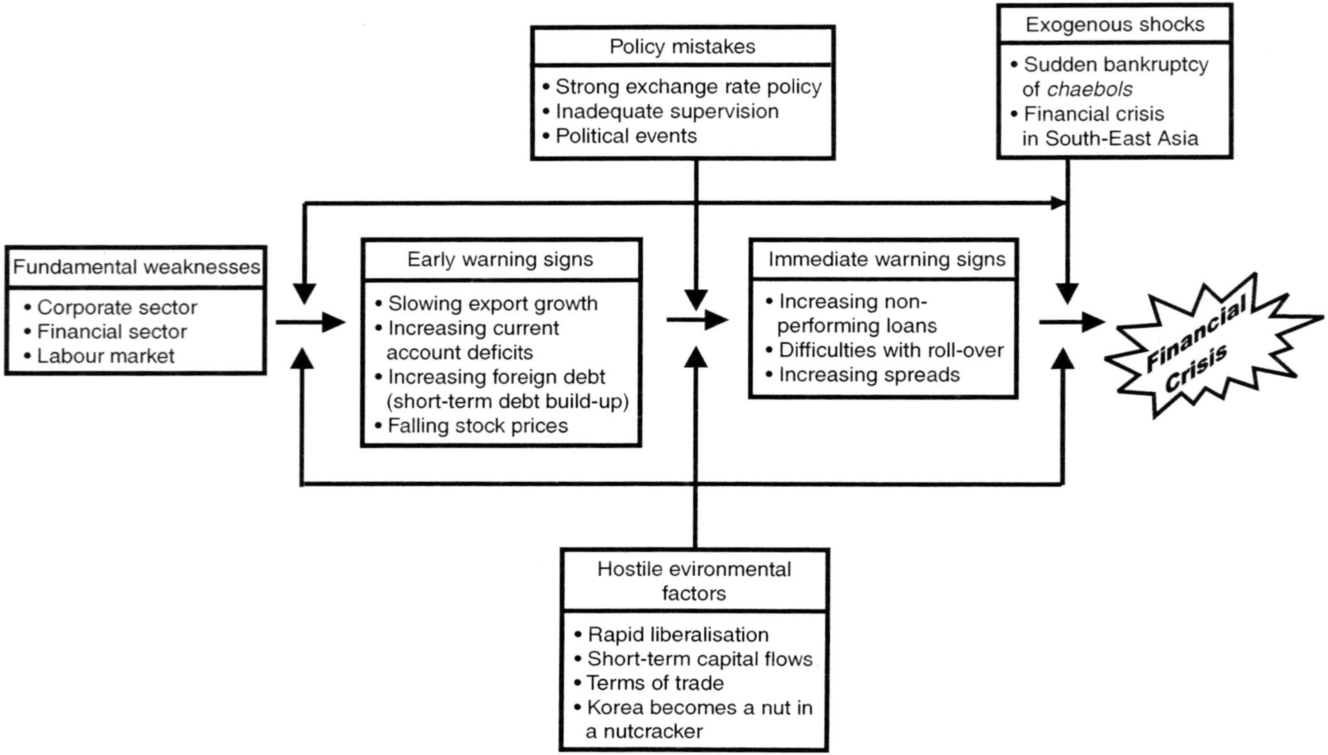

Figure 4.2 The financial crisis framework

to Korea. By 30 November the won had depreciated by about 20 per cent against the US dollar and the stock market index had fallen by about 30 per cent to a ten-year low. Furthermore Korea's useable foreign currency reserves declined sharply when the Bank of Korea financed the repayment of short-term debts of commercial banks' offshore branches.

Korea finally had to turn to the IMF on 21 November 1997 as the roll-over ratio of short-term external borrowings by domestic financial institutions kept falling and the country's usable foreign currency reserves had plummeted to $7.3 billion from $22.3 billion only a month previously.

Thus, like a human stroke, the Korean crisis was triggered by two exogenous shocks. It should be noted here that the self-reinforcing flight of capital was not a cause but a symptom of the financial crisis, a symptom that erupted in response to fundamental weaknesses, an unfriendly international environment, policy mistakes and exogenous shocks.

4.4 The IMF aid package[17]

On 3 December 1997 Korea and the IMF signed an agreement for a financial aid package totalling $58.3 billion. This was subject to a broad range of conditions, including macroeconomic stabilisation and structural reform. The IMF committed $21 billion, the World Bank and the Asian Development Bank $14 billion, and the USA, Japan, Australia and other interested countries $23.3 billion. It was expected that the announcement of such a large financing package, in conjunction with a reform plan, would be enough to calm and turn around the troubled financial market. A key objective was therefore to stabilise the exchange rate and to choke off any second-round inflation effects from the currency depreciation. Accordingly only $5.5 billion was initially disbursed, and there was no attempt to discuss debt rescheduling with international creditors.

Under the terms of the IMF agreement the Korean government was required to implement tough measures, including tight monetary policy and fiscal austerity, in conformity with the prevailing exchange rate of 1100 won to the dollar and the agreement's projections for GDP growth, inflation and the current account for 1998.[18] The initial programme and subsequent amendments are summarised in Table 4.3. The terms also included the immediate closure of insolvent financial institutions. As an emergency measure the government was asked to raise interest rates sharply to stem the outflow of foreign funds and the rapid depreciation of the exchange rate, and to build up its usable foreign exchange reserves. The call rate was raised from 12.3 per cent on 1 December 1997 to 20.7 per cent on 3 December and 30.1 per cent on 23 December.[19] As a consequence yields on three-year corporate bonds soared from around

Table 4.3 The IMF's macroeconomic projections and actual results for 1998

	Original programme (12/97)	**First quarterly programme (2/98)**	**Second quarterly programme (5/98)**	**Third quarterly programme (7/98)**	**Fourth quarterly programme (11/98)**	**Actual results (12/98)**
Real GDP growth rate (%)	3.0	1.0	–1.0	–4.0	n.a.	–5.80
Inflation rate (%)	Below 5.0	Below 10.0	Below 10.0	9.0	n.a.	7.5
Exchange rate (W/$)	1186	1426	1417	1440	1425	1399
Current account	n.a.	Surplus of $8 bn	Surplus of $23 bn	Surplus of $35 bn	n.a.	Surplus of $40.3 bn
% of GDP	Below 1.0	2.50	7.0	n.a.	n.a.	10.60
Fiscal target (% of GDP)	Surplus of 0.20	Deficit of 1.50	n.a.	Deficit of 4.0	Deficit of 5.0	Deficit of 5.0

Sources: IMF; Ministry of Finance and Economy.

14 per cent before the crisis to above 30 per cent, and yields on 91-day commercial paper rose sharply from 13–14 per cent to a peak of 40.8 per cent on 31 December. Broad money growth (M3) had fallen to 13.9 per cent by the end of December, down from 16.3 per cent at the end of November.

The agreement also included significant fiscal restraints aimed at limiting the deterioration of public finances in 1998. The IMF asked Korea to achieve a fiscal surplus of 0.2 per cent of GDP in 1998 by making the necessary contractionary adjustments. Sound fiscal policy had long been a hallmark of Korea, where the use of public finances for macroeconomic management purposes or to attain income distribution objectives had long been avoided. The initial budget for 1998, based on projected real growth of about 6 per cent, envisaged a zero deficit, but was thrown off course by the severity of the ensuing economic crisis due to declining tax revenues, increased payments to the unemployed and the cost of financial sector restructuring. Despite the economic crisis the balanced budget objective for 1998 was maintained, although the growth projection under the IMF programme was sharply reduced to about 3 per cent. Maintaining a balanced budget was considered necessary to alleviate the burden on monetary policy and to provide for the still uncertain cost of restructuring the financial sector. As it became apparent that the economy was much weaker than initially projected, the 1998 budget target was revised to a deficit of about 1.5 per cent of GDP. At the end of July the government, in consultation with the IMF, further revised the target to 4 per cent of GDP and submitted a second supplementary budget to the National Assembly.

The IMF agreement also contained detailed specifications of microeconomic reforms aimed at opening up the Korean economy to greater domestic and world competition, the reform of corporate governance structures and practices, and the improvement of transparency and reporting procedures. The principal intention of these initiatives was to speed the pace of restructuring and reform of the financial system and the *chaebols*. These initiatives were supported by measures to increase labour market flexibility, change Korea's outdated bankruptcy procedures and open up corporate control to foreign capital. (Developments in these areas are discussed in the following chapter.) Some analysts criticised the programme for misplaced emphasis on structural reforms, arguing that the key problem was a temporary, albeit severe, shortage of foreign exchange, and for going beyond the remit of the IMF[20]. In defence of the IMF the OECD argued that the Korean authorities' demand for emergency aid had been made very late in the day when the country was on the brink of default (OECD, 1998, p. 40). Rehabilitating the financial system, according to the OECD, and resolving the corporate debt situation were the essential preconditions for rapidly restoring confidence in the financial market and ending the economic crisis.

Troubled financial institutions would be closed, and those deemed viable would be restructured and/or recapitalised. Nine insolvent merchant banks that had been suspended on 2 December 1997 were required to submit a rehabilitation plan within 30 days. If these plans were not approved the institutions' licenses would be revoked. The remaining merchant banks were required to submit a recapitalisation programme by 31 December 1997, and to meet a capital adequacy radio of at least 4 per cent, as stipulated by the Bank for International Settlements (BIS), by 31 March 1998. Commercial banks were also required to prepare a plan to meet the BIS 8 per cent minimum requirement by September 1998. In addition, virtually all capital account restrictions on foreign investors' access to the bond markets were to be lifted from 1 January 1998.

Despite the IMF agreement the financial market deteriorated further. The roll-over ratio of short-term debt declined sharply and usable official reserves were almost depleted by mid December. For example the roll-over ratio of the seven largest commercial banks fell to 32.2 per cent in December from 58.8 per cent in November and 86.5 per cent in October. The Korea Stock Price Index, after a brief increase to 435 on 6 December from 379 on 3 December, kept sliding, reaching 351 on 24 December. As the speed of depreciation accelerated the exchange rate plummeted from about 1150 won/US$ at the beginning of the month to almost 2000 won/US$ at the end of the year.[21] All these developments were much worse than the IMF and indeed the Korean government had predicted.

Korea was facing imminent default by 24 December so the IMF decided to force foreign commercial banks to roll-over their short-term credits and made comprehensive debt roll-over a precondition for further disbursements of IMF funds. Initially the banks and the government announced a freeze on debt servicing, then on 16 January 1998 formally agreed to a complete roll-over of all short-term debts falling due in the first quarter of that year. On 28 January an agreement was reached to convert $24 billion of short-term debt into maturities of between one and three years (Radelet and Sachs, 1998b, p. 30). The new arrangements put a brake on the falling won and on the decline of the stock market (Figures 4.3 and 4.4).

Although the financial market stabilised in early 1998 the economy entered a deep recession, with output falling by almost 6 per cent during the course of the year. The call interest rate remained above 20 per cent until April (Figure 4.3), and was even higher in real terms since domestic prices and wages began to fall in March. The rise in interest rates had a severe impact on the corporate sector. In the manufacturing sector interest costs surged to 10.7 per cent of sales in the first half of the year and losses rose to 5 per cent. By February the number of bankruptcies had risen to more than three times the precrisis level. Surviving firms

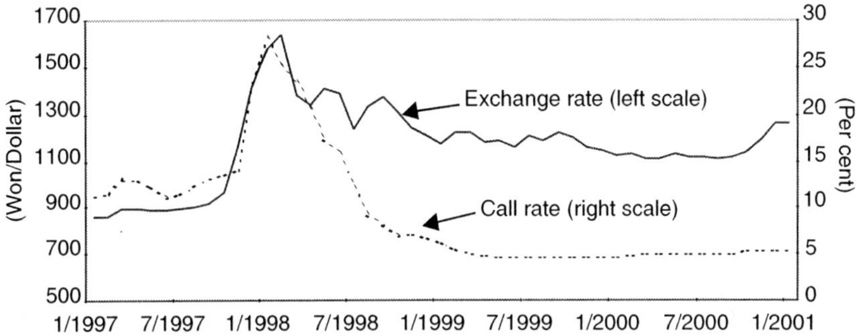

Source: Bank of Korea.

Figure 4.3 Exchange rate and interest rate movements, January 1997 to January 2001

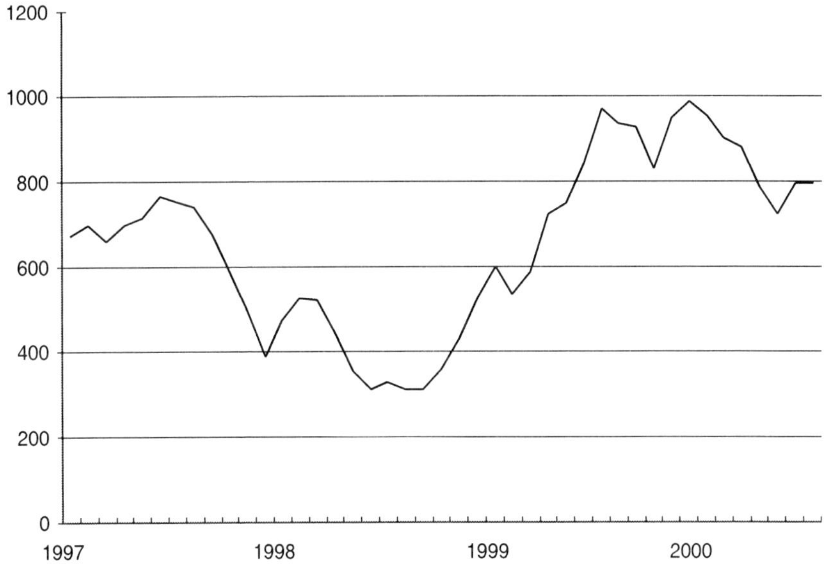

Source: Bank of Korea.

Figure 4.4 Stock price index, KOSPI, 1997–2001 (4 January 1980 = 100)

responded to the cash flow squeeze by slashing investment, reducing their inventories and cutting labour costs.

4.4.1 The consequences of the IMF programme

The original criteria were quickly overtaken by events and the IMF pragmatically revised them in subsequent quarterly performance reviews (Table 4.3). As market interest rates soared to the 30–40 per cent level the financial difficulties of corporations deepened and investment collapsed. Because the IMF programme required financial institutions to meet the BIS capital adequacy ratios they were reluctant to provide corporations with funds for fear of incurring new non-performing loans. Even strong banks came under intense pressure as foreign creditors refused to roll over loans and domestic depositors fled to foreign owned banks. The merchant banks, which formerly provided corporations with short-term funds, virtually suspended new lending to corporations and tended to refuse to roll over loans that fell due. This made the situation even worse for debt-ridden corporations and boosted the number of insolvencies (especially in the case of small and medium-sized companies) to three times the precrisis level. There were 3197 bankruptcies in December 1997, 3323 in January 1998 and 2749 in March 1998. The sharp deterioration in economic circumstances and tight credit conditions threatened the economic restructuring efforts. In June 1998 bank loans were 1.5 per cent below their February level, the brunt of the decline being borne by SMEs, as reflected in the high rate of insolvency. The ratio of dishonoured bills rose drastically to 2.1 per cent in December 1997 from 0.5 per cent the previous month. The contractionary IMF prescriptions also led to a dramatic reduction in consumption, with domestic demand falling by 29 per cent in the first quarter of 1998. As a consequence the external liquidity crisis became a fully fledged economic crisis when the full extent of the collateral damage to the real sector became apparent.

In 1998 real GDP dropped 5.8 per cent on a year-on-year basis, with the manufacturing and construction industries being most severely affected. In 1998 manufacturing output fell by 7.2 per cent, agriculture, forestry and fishing output by 6.3 per cent, and service sector output by 5.4 per cent. Almost 1.66 million jobs were lost in 1998, boosting the unemployment rate to 6.8 per cent compared with 2.6 per cent in 1997. Per capita GDP was \$6843 in 1998, down sharply from \$10363 in 1997 and \$11417 in 1996, and only marginally above the \$6816 recorded in 1991.[22] In 1998 the current account reached a surplus of \$40.6 billion, the largest in history. However this was mainly brought about by a decline in imports rather than an increase in exports. (A more detailed discussion of these macroeconomic developments is conducted in Section 4.5.)

4.4.2 Was the IMF's diagnosis and prognosis correct?

The IMF later admitted that the initial targets had been wrong as key economic variables such as the real GDP growth rate and the unemployment rate turned out to be far worse than predicted. The depth of the ensuing slowdown had not been foreseen in the initial programme projections, and major macroeconomic projections were revised sharply and successively downward during the course of the programme (Table 4.3).[23] The sharp revisions to the projections for growth and exchange rates suggests that the IMF programme, especially in its original form, was inappropriate for and could not adequately deal with the Korean financial crisis. In fact, as will be discussed below, the wrong projections led to inappropriate measures and these obviously contributed to the recession. As Jack Boorman (director of the IMF's Policy Development and Review Department) admitted, 'the original IMF program was based on the view that the Korean economy would experience a slowdown in growth, but not a deep recession'.[24] So the adoption of tight monetary and fiscal policy and high interest rates contributed to the recession, and even though they were reversed when the recession turned out to be deeper than expected[25] this reversal was too late as the IMF measures had already put too heavy a strain on the troubled real economy and caused the economic contraction to become fully fledged.

Why did the IMF's initial, and to a lesser extent subsequent, macroeconomic projections turn out to be so wrong? Hubert Neiss (director of the IMF's Asia and Pacific Department) argued that it was because 'important decisions in several complex and painful areas had to be made almost overnight and without full information'.[26] This argument may hold for the original projections, but why was it necessary for the projections to be significantly changed five times in less than one year? The IMF claimed that this reflected the flexibility of the programme, but this raises questions about the credibility of the IMF as a doctor.

4.4.3 Did the programme help stabilise the financial market?

Some of the initial programme measures not only failed to restore market confidence, they also intensified the panic among international investors. In the first few weeks after the IMF arrangement was announced the exchange rate depreciated and did not show signs of stabilising until early January 1998 (Figure 4.3). There were many reasons for this. First, based on its naive projection of the economy the IMF did not attempt to force foreign commercial banks to roll over their short-term credits. Only when the situation became even worse did it insist on a comprehensive debt roll over as a precondition for further disbursements of IMF funds. In retrospect, some debt relief in the shape of loan roll-overs and debt restructuring were necessary to allow more time for loan repayment by domestic financial institutions and corporations.

Second, despite pledging \$58.3 billion in emergency funds only a limited amount was actually disbursed – \$5.5 billion upon announcement of the package and a further \$7.7 billion at the end of 1997. Of the total emergency funds, \$22 billion was viewed as a 'second line of defence', and the precise terms and conditions under which these contingency funds would be made available were very unclear. IMF economists *Lane et al.* (1999) admit that uncertainty about the availability of the contingency funds may have influenced market participants' decision to continue to exit.

Third, the recommendations on tight budgets, bank closures and high interest rates contributed to even higher numbers of business insolvencies, and this in turn worsened investors' perception of Korea's creditworthiness. This point deserves detailed discussion as the IMF has pointed to the ultimate steady appreciation of the won as proof of the correctness of its prescriptions.

When domestic and foreign currency bonds are imperfect substitutes the foreign exchange rate is in equilibrium only if the interest parity condition holds:

$$R_w = R_\$ + (E^e_{w/\$} - E_{w/\$})/E_{w/\$} + \pi$$

where R_w is the interest rate on domestic currency (won) deposits, $R_\$$ is the interest rate on foreign currency (US dollar) deposits, $E^e_{w/\$}$ is the expected future won/dollar exchange rate, $E_{w/\$}$ is the current won/dollar exchange rate and π is a risk premium that reflects the difference between the riskiness of domestic and foreign bonds.

If the IMF had been right a sharp increase in interest rates would have stabilised the exchange rate. As seen in Figure 4.3, however, the exchange rate quickly fell far below the targets set in the programme and the tight money supply and high interest rates triggered further corporate failures. This, of course, far from restored public confidence. The resulting financial instability and unrest might have caused the risk premium, π, to rise sharply, resulting in a net capital outflow instead of an inflow. This may have contributed to the fall of the won.

Furthermore there is little evidence that the interest rate hikes brought about a capital inflow. For instance during the first quarter of 1998 net foreign portfolio investment was a mere \$7.5 billion, which was too little to stabilise the exchange rate. As a matter of fact the Korean won appreciated during the same period because of international financial assistance of \$21.4 billion, success in rolling over most short-term external debt (totalling \$21.8 billion in March 1998) and a record trade surplus of \$12.3 billion.

As Radelet and Sachs (1998b) point out, the first signs of the end of the currency free-fall only came on 24 December 1997, when the IMF changed its strategy. Its revised approach was based on debt restructuring, accelerated disbursements of international funding, and a more comprehensive and rational restructuring of the financial sector.

4.4.4 Did the programme help prevent complications?

As noted above the IMF programme was based on seriously inaccurate projections that resulted in the implementation of measures such as the immediate closure of a number of financial institutions, tight budgets and high interest rates. These measures were mainly designed to stabilise the financial market, but as pointed out previously they failed to reduce the perception of risk in the Korean economy. Instead they needlessly aggravated the problems of the real sector and intensified the crisis, as the much higher interest rates and cuts in domestic demand caused many profitable but high debt-to-equity firms to go into bankruptcy. Thus the external liquidity crisis became a fully fledged economic crisis when the full extent of the damage to the real sector became apparent. Even in the USA, or any other advanced economy, many firms would experience severe financial difficulties if market interest rates were over 30 per cent.

Of course the opposite approach would not have been desirable either. Pursuing an expansionary monetary policy and lowering interest rates would have caused the exchange rate to overdepreciate, led to hyperinflation and damaged companies with large foreign debts. The point here is that the initial programme should have avoided excessive tightening and concentrated on rescheduling foreign debt. In addition, instead of using most of the emergency IMF loans to meet the debt servicing obligations falling due, a portion should have been used to help finance credits for manufacturers and exporters, who were facing a sharp credit squeeze because of the financial crisis.

In sum the IMF programme served to deepen the woes of the troubled Korean economy.

4.4.5 Did the programme properly address the fundamental causes?

As discussed in Chapter 3 the Korean crisis was rooted in the weakened fundamentals of the economy. Therefore attempting to stabilise only the financial market without addressing structural reform would have been like treating the symptoms without addressing the cause. Hence the IMF programme placed strong emphasis on structural reform of the banking sector, the capital market, the corporate sector, the labour market and the public sector in order to facilitate the return of sustained growth. The details of these reforms are discussed in Chapter 5, but two points need to be made here with regard to the timing of the IMF measures.

First, when the programme was implemented in December 1997 it should have concentrated on helping Korea to cope with its foreign exchange shortages and to regain access to the international capital markets, and the rescue fund should not have been made contingent upon economic reform. This is not because the economy was fundamentally healthy and structural reform was not necessary, but because emergency stabilisation measures should have come first to prevent unnecessary complications arising from the crisis. Only then should attention have been turned to the long-term goal of structural reform.

Second, as a precondition for financial aid the IMF required Korea to undertake reforms that had little to do with restoring market confidence or with the country's ability to repay its debts. Specifically, a timetable for trade liberalisation was required to be set in order to eliminate trade-related subsidies, restrictive import licensing and the import diversification programme. A key question is how this could have helped Korea, which would have required enormous current account surpluses to repay its foreign debts and recover from the crisis. The IMF insisted that trade liberalisation would enhance domestic competition, but this should have been pursued at a later stage because manufacturers were already suffering severely from high interest rates, credit crunches and a drastic fall in demand for their products.

4.5 Economic developments in the aftermath of the crisis 1998–2001

4.5.1 Developments in 1998

The financial crisis developed into a severe economic recession during the first half of 1998.[27] This recession was so severe that it also resulted in a social crisis, characterised by a dramatic rise in unemployment and poverty. As indicated in Table 4.4 and Figure 4.5, the economy went into a sharp nosedive in the first half of 1998. The high interest rate policy (see Figure 4.3) had a major impact on the economy at that time in that it contributed to declining consumer confidence and a severe decline in private

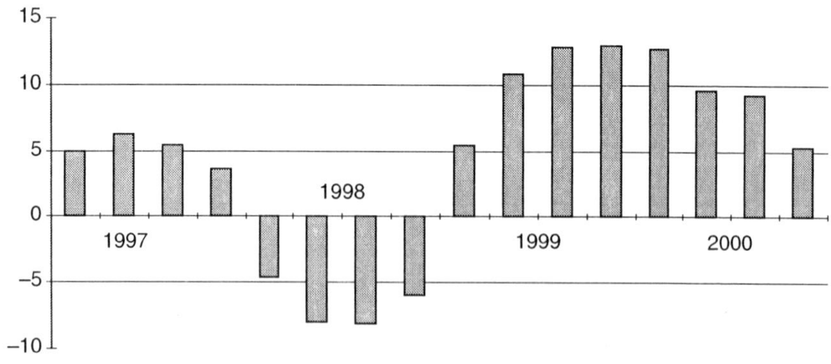

Source: Bank of Korea.

Figure 4.5 Quarterly GDP growth rate, 1997–2000 (per cent)

Table 4.4 Demand and output conditions, 1990–2001 (percentage change)

				1998					1999					2000				
	1990–99	**1997**	**1998**	**Q1**	**Q2**	**Q3**	**Q4**	**1999**	**Q1**	**Q2**	**Q3**	**Q4**	**2000**	**Q1**	**Q2**	**Q3**	**Q4**	**2001**
Private consumption	7.1	3.5	–11.7	–9.9	–11.0	–10.4	–6.9	11.0	6.7	10.3	12.1	12.1	7.1	5.8	4.8	1.3	1.2	4.2
Government consumption	4.6	1.5	–0.4	1.3	–0.7	–0.6	–0.4	1.3	–2.0	–1.7	0.1	0.8	1.3	1.9	1.2	0.3	3.5	0.2
Gross fixed capital formation:	7.7	–2.2	–21.2	–21.0	–24.0	–22.2	–17.9	3.7	–4.2	4.9	7.0	7.6	11.0	30.1	–4.6	–3.5	–18.1	–1.7
Construction	7.7	2.3	–10.1	–5.9	–7.8	–12.0	–13.7	–10.3	–13.6	–8.5	–9.8	–10.2	–4.1	–3.4	2.9	–5.0	–3.1	5.8
Machinery and equipment	10.1	–8.7	–38.8	–38.0	–46	–39.3	–27.4	36.3	13.0	37.3	48.5	55.1	34.3	83.3	–12.1	–1.8	–32.4	–9.8
Final domestic demand	7.0	1.2	–14.0	–12.0	–15	–13.6	–10.2	7.6	2.4	7.2	9.1	9.3	7.7	12.6	1.3	–0.3	–5.1	na[2]
Increase in stocks[1]	0.2	–2.0	–5.5	–9.3	–6.4	–5.3	–2.2	5.4	5.9	5.6	5.7	5.0	–0.9	–14.6	–1.9	5.0	1.4	na[2]
Total domestic demand	7.2	–0.8	–19.8	–22.0	–22	–19.6	–12.5	14.7	10.6	14.7	15.4	14.0	6.7	–5.5	–0.8	5.5	–3.6	na[2]
Exports	13.3	21.4	14.1	25.7	13.2	8.0	8.8	15.8	9.2	14.6	20.0	21.0	21.6	47.6	1.4	18.8	–2.8	1.0
Imports	13.6	3.2	–22.1	–27.0	–26.0	–25.9	–9.0	28.8	27.3	28.3	32.3	28.0	20.0	25.7	–5.1	27.2	–6.6	–2.8
Foreign balance[1]	–0.1	5.7	12.5	18.6	13.0	11.6	6.0	–1.0	–3.3	–1.3	–0.1	1.0	3.5	11.8	2.6	0.4	1.0	na[2]
GDP	7.1	5.0	–6.7	–3.6	–7.2	–7.1	–5.3	10.9	5.4	10.8	12.8	13.0	8.8	6.6	6.4	9.8	–1.7	3.0

Notes:
1. Contribution to growth.
2. Not available.
Source: Bank of Korea.

consumption expenditure by 10 per cent per annum in the first quarter of 1998 and 11 per cent in the second quarter.

The rise in interest rates also had a severe impact on the corporate sector. Interest costs surged to 10.7 per cent of sales in the first half of 1998 in the manufacturing sector, while losses grew by 5 per cent. Firms that managed to survive bankruptcy responded to the cash flow squeeze by slashing investment, reducing their stock and cutting labour costs. The biggest decline occurred in investment, with gross capital formation falling by over 20 per cent in 1998. This was a consequence of high interest rates, credit crunch conditions (which emerged when banks changed their lending behaviour in an effort to boost their capital adequacy ratios) and declining profitability. Capital formation was also discouraged by the uncertain economic outlook and the growth of excess capacity following the collapse of domestic demand. In the construction sector investment in machinery and equipment declined by over 40 per cent in the first half of 1998 and by over a third for the year as a whole. R&D expenditure was also cut in 1998, with outlays in the private sector falling by 8 per cent. Only government spending was weakly expansionary in the first quarter of 1998.

The decline in stock made a negative contribution of 5.5 per cent to growth in 1998. By the end of the year the value of the stock held by firms was 18 per cent lower than it had been a year earlier, for four reasons. First, the high interest rates prevailing during much of 1998 raised the cost of holding stock. Second, firms in financial distress sold off their stock to raise cash. Third, because of the gloomy economic outlook firms reduced their output by more than the fall in demand. Finally, the difficulty of obtaining trade finance forced producers to run down their stock of raw materials and intermediate goods.

Firms also responded to the crisis by cutting labour costs by reducing their staffing level, wages and hours of work (Table 4.5). Dependent employment (not self-employed and family workers) declined by almost 8 per cent, the sharpest falls being recorded in the manufacturing and construction sectors. The drop in employment was facilitated by the February 1998 revision of the Labour Standards Act, which permitted layoffs for managerial reasons. During 1998, 120 000 workers (almost 1 per cent of employees) were laid off and a further 260 000 opted for early retirement. The reduction in employment was accompanied by a 2.5 per cent decline in nominal earnings, reflecting the exceptional degree of flexibility in wages in Korea. The latter was primarily due to the importance of overtime and bonus payments, which usually accounted for a third of employees' earnings. However in 1998 these two types of payment fell by more than 15 per cent. In addition the annual economy-wide wage rise was cut from 9 per cent to 4 per cent. Finally, working hours were reduced by 1.9 per cent in 1998 due to large overtime cuts.

Table 4.5 Labour market developments, 1990–2001 (percentage change from previous year)

	1990–96	1997	1998	1999	2000	2001
Employment						
Total	2.3	1.4	–5.3	1.4	3.8	1.4
By sector:						
Agriculture	–4.9	–1.8	4	–5.3	–2.6	–4.2
Construction	6.5	1.7	–21.3	–6.5	7.2	–0.4
Manufacturing	–0.8	–4.5	–13	2.8	5.9	–1.0
Services	5.4	4.3	–1.6	3.4	4.0	na
By type of employment:						
Self employed	2.3	2.9	–3.4	1.1	2.7	2.8
Family workers	–1.0	–2.2	6.8	–5.4	0.1	–3.3
Employees	2.9	1.2	–7.8	2.7	5.0	1.5
Regular		–3.4	–9.8	–6.3	3.3	4.0
Temporary	3.5	8.5	–4.3	4.6	7.8	2.0
Daily	–0.3	4.9	–8.3	31.9	3.9	–5.9
Unemployment						
Labour force	2.1	2.0	–1.0	0.8	1.5	1.1
Unemployment rate[1]	2.4	2.6	6.8	6.3	4.1	3.7
Participation						
Population 15 years and over	1.7	1.6	1.5	1.1	1.0	1.0
Employment/Population (%)	43.9	45.9	43.1	43.3	44.2	na
Total participation rate[2]	61.2	62.2	60.7	60.5	60.7	60.8
Men[2]	75.6	75.6	75.2	74.4	74.0	73.6
Women[2]	47.7	49.5	47.0	47.4	48.3	48.8

(continued)

Table 4.5 Labour market developments, 1990–2001 (percentage change from previous year) (*continued*)

	1990–96	1997	1998	1999	2000	2001
Wages						
Total economy:						
Earnings	12.6	7	–2.5	12.1	8.0	5.6
Hours worked	–0.3	–1.3	–1.9	4.5	–0.9	–1.1
Earnings per hour	12.9	8.4	–0.6	7.3	9.0	na
Real earnings per hour[3]	7.1	3.6	–7.5	6.4	6.6	na
Manufacturing sector:						
Earnings	12.6	5.2	–3.1	14.9	8.5	6.3
Hours worked	–0.3	–1.2	–3.7	8.6	–1.5	–2.0
Earnings per hour	12.9	6.4	0.5	5.7	na	na
Real earnings per hour[3]	7.1	1.9	–6.4	4.8	na	na
Total labour input[4]	–1.0	–9.0	–16.5	4.9	na	na
Output	7.7	4.5	–6.6	25.0	na	na
Productivity	8.8	14.8	11.8	19.2	na	na
Unit labour costs	4.1	–7.3	–10.1	–9.6	–1.5	na

Notes:
1. As percent of the labour force.
2. As percent of population over the age of 15.
3. Deflated by the consumer price index.
4. Number of workers in the manufacturing sector times hours worked.
na = not available.

Source: Bank of Korea, National Statistical Office and Ministry of Labour.

The decline in employment and wages sharply reduced household income. This squeeze on income was reflected in a tenfold rise in the number of individuals filing for bankruptcy in 1998. In addition household wealth was significantly reduced by a fall of about 13 per cent in land and housing prices. Although the stock price index rose by 50 per cent during the course of 1998 (Figure 4.4), by the end of December it was still 14 per cent below its 1997 average. However stock price movements had little impact since only about 4 per cent of the population owned equities. Faced with falling income and wealth, households cut their domestic consumption expenditure by almost 10 per cent in real terms in 1998, led by a one third decline in the purchase of durable goods. Most notably, car sales fell by half.

In 1998 the number of unemployed almost tripled to 1.5 million, an unemployment rate of 6.8 per cent compared with 2 per cent prior to the crisis. The unemployment problem, however, was even more severe than suggested by these indicators. First, the long-term upward trend in the participation rate was reversed in 1998. Second, there was an increase in underemployment. Third, even though the government created about 440 000 public works jobs in 1998 (equivalent to 1.2 per cent of the working age population) to assist the newly unemployed, the participation rate fell from 62.2 per cent in 1997 to 60.7 per cent in 1998 (Table 4.5). With the entry of about 400 000 new graduates into the labour market in early 1999, the unemployment rate increased further to 8.4 per cent before falling to 6.5 per cent in May.

The large decline in domestic demand helped to limit the inflationary pressure arising from the sharp depreciation of the won at the end of 1997. While import prices jumped more than 50 per cent in the first quarter of 1998, most of this increase was not passed on to consumers. The price level remained basically unchanged due to weak demand, falling wages, a one third cut in the price of oil and some recovery in the exchange rate. The overall increase in the CPI was limited to 7.5 per cent for 1998 as a whole.

Following a deficit of $8.2 billion in 1997, Korea recorded a $40.4 billion current account surplus in 1998 – a swing of almost $50 billion in one year (Table 4.6). This surplus was primarily due to a fall in imports almost equivalent to 13 per cent of GDP. Imports fell 35.5 per cent in dollar terms (Table 4.7) due to a 25 per cent drop in volume (Table 4.8), a decline in the dollar prices of oil and other commodities, weak domestic demand, and reduced trade lending by financial institutions. By region the sharpest declines – more than 40 per cent – were recorded for imports from Japan and the EU. Consumer products were especially hard hit, with imports of non-durable items falling by more than 60 per cent. In addition to the trade balance, two other factors contributed to the large current account surplus in 1998. First, a decline in overseas travel by Koreans pushed the non-factor service balance into surplus. Second, a jump in private transfer inflows offset the deterioration in the investment income balance. In early 1999, however, imports began to increase as output growth resumed.

Table 4.6 Current account balance, 1990–2001 ($billion)

	1990–96	1997	1998	1999	2000	2001
Merchandise trade:						
Exports	91.7	138.6	132.1	145.2	175.8	151.4
Imports	96.1	141.8	90.5	116.8	159.2	138.0
Balance	–4.4	–3.2	41.6	28.4	16.6	13.4
Non factor Services:						
Exports	15.2	26.3	25.6	26.5	29.7	29.6
Imports	17.9	29.5	24.5	27.2	33.7	33.1
Balance	–2.7	–3.2	1.0	–0.7	–4.0	–3.5
Investment Income:						
Credit	2.9	3.9	2.7	3.2	6.8	7.0
Debit	3.6	6.3	8.3	8.4	9.0	7.9
Balance	–0.7	–2.5	–5.6	–5.2	–2.2	–0.9
Transfers, net						
Public	–0.1	–0.4	–0.4	–0.3	–0.4	–0.2
Private	1.0	1.0	3.8	2.3	1.0	–0.1
Current account	–7.0	–8.2	40.4	24.5	11.0	8.6
% of GDP	–1.7	–1.5	12.7	6.0	2.4	2.0

Source: Bank of Korea.

Table 4.7 Developments in Korea's exports and imports, by value, 1997–2001 (percentage change)

	2000 Share in	1997	1998	1999	2000	2001
Total exports:	100.0	5.0	–2.8	8.6	19.9	–12.7
Food and consumer goods	1.6	–2.3	–8.9	7.5	–5.4	na
Fuel and raw material	6.7	26.0	–4.2	6.2	47.5	na
Light industry	17.6	3.3	–3.7	–8.5	1.9	–13.1
Heavy industry:	74.1	4.4	–2.2	15.0	23.7	–12.6
Passenger cars	6.4	4.6	–5.4	15.3	17.9	3.1
Electronic products	36.0	8.0	–6.7	33.6	35.4	–23.7
Exports as a share of GDP		28.6	41.6	35.4	37.7	35.6
Total imports:	100.0	–3.8	–35.5	28.4	34.0	–12.1
Consumer goods	10.0	–1.9	–39.5	10.7	14.7	3.5
Industrial materials and fuels	49.2	1.2	–34.3	25.6	39.9	–8.9
Capital goods	40.8	–10.1	–35.5	38.4	34.9	–19.7
Imports as a share of GDP		30.3	29.4	29.5	35.1	33.4

Notes:
Light industry includes textiles, apparel, and rubber products; heavy industry includes all other manufactured products, except food.
na – not available.

Source: Bank of Korea, National Statistical Office.

Table 4.8 Developments in Korea's exports and imports, by volume, 1997–2001 (percentage change)

	1997	1998	1999	2000	2001
Total exports:	14.6	19.2	12.0	20.9	0.7
Light industry[1]	8.4	9.6	–4.9	–1.1	–5.5
Heavy industry[2]:	16.4	23.1	23.4	33.2	2.4
Passenger cars	13.8	8.1	15.0	13.9	–3.0
Electronic products	23.1	26.7	60.0	51.6	–0.1
Semiconductors	36.4	67.8	28.3	33.7	18.6
Telecommunication goods	27.4	24.4	78.1	93.2	10.2
Total imports:	1.9	–25	29.1	18.9	–2.3
Consumer goods	15.4	–31.7	22.4	14.4	8.9
Industrial materials and fuels	5.4	–16.1	23.6	6.2	–0.4
Capital goods	–7.3	–35.4	41.6	43.3	–8.2
Imports as a share of GDP[3]	33.3	27.8	32.3	35.7	na

Notes:
1. Light industry includes textiles, apparel and rubber products.
2. Heavy industry includes all other manufactured products, except food.
3. On a national accounts basis using 1995 prices.
4. na – not available.

Source: Bank of Korea, National Statistical Office.

Korean exports increased by 19.2 per cent in volume terms in 1998 (Table 4.8), sustained by the competitiveness gains that arose from the decline of the currency. In trade-weighted terms the won fell by 30 per cent in 1998. The gain in competitiveness was even larger, given the cut in wages, in terms of relative unit labour costs, measured in a common currency, which improved by more than a third. Consequently export prices fell by 17 per cent in dollar terms, helping to sustain the volume of shipments overseas. However, given the large decline in prices the value of total exports actually fell by 2.8 per cent (Table 4.7).

The rise in exports following the improvement in price competitiveness was partially offset by a sharp drop in demand in overseas markets. In 1998 Korea's overall export market growth for manufactured products fell to 2 per cent from 11 per cent the previous year, reflecting the impact of the Asian financial crisis. Asia's share of Korean exports had increased markedly prior to the crisis, and by 1997 South-East Asia and China were purchasing more than a fourth of total exports while Japan accounted for another 10 per cent in US dollar terms. In 1998, however, Korea's exports to South-East Asia fell by 25 per cent in dollar terms, while those to Japan and China fell by 17 per cent and 12 per cent respectively. These declines were partially offset by increased exports to the USA and EU. Consequently Korea's export performance was markedly superior to that of other Asian countries, despite the lack of trade financing and a rise in foreign restrictions on Korean exports.

The large current account surplus and the rise in Korea's foreign exchange reserves helped to restore the confidence of foreign investors. In 1996 investment from abroad had totalled almost $50 billion. By the last quarter of 1997, however, this had swung to an outflow of more than $15 billion at an annual rate. An even larger outflow took place in the third quarter of 1998 following the crisis in Russia. However the total outflow of foreign investment was limited to $2.6 billion as a sharp rise in FDI almost offset the reduction in foreign loans. In addition foreigners made a net purchase of $4 billion of Korean equities in 1998, boosting their holdings to 19 per cent of total market capitalisation and contributing to the recovery of the stock price index in the second half of the year. Korea's capital account swung from a net inflow of $23 billion in 1996 to a net outflow of almost $4 billion in 1998.

The surge in FDI in 1998 was encouraged by the government's efforts to simplify the regulatory and administrative procedures for foreign investors. This contributed to a 27 per cent rise in FDI on a notification basis to a record high of $8.9 billion. Much of the increase was concentrated in the manufacturing sector, notably in electronics. The USA and Europe each accounted for about a third of total FDI, but Japan's share remained quite modest. The growing participation of foreign firms was expected to boost competition and lead to significant efficiency gains.[28]

From mid 1998 signs of economic recovery began to emerge. For example the downturn in GDP growth was reversed, the exchange rate strengthened (Figure 4.3) and interest rates fell to levels well below those which had prevailed before the crisis erupted (Figure 4.3). The Korea Stock Price Index rose to almost 600 points, up from a low of 298 in June 1998 (Figure 4.4). At the end of 1998 short-term debt accounted for just 21 per cent of total debt and the usable foreign exchange reserves surpassed $50 billion.

4.5.2 Developments in 1999

By the latter half of 1998 improvement in a broad range of indicators signalled an economic turnaround. The recovery between 1999, only two years after the financial crisis, and mid 2000 was outstanding by almost any measure and much stronger than expected. In contrast to the 2 per cent growth rate projected in the government's 1999 budget, output rose by almost 11 per cent, giving the GDP growth trajectory a distinct V shape (Figure 4.5). The resumption of job creation reduced the unemployment rate from its peak of 8.5 per cent in February 1999 to 4.8 per cent in December 1999.[29] Inflation in 1999 fell below 1 per cent – the lowest ever recorded in Korea – thanks to an appreciation of the won and continued slack in the economy. Massive current account surpluses in two consecutive years (1998 and 1999) helped boost the foreign exchange holdings to $90 billion by the end of June 2000.

The recovery was led by private consumption (Table 4.4), fuelled by pent-up demand and rising overtime payments. The corporate sector, having slashed employment and wages and reduced its debt burden, recorded profit gains, leading to a rise in fixed investments. Another important factor was a reduction in destocking, which made a large contribution to growth. Export growth also picked up, reflecting Korea's increased competitiveness following the deprecation of the won. Output increased by almost 11 per cent in 1999 – despite the problems resulting from the mid-year collapse of Daewoo, the second largest *chaebol* – and continued to expand at a robust pace into the early part of 2000. The consumer price increase in 1999 was 0.8 per cent, a record low. During the first half of 2000 it climbed to 1.5 per cent, although core inflation (excluding energy and most agricultural products) was about 1 per cent.

Korea's early and strong rebound from the crisis was due to a number of factors. First, there was a recovery in confidence following the build-up of foreign exchange reserves as a result of the large current account surplus. This increased confidence boosted capital inflows, notably in the form of FDI, which rose from $8.8 billion in 1998 to an all-time high of $15.5 billion in 1999, thus further increasing the foreign exchange reserves. The capital inflows, combined with the large current account surplus, also helped the exchange rate to recover and resulted in the upgrading of Korea's sovereign debt rating.

Second, a broad range of structural reforms were implemented to address the weaknesses that had made Korea vulnerable to contagion from the financial crisis. These reforms, which included significant changes in the financial system, the corporate sector, the labour market and government regulations, had a positive affect on confidence both within Korea and abroad concerning the country's prospects (these reforms are discussed in greater detail in Chapter 5).

Third, the recovery and stabilisation of the currency facilitated the easing of monetary and fiscal policies, which had been tightened after the onset of the crisis. A key measure was the reduction of short-term interest rates from over 30 per cent to less than 5 per cent in 1999, and the long-term bond rate remained in single digits during most of the year. The lower interest rates were extremely beneficial to Korea's highly indebted corporate sector and boosted banks' operating profits. Government spending increased by about a fifth between 1997 and 1999. This added expenditure was focused on assisting the unemployed, helping SMEs to overcome the credit crunch, and rehabilitating the financial sector. Consequently the consolidated central government budget, which had typically been kept in balance prior to the crisis, recorded a deficit that was equal to 4 per cent of GDP in 1999 (these developments are discussed in more detail in Chapter 5).

Fourth, favourable external conditions supported the strong recovery. The significant decline in the effective exchange rate in 1998 was only partially reversed the following year. In addition trade in overseas markets picked up and a strong demand for electronic goods boosted Korean exports. Fifth, technical factors, notably inventory adjustment, added to the strength of the expansion in 1999. Finally, there was a sharp expansion of the information and communications sectors, which by 1999 accounted for almost 8 per cent of GDP. These sectors' output grew by more than 40 per cent in 1999, accounting for about 4 per cent of GDP growth (this is discussed further in Chapter 6).

After a steep decline of almost a fifth in 1998 total domestic demand bounced back strongly in 1999, rising by 14.7 per cent, and continued to expand at a rapid pace into early 2000 (Table 4.4). The driving forces of the upturn, which started in the third quarter of 1998, were buoyant private consumption, a turnaround in equipment investment and a slowing of the pace of inventory decumulation.

The fall in income and wealth, which had severely curtailed private consumption during the crisis, was reversed in 1999. Urban households' average income rose by 6.5 per cent in real terms, while land prices increased slightly after falling by 14 per cent in 1998. The upward trend in the stock market in 1999 (Figure 4.4) also encouraged consumption, although its impact was limited by the fact that less than 15 per cent of households owned equities. In addition the government reduced the special consumption tax on cars and some household appliances in July 1998 to encourage consumption. These factors, combined with a large degree of pent-up demand, led to a double-digit rise in consumption that accounted for half of the economic growth recorded in 1999. This surge in consumption was led by durable goods purchases. In particular the sale of domestic cars jumped by 84 per cent and personal computers by 55 per cent. A rise in service spending was also important, given that services' share of private consumption had increased from 40 per cent to almost 60 per cent over the past decade.

Fixed capital formation recovered less strongly from its sharp contraction in 1998, rising by 3.7 per cent in 1999 and contributing 1 per cent to growth. Investment in machinery and equipment contributed significantly to the turnaround – after falling by 38.8 per cent in 1998 it increased by almost the same amount in 1999. In contrast construction investment declined by 10 per cent for the second consecutive year, reflecting the depressed state of private construction activities. Housing construction was particularly curtailed as the number of permits issued had been halved in 1998, although this decline was compensated by a 15 per cent rise in social capital projects.

The turnaround in fixed asset investment was primarily due to an upturn in corporate profitability. The ratio of net income to total assets, which was strongly negative in 1997 and 1998 for listed non-financial firms, recovered to 3.5 per cent owing to the economic recovery and the reduction in interest costs. The 30 largest *chaebols* reduced their indebtedness in line with their obligation to lower their debt to equity ratios to less than 200 per cent by the end of 1999. Consequently the total borrowing to assets ratio for listed manufacturing companies fell significantly from its 1997 peak of 58 per cent to less than 40 per cent in 1999. This decline in debt helped to reduce interest expenses as a share of sales. Interest expenses were also lowered by a 1 per cent reduction of the average interest rate charged on loans by nationwide commercial banks to just under 10 per cent in the first half of 1999. The recovery in investment was also encouraged by new opportunities in emerging industries, notably information and communications. In addition venture businesses, a category created in 1997, numbered over 5000 by 1999, boosted by a doubling of the number of Internet start-up companies to about 2400.

A number of interesting developments took place in terms of investment. First, SMEs accounted for 46 per cent of new bank loans in 1999 compared with only 8 per cent for large companies. Second, the top 30 *chaebols'* share of loans from the financial institutions fell markedly from 35 per cent at the end of 1998 to 25 per cent a year later. Third, the manufacturing sector's share of outstanding loans declined from 35 per cent to 32 per cent over the same period. Fourth, smaller companies began to play a larger role in total R&D activities. SMEs' share of such expenditure increased from 9 per cent in 1997 to 15 per cent in 1999, with a corresponding decline in the share of large companies.

Stock-building made a large contribution of 5.4 per cent to GDP growth in 1999, reversing the negative trend during the preceding year. Stock in the industrial sector had fallen by 17 per cent in 1998, reflecting high interest rates, distress sales of inventory by troubled firms and the difficulty of obtaining trade finance, which forced producers to run down their stock of raw materials and intermediate goods. As production expanded in the first half of 1999 the pace of inventory decumulation stabilised, thus making a positive contribution to output growth. By the end of the year inventory growth had turned positive for the first time since the crisis. As shipments rose sharply in 1999 the decrease in inventories for the year as a whole reduced the inventory to shipment ratio to the lowest level on record.

Although inflation was very low in 1999, double-digit output growth, coupled with the decline in the unemployment rate and the sharp hike in oil prices, prompted concern about the risk of inflationary pressure. As mentioned earlier the increase in consumer prices was limited to 0.8 per cent in 1999, despite a 2.2 per cent rise in the price of publicly provided services, which accounted for about 13 per cent of the consumer price index. Moreover the record low inflation rate was achieved in spite of a 2.8 per cent rise in food prices. Excluding food, consumer prices actually fell in 1999. Perhaps the most important factor was the extent of slack in the economy, as reflected in low capacity utilisation rates and high unemployment. In addition the sustained appreciation of the won from its trough at the end of 1997 put downward pressure on prices (Figure 4.3). Import liberalisation, notably the ending of the ban on certain Japanese products, also enhanced competition in the retail sector. Finally, restructuring in the distribution sector, including the growth of electronic commerce and the establishment of large-scale discount stores, helped to reduce inflation.

With the sharp rise in industrial production employment growth resumed, reaching 1.4 per cent in 1999 (Table 4.5).[30] This increase was solely accounted for by the manufacturing and service sectors, and employment in the construction sector contracted for the second consecutive year. While the number of employees bounced back from the sharp decline recorded in 1998 the number of regular workers[31] continued to fall. The proportion of temporary and daily workers rose from 46 per cent of employees in 1997 to 52 per cent in 1999 for several reasons. First, firms tended to prefer to hire such workers as they were less expensive than regular workers and easier to lay off. Second, the public works programmes continued into 1999, employing an average of 380 000 persons per day in short-term jobs. Finally, the decision in 1998 to allow job agencies to supply temporary workers for 26 occupational categories encouraged the use of such employees.

The resumption of employment growth reduced the unemployment rate from a peak of 8.4 per cent in the first quarter of 1999 to under 4 per cent in May 2000. Nevertheless unemployment was still considerably higher than the 2 per cent level that had prevailed in 1995 and 1996, suggesting that some degree of slack remained in the labour market. While a return to the precrisis unemployment rate appeared infeasible in the new economic environment, there was room for a further decline without provoking inflationary pressure. There was also a significant fall in the participation rate after the crisis, suggesting an even greater degree of slack in the labour market. Indeed the participation rate in 1999 was 1.7 per cent below its 1997 level, with the decline concentrated among women (Table 4.5).

The improvement in labour market conditions was accompanied by a rise in wages, although this was balanced by an increase in productivity. Following a 2.5 per cent fall in 1998, wages rose by 12 per cent in 1999. While the double-digit hike caused concern about cost-push inflationary pressure, much of the increase was due to a rise in overtime pay of nearly one third as firms preferred to increase their employees' working hours rather than hire additional workers. The number of hours worked increased by more than eight hours a month or about 4.5 per cent in 1999 (Table 4.5). With productivity, adjusted for hours worked, rising at double-digit rates, unit labour costs dropped significantly for the third consecutive year in the manufacturing sector.

Asset prices recovered in 1999, reflecting renewed economic growth and low interest rates. Both land and house prices rose by 3 per cent, but remained around 10 per cent below their precrisis levels. The Korea Stock price index (KOSPI) nearly doubled in 1999 (Figure 4.4), partly as a result of $5.6 billion of net purchases from abroad, boosting foreigners' share of total capitalisation to 21.9 per cent compared with 18.6 per cent in 1998. Meanwhile the Korea Securities Dealers Automated Quotation (KOSDAQ) market, the Korean equivalent of NASDAQ established in 1996 to facilitate fund-raising by SMEs and venture companies, more than tripled, reflecting the boom in the information and telecommunications sectors. With the increase in prices and the addition of another 100 companies, the total capitalisation of KOSDAQ soared from 7 trillion won in 1997 to over 100 trillion won (21 per cent of GDP) at the end of 1999. The sharp increase in stock prices caused some concern about a possible bubble. Even with the rebound in 1999, however, the KOSPI was still below the 1994 level. Furthermore a correction during early 2000 reduced the index by about one fourth by the end of May. The KOSDAQ experienced an even sharper correction in prices in the spring of 2000 that reduced the index by almost half between February and May.

The recovery of the won continued in 1999, with an 18 per cent rise in the yearly average rate relative to the dollar and a 15 per cent appreciation on a trade weighted basis (Figure 4.3). In 1999 import prices (in won) fell by 17 per cent, partially reversing the 28 per cent rise in 1998 and helping to keep inflation below 1 per cent. Much of the appreciation of the won occurred in the latter part of 1999 and continued into 2000. Currency appreciation was driven by the large current account surplus and capital inflows, particularly into the stock market. As well as portfolio inflows, FDI inflows surged by 62 per cent in 1999 to $8.8 billion, led by mergers and acquisitions involving foreign firms. More than half of FDI, measured on a notification basis, was linked to the restructuring of financial institutions and *chaebols*. The surpluses on FDI and portfolio investment were partially offset by an outflow of short-term foreign debt repayments. Nevertheless total capital inflows, after turning negative in 1998, were positive once again, although the scale of inflows, at around $5 billion, was only a fraction of the nearly $50 billion recorded in 1996. When capital outflows resumed in 1999 the net result was a small capital account surplus of less than $1 billion.

The strong recovery of domestic demand stimulated an increase in imports that halved the current account surplus from almost 13 per cent of GDP in 1998 to 6 per cent in 1999, although the current account surplus still amounted to some $24.5 billion (Table 4.6). Consequently the external balance made a negative contribution to growth in 1999. About half of the 29 per cent rise in imports, in dollar terms, was related to GDP growth,[32] while the other half was due to special factors, notably renewed demand following the postponement of foreign purchases. Another special factor was the termination of the Import Diversification Programme, which had restricted imports of certain products from Japan.

The phasing out of this scheme, which was completed by mid 1999, contributed to a 43 per cent rise in imports from Japan that year. Meanwhile progressive trade liberalisation had helped boost imports from 27 per cent of GDP in 1993 to around 30 per cent in 1999. This expansion of imports was led by capital goods, reflecting renewed investment in machinery and other equipment. The growth of imported consumer goods was relatively subdued in value terms (Table 4.7) but strong in volume terms (Table 4.8). Indeed imports of consumer products remained one third below their precrisis level. A 24 per cent jump in the price of crude oil in 1999 also boosted imports.

Export volume growth was relatively buoyant at 12 per cent in 1999, despite the collapse of the Daewoo group (which had accounted for 15 per cent of export revenue) and some attenuation of the competitiveness gains realised after the crisis. The appreciation of the won in 1999 more than offset the further decline in unit labour costs in manufacturing, resulting in a 10 per cent rise in Korea's labour costs relative to those of other countries. Nevertheless Korea remained in a strong competitive position as its relative labour costs were one fourth below their 1997 level. This helped export volume significantly to outpace the growth of Korea's exports by value for the fourth consecutive year. Indeed Korea's export performance since 1995 had surpassed that of all OECD countries with the exception of Hungary. Export growth in 1999 was led by a 30 per cent gain in shipments to the USA and to Japan. There was, however, a dichotomy between (a) the decline in export volume and the value of light industry products and (b) the strong increase in export volume and value of heavy industrial products, including electronic products. The largest gains were recorded in portable telephones (104 per cent) and computers (89 per cent). The export increase was achieved despite a rise in the number of import restrictions imposed by other countries from 76 in 1998 to 96 in 1999.

4.5.3 Developments in 2000

In early 2000 it seemed as though the Korean economy had overcome the worst of the crisis, with the strong global demand for Korean exports, particularly in the ICT sector, and the competitive domestic exchange rate maintaining the growth momentum. However in the second quarter of the year economic growth slowed and capacity utilisation and investment declined (Table 4.4). Private consumption also slowed, as did the other major source of growth during the expansionary period, exports, although a concurrent slowdown in imports enabled the maintenance of a substantial current account balance. In the third quarter there was a temporary reversal, due primarily to a sizable degree of stock-building and a recovery in export growth, but in the fourth quarter output declined by a seasonally adjusted rate of 1.7 per cent. Hence the economy again began to show some instability due to the slowdown of growth and bearish movements of the stock market. Some have argued that this was mainly because rapid economic recovery had taken place without the necessary restructuring of the financial and corporate sectors.

The downturn was the consequence of both domestic and external factors. On the domestic front there was a noticeable deterioration in confidence among the household and business sectors during the year. This was reflected in the stagnation of private consumption in the second half of 2000 and a rapid reduction in investment, in machinery and equipment, particularly in the last quarter. This loss of confidence was due to a number of factors. First, there was a delay in providing public funds for financial restructuring due to the spring elections and political disputes later in the year. This delay served to worsen the *chaebols'* financial problems. For example seven of the top 30 *chaebols* did not earn enough profits to pay even the interest on their debts, let alone repay the principal. The problems in the corporate sector in turn threatened the health of the financial sector. Banks experienced a continual increase in non-performing assets, while the bond market was closed to most companies in 2000.

Second, the work-out programme for Daewoo-affiliated companies revealed considerably higher than expected levels of debt and the negotiations to sell Daewoo Motors to Ford collapsed in September 2000. In addition the revelation of financial ill-health among some Hyundai subsidiaries in mid 2000 added to uncertainty in the financial markets, and this seemed to mark the turning point from economic recovery to slowdown. Third, labour unrest indicated that there was significant opposition to restructuring. Fourth, the corporate sector, including some companies affiliated to the largest *chaebols*, continued to experience balance sheet problems, despite buoyant growth. The overall deterioration in confidence was reflected in a fall in the KOSPI in 2000, despite record net purchases of Korean equities by foreigners. This negative wealth effect, in conjunction with declining household income and business profits, contributed to the decline in both consumption and investment spending.

On the external side, the sharp rise in oil prices in mid 1999 had a major impact on Korea, which relied on oil imports for about half of its energy needs. Higher oil prices increased the import bill by $11 billion in 2000, equivalent to 2.25 per cent of GDP. This was accompanied by a deceleration of world economic growth, particularly in the USA, which accounted for over a quarter of Korea's total exports and a third of its ICT exports. Declining demand for Korean exports, particularly from the ICT sector[33] was matched by a downward trend in the price of semiconductors,[34] the country's number one export item.[35] After rising at an annual rate of 21 per cent during the first three quarters of 2000, exports fell by almost 3 per cent in the final quarter. Global semiconductor sales, which had increased by 60 per cent in dollar terms in mid 2000, turned negative by the end of the year.

Despite the economic downturn, during 2000 unemployment fell to 4.1 per cent, compared with 6.3 per cent in 1999. Employment growth was quite strong in the first half of the year, reducing the unemployment rate to a low of 3.5 per cent at one point, although it rose again in the second half of the year as a result of the economic slowdown. The participation rate increased in the second half of the year, mainly because of an increase in the number of female workers. Unit labour costs in the manufacturing sector declined further in 2000.

Despite the downturn in the global economy, export growth remained strong in 2000. In value terms, merchandise exports increased from $145.2 billion in 1999 to $175.8 billion in 2000 (Table 4.6), a 21.1 per cent increase. This was due to a high demand in overseas markets in the first and third quarters of 2000, and Korea's strong competitive position. Export growth was stronger for heavy industrial products – including electronic products, semiconductors and particularly telecommunications products – than for light industrial products, in both value and volume terms (Tables 4.7 and 4.8). Merchandise imports also continued to surge, rising from $116.8 billion in 1999 to $159.2 billion in 2000, a 36.3 per cent increase (Table 4.6). In volume terms, imports of capital goods experienced the largest increase and industrial materials and fuels experienced the smallest (Table 4.8).

Inflationary pressures began to re-emerge during 2000. Consumer prices showed a sharply rising trend after June 2000, mainly due to the higher oil prices, increased public service charges and higher prices for farm livestock-fisheries products. However inflation remained well below its pre-crisis rate.

The financial markets exhibited large fluctuations (Figure 4.4) due to a combination of factors, including the rapid rise in international oil prices, the drop in semiconductor prices and the breakdown of the planned sale of Daewoo to Ford. However market apprehensions subsided somewhat following the stabilisation of oil prices and the publication of the government's plan for further corporate and financial restructuring.

4.5.4 Developments in 2001

The slowdown in the economy in the last quarter of 2000 continued into the first quarter of 2001. However, there were optimistic signs in the first half of the year, including a recovery of GDP growth, a fall of 3.5 per cent in the unemployment rate and a renewal of business and household confidence. As indicated in Table 4.4, investment remained uncertain given the country's low rate of capacity utilisation in the industrial sector and the difficult credit environment facing enterprises. Investment in machinery and equipment remained weak, but the construction sector showed signs of recovery. Consumption expenditure also remained weak. Export growth increased and was expected to play a leading role in the ongoing recovery, but the extent of this depended on the recovery of the US economy and the maintenance of a competitive exchange rate. Stock-building remained weak, although it was expected to begin to make a positive contribution to growth during 2001.

There were risks, both domestic and external, attached to continued expansion of the economy. On the domestic side the major risk appeared to be financial market turbulence, with the possibility that the bankruptcy of even more large companies would trigger difficulties among financial institutions. On the external side there remained a risk of destabilising flows of portfolio investment. Realisation of the benefits of opening the equity and bond markets required policies that would maintain the confidence of foreign investors. However the stock market in Korea showed a close correlation with that in the USA, so a sharp correction in US share prices, resulting from a slowdown in the US economy, could lead to a further decline in the Korean market, which had fallen by about 20 per cent from its peak at the end of 1999. Such a correction could reduce growth in Korea through the negative wealth effect, as well as through slower growth in Korea's major export markets. Finally a depreciation of key Asian currencies might also undermine Korea's export growth. The slowing of the US economy posed a major threat to Korean exports, and in the second half of the year this threat became even more potent as the domestic and global environment deteriorated considerably, particularly after the terrorist attack on the World Trade Centre on 11 September. At the time of writing the global prospects look particularly bleak, and this of course is of considerable concern to an export-dependent economy such as Korea, and indeed the whole East Asian region.

4.6 Summary and conclusions

The Korean economy is still recovering from the financial crisis that hit the country late in 1997 following years of structural weaknesses, policy mistakes and an increasingly hostile international environment. The crisis was triggered internally by an unprecedented number of business insolvencies and externally by the South-East Asian financial crisis and its spread to other countries in East Asia.

By drawing an analogy between the economy's financial system and the human circulatory system this chapter has shown how numerous factors systematically intertwined to spark off the crisis. The 'stroke hypothesis' encapsulates the key ingredients of the crisis, its triggers and the warning signs that existed before its onset. This approach enabled a systematic evaluation of the crisis and the IMF's structural reform programme.[36]

The crisis was initially badly handled by the IMF, whose policy response – in the form of tight monetary and fiscal policies and a severe interest rate hike – turned the financial crisis into an economic and social crisis. While the structural reforms required by the IMF were of considerable importance to long-term economic growth, emphasis on these, in the context of an economy experiencing a temporary liquidity shortage, merely detracted from the immediate problems and served to compound Korea's difficulties.

While the crisis can be attributed to structural weaknesses and policy distortions, foreign investors can be held responsible for deepening the crisis by overreacting to the deteriorating circumstances of corporations and financial institutions. One could ask whether Korea could have avoided the trauma if the channels of contagion had been blocked through multilateral cooperation at an earlier stage. The rapid recovery of the economy in 1999 suggests that it could have, and there is empirical evidence to support this view.

A number of recent studies on contagion claim that macroeconomic similarities and strong trade and financial linkages between countries are important factors in the spread of crises from one country to another. However the East Asian NIEs shared few macroeconomic similarities with the ASEAN 4, they were not linked to the South-East Asian countries in terms of capital account transactions, and although their exports to the region were growing their trade linkages with the ASEAN 4 were not strong enough to serve as major channels of contagion. This leads to the conclusion that financial panic and herd behaviour spread the Thai crisis to the NIE 4. The fallout from the crisis in the ASEAN 4 could have been contained if foreign institutional investors had been less frightened about financial instability arising in Taiwan, but once they saw the vulnerability of Taiwan to crisis it appears they concluded that Hong Kong and Korea were equally assailable.

In 1998 Korea suffered its worse recession in the postwar era, but in the latter half of the year it staged a remarkable recovery that continued into 1999 and 2000. Strong economic growth in conjunction with rising foreign exchange reserves greatly enhanced both domestic and international confidence in the country. This resulted in the return of foreign investment, both in the equities market and in the form of FDI, which bodes well for the future.

However the country is not yet out of the woods as there is concern about the US economy, a major market for Korean exports, and about the Japanese and EU economies. The country still has a shaky financial system, a corporate sector that seems reluctant to restructure, a labour market that is still subject to rigidities and a public sector whose efficiency must be improved. Reform of these areas is discussed in the following chapter, where the progress made to date will be identified and evaluated.

Part III

5
The Post-Crisis Macroeconomic Policy Framework and Structural Reform: Reviving the Old Economy

5.1 Introduction

This chapter reviews and assesses the macroeconomic management and restructuring measures implemented in the wake of the financial crisis. Section 2 discusses the macroeconomic policy framework adopted by the monetary authorities in an effort to stabilise the currency and regain macroeconomic stability. This is followed in Section 3 by a discussion of the structural reform process pursued by the government in an effort to address more fundamental weaknesses in the economy. The main focus is on reform of the financial, corporate and public sectors and the labour market. Section 4 considers the performance of the economy during the period of reform and the challenges still to be faced. Finally, Section 5 presents some concluding remarks.

5.2 The macroeconomic policy framework

5.2.1 Monetary and exchange rate policies

During the crisis the Bank of Korea adopted a flexible monetary policy to assist the government's drive to stabilise the financial markets and implement structural reforms. It also helped to fund the restructuring of the financial sector. When the financial markets regained their stability and the economy began to revive, the Bank turned its attention to building a firm basis for price stability.

Foreign exchange market stabilisation

When the crisis erupted the Bank judged that the most urgent task was to stabilise the foreign exchange and financial markets. To help stabilise the foreign exchange market and curb capital outflows the Bank duly pushed up its market intervention rate to 35 per cent per annum. In tandem with this the government negotiated a prolongation of financial institutions' short-term external debts and issued foreign-currency-denominated government bonds. While these measures apparently calmed the foreign exchange market and resulted in a surplus in the current account from early 1998, Goldfajn and Baig (1998) and Park and Choi (1999) claim that the interest rate hike did not significantly affect the devaluation of the exchange rate although Cho and West (1999) and Basurte and Ghosh (2000) claim the opposite. In particular, Oh (2000c) considers that the positive correlation between the interest rate and the exchange rate obtained for Korea, which is contrary to the traditional theory of the interest rate parity condition, was mainly due to the fact that the stock market was more developed and active than the bond market. Also as we argued in Chapter 4, the IMF's high interest rate policy increased the country risk premium and contributed to the free fall of the Korean currency.

In fact the high interest rate policy had a number of pernicious side effects: it exacerbated the slowdown in economic activity by reducing consumption and investment, and it greatly increased the incidence of corporate failure and the accumulation of bad debts by financial institutions. In response, from the second quarter of 1998 the Bank shifted its attention from stabilising the foreign exchange market to preventing the economy from contracting too deeply. It steadily lowered its market intervention rate from the second quarter, when foreign exchange market conditions had improved considerably thanks to the sustained current account surplus, the arrival of support funds from international financial institutions and renewed inflows of foreign investment capital. The scale and pace of the interest rate reduction was conducted cautiously, taking into consideration developments in the real economy and the foreign exchange market, since the external environment was still unsettled and the international financial markets were in turmoil. The call rate consequently dropped to 8.5 per cent at the end of August 1998 and 6.5 per cent at the end of December. In addition, in September 1998 the interest rate on the aggregate credit the Bank supplied to commercial banks was reduced from 5 per cent to 3 per cent, thus inducing them to reduce their lending rates. This effectively brought about a steady reduction both in market interest rates and in the lending rates charged by financial institutions (see Chapter 4, Figure 4.3).

During the first half of 1999 the financial and foreign exchange markets achieved a fair degree of stability, but during the second half the financial market experienced increasing uncertainty and its restabilisation became a prime consideration for policy makers. In particular the difficulties of the troubled Daewoo group and investment trust companies led to a renewed focus on financial market stability when framing interest rate policy from August onwards. The Bank therefore reduced the call rate step by step to 4.75 per cent in May 1999, where it was maintained until January 2000.

The inflation targeting system

With the attainment of financial market stability and the economy on the upturn, the Bank turned its attention to building a firm basis for price stability. The monetary policy framework had been fundamentally changed after the crisis and an inflation targeting system was introduced under the provisions of the revised Bank of Korea Act of 1997.[1] The Act was concerned with establishing the neutrality and autonomy of monetary policy, and under its provisions the Bank was required to set and strive to achieve an annual inflation target.

The Bank adopted the consumer price index (CPI) as its benchmark indicator when the inflation targeting system was implemented in 1998, but as the CPI could be seriously affected by temporary or transitory shocks such as natural disasters or sharp fluctuations in the international price of oil, in 2000 the Bank decided that monetary policy should be formulated and implemented on the basis of the underlying trend of prices. There are various methods of adjusting the CPI to find the underlying trend of prices, such as adjustment by exclusion and the trimmed mean method. The Bank decided that adjustment by exclusion best suited the situation in Korea,[2] and from 2000 onwards employed the underlying inflation rate, which strips out from the CPI index price changes relating to petroleum and agricultural products, with the exception of cereals.

The Bank used a short-term inflation target with a one-year time horizon when it established the inflation targets for 1998 and 1999. To account for a time lag in the monetary transmission mechanism, the Bank decided to set, in addition to the annual inflation target a mid-term target of 2.5 per cent from 2001 onwards in order to maintain the consistency of monetary policy in the medium term (Figure 5.1).[3] It also introduced a number of measures to enhance the transparency, credibility and accountability of monetary policy.[4]

At the time of writing three years had passed since the inflation targeting system was introduced so it was too early to assess the performance of the new system. Nevertheless a few observations can be made. First, the average inflation rate was much lower after the adoption of the inflation targeting system than before it was introduced. In 1998 and 1999 inflation remained far below the targets due to strong deflationary factors: the cost of imports fell in line with the continuing appreciation of the won; the financial costs borne by business firms were reduced owing to improved financial structures and the easing of interest rates; manpower costs fell as a result of improved labour productivity and labour market flexibility; and price competition between retailers became intense in the struggle to secure customers in the severe economic depression after the crisis.

In 2000 the economy seemed to return to normal. In particular the effects of the sharp rebound of the Korean won after its depreciation during the crisis, which had helped to ensure that the inflation rate remained

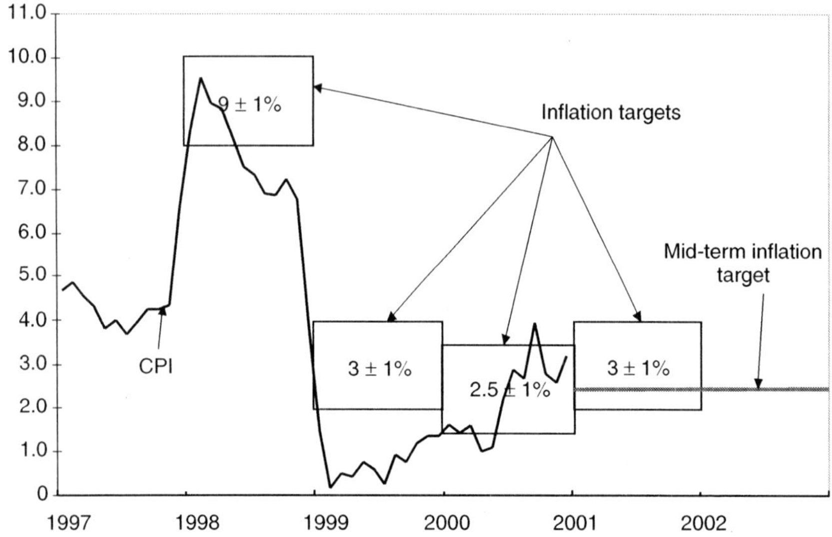

Source: Bank of Korea.

Figure 5.1 Inflation targets and inflation rates, January 1997 to January 2002 (per cent)

below the lower bound of the inflation targets in 1998 and 1999, had been almost fully absorbed. Nevertheless in 2000 the inflation rate remained within the target band.

Second, because of the ongoing financial and corporate sector restructuring and reform the Bank had to take financial stability into account when implementing its monetary policies. Upon the outbreak of the currency crisis the Bank dramatically raised its market intervention rate, in consultation with the IMF, to 35 per cent in order to engineer a rapid stabilisation of the exchange rate. Accordingly the major market interest rates rose to 30–40 per cent at the end of 1997, followed by a fall to around 20 per cent, where they remained until March 1998. In 2000 inflationary pressure increased so the Bank gradually raised the call rate in steps of 0.25 per cent. In 2001 the economy entered a recession so the Bank gradually reduced the target rate.

5.2.2 Fiscal policy

An expansionary fiscal policy in 1997 and 1998 (Table 5.1), along with the easing of monetary policy, contributed to Korea's economic recovery. Government spending was increased to assist the unemployed and SMEs. This, together with support for financial sector restructuring, resulted in a large fiscal deficit of just over 4 per cent of GDP in 1998 (Table 5.2). In

Table 5.1 Fiscal impulse indicator, 1995–2000 (per cent)

1995	1996	1997	1998	1999	2000
0.2	0.0	1.7	0.7	−0.3	−3.1

Note: A positive value denotes an expansionary fiscal policy, a minus value indicates a tightening of fiscal policy.

Source: Oh *et al.* (2001).

Table 5.2 Consolidated government budget balance, 1996–2000 (trillion won)

	1996	1997	1998	1999	2000
Consolidated budget balance	1.1	−7.0	−18.8	−13.1	6.5
Ratio to GDP (%)	0.3	−1.5	−4.2	−2.7	1.3

Source: Ministry of Planning and Budget.

order to reduce this deficit the government tightened its fiscal policy from the second half of 1999 when the economy underwent a sharp recovery and unemployment fell. In 2000 an unexpectedly high increase in tax revenue and reduced spending on the unemployed combined with the results of tight fiscal policy to provide a budget surplus of 1.3 per cent of GDP.

The issuing of government bonds was increased substantially to finance the budget deficits during the worst of the crisis in 1997–98, so government debt rose accordingly. The gross debt of central and local government rose from 14.4 per cent of GDP in 1997 to 23.1 per cent in 2000 (Table 5.3), although this was still well below the OECD average of about 70 per cent of GDP. However government-guaranteed debt also increased from 3 per cent of GDP in 1997 to 14 per cent in 2000, and as a consequence the overall

Table 5.3 Government debt, 1997–2000 (trillion won)

	1997	1998	1999	2000
Central government debt	50.5	71.4	89.7	100.9
Ratio to GDP (%)	11.1	15.9	18.6	19.5
General government* debt	65.6	87.6	107.7	119.7
Ratio to GDP (%)	14.4	19.5	22.3	23.1
Including government guaranteed debt	78.6	159.6	189.2	194.2
Ratio to GDP (%)	17.3	35.5	39.2	37.5

* Central government and local government.
Source: Ministry of Planning and Budget.

debt ratio reached nearly 38 per cent of GDP at the end of 2000. The impact on the budget of this indebtedness was reflected in a sharp increase in interest payments. Limiting the rise in government debt became an important task, given the pressure for increased social welfare spending and the need for further resources to be devoted to financial restructuring.

Prior to the crisis large-scale issues of government bonds had been unusual and the bonds had been absorbed either by the Bank of Korea or by financial institutions at a predetermined price, therefore their prices had not incorporated market interest rates and market liquidity conditions. From 1998 government and public bonds were issued through competitive bidding among financial institutions. Since then the interest rate on Treasury bonds has acted as a benchmark for investment decisions in the domestic bond market, which also facilitates efficient monetary policy implementation.

5.3 Structural reforms

Because the roots of the Korean crisis lay in the economy's weak fundamentals, attempting to stabilise the financial markets without making structural reforms would have been akin to treating the symptoms without addressing the cause.[5] Accordingly, from the onset of the crisis in 1997 the government set out to make structural reforms in almost all areas of the economy. This section focuses on the reforms conducted in five key sectors: the financial sector, the corporate sector, the labour market, the public sector, and the capital and foreign exchange markets.

5.3.1 Financial sector restructuring

In the wake of the crisis the government launched a financial sector restructuring and reform programme aimed at instituting a properly functioning, market-oriented financial system. In the short term the reforms were aimed at stabilising the financial system by eradicating non-performing assets, restructuring or closing insolvent financial institutions and rehabilitating viable ones, and ensuring that a forward-looking loan classification system was introduced. In the long term the focus was on attaining international standards in the governance, soundness and efficiency of financial institutions and the regulatory and supervisory institutions, and making the system more market oriented. In order to improve financial supervision two financial supervisory authorities – the Financial Supervisory Commission (FSC)[6] and the Financial Supervisory Service (FSS) – were created in early 1998, and to facilitate financial sector reform the Korea Asset Management Corporation (KAMCO)[7] and the Korea Deposit Insurance Corporation (KDIC) were reorganised.

In the immediate aftermath of the crisis the authorities closed or suspended the operations of a number of non-viable financial institutions, including, most notably, a number of merchant banks. Merchant banks were wholesale financial institutions engaged in underwriting primary capital market issues, leasing and short-term unsecured lending, and a key part of their funding activities involved borrowing in foreign markets. At the end of 1997 there were 30 merchant banks operating in Korea. They often competed directly with commercial banks but were subject to less stringent regulatory regimes. They were not subject to the same ownership limitations as commercial banks, and many were in fact owned by the large industrial groups to whom they provided finance. They were permitted to assume much higher interest rates and currency risk than the commercial banks. They usually lent without collateral and therefore had less protection in the event of default. Korea's merchant banks had become very aggressive lenders before the crisis, relying heavily on foreign currency funding, and hence their currency mismatches were larger than those of commercial banks. Internationally the merchant banks also had considerable loan exposure to South-East Asia and other emerging markets that were badly affected by the 1997 crisis. Other non-bank financial institutions, including securities companies and investment trust companies, all had significant exposure to the currency, bond and equity markets.

In November and December 1997 KAMCO bought 3 trillion won of impaired loans from the merchant banks and reimbursed depositors to the tune of 5 trillion won. Also in December, the operations of 14 of the merchant banks were suspended and all 30 banks were ordered to submit restructuring plans by the end of the month. These plans had to specify how they would attain BIS capitalisation ratios of 4 per cent by March 1998, 6 per cent by June 1998 and 8 per cent by June 1999. If their rehabilitation plans were accepted the banks were obliged to sign a managerial contract with the government, including an explicit commitment to meet the deadlines and achieve other performance indicators. If the plans were not approved their licenses were revoked – 14 merchant banks were closed when their plans were judged to be unacceptable. If the remaining banks did not meet the performance criteria specified in their agreements corrective measures would be applied, including closure. Because of the declining financial strength of these banks it was inevitable that further fatalities would occur, and indeed by the end of 2000 only 10 remained (Table 5.4).

As for the 33 commercial banks, at the end of 1997, 14 had less than the 8 per cent minimum capital asset ratio. Korea First Bank's capital was in fact negative, while Seoul Bank's was less than 1 per cent. In January 1998 these two banks were recapitalised with public funds and effectively nationalised.[8] Korea First Bank was subsequently sold to a foreign consortium. The remaining 12 banks whose capital adequacy ratios had fallen short of 8 per cent were required to prepare a rehabilitation plan by 15 April to demonstrate how they would achieve the required ratio of 8 per cent within two years. They were also required to sign contracts with

Table 5.4 Number of financial institutions[1] in Korea, 1997–2000

		1998			1999			2000			
	End of 1997	Closed	Merged[2]	Newly installed	Closed	Merged[2]	Newly installed	Closed	Merged[2]	Newly installed	End of 2000
Commercial banks	33	5	3	–	–	2	–	–	1	–	22
Merchant banks	30	16	–	–	1	3	–	1	–	1	10
Securities companies	36	6	–	1	–	–	1	–	1	12	43
Investment trust companies	31	6	–	–	–	1	–	–	–	3	27
Insurance companies	45	4	1	–	–	–	–	1	5	–	34
Other[3]	1897	91	16	13	126	55	6	111	55	2	1464
Total	2072	128	20	14	127	61	7	113	62	18	1600

Notes:
1. Branches of foreign companies excluded.
2. Number of companies reduced due to merger.
3. Mutual savings and finance companies, and credit unions.

Source: Bank of Korea (2001b).

internationally recognised accounting firms to conduct diagnostic reviews and provide an assessment of their recapitalisation plans. These subsequently formed part of the FSC's assessment of the banks.

On 29 June the FSC announced that five insolvent, or 'disapproved', commercial banks would be closed or absorbed by healthier banks the following month. The seven 'conditionally approved' banks took the corrective measures imposed by the FSC to improve their soundness, and were monitored closely thereafter. The FSC also signalled that a similar review of all banks would take place in the future, and any whose capital adequacy ratio fell below 8 per cent would be obliged to submit to the restructuring procedures already enforced on the 12 undercapitalised banks. At the end of 2000 only 22 of the original 33 were still operating (Table 5.4).

The public sector's financial contribution to the restructuring of the financial sector was enormous. At the beginning of the crisis the government allocated 64 trillion won ($53.3 billion) in public funds to the restructuring effort, and by the end of 1999 the entire allocation had been used to purchase 20.5 trillion won ($17.1 billion) of non-performing loans from banks and secondary financial institutions through KAMCO, and to provide 43.5 trillion won ($36.2 billion) of recapitalisation and deposit repayment support through the KDIC. In 2000 an additional 35 trillion won ($29.2 billion) was injected. By August 2000 a total of 91 trillion won had been spent, or 17.6 per cent of GDP (Table 5.5), primarily to recapitalise viable financial institutions and address the non-performing loans problem. By March 2001 the total net outlay had increased to 107.5 trillion won, equivalent to 20.8 per cent of GDP (Table 5.5). The bulk of these funds was spent on commercial banks but a significant amount went to non-bank institutions, whose number also fell between 1997 and 2000, with the exception of securities companies, which increased from 36 to 43 (Table 5.4).

The restructuring programme achieved some success, and a number of privately owned banks secured strong balance sheets and could meet tough prudential standards. However the government remained the owner of a number of weaker banks encumbered with non-performing loans and weak profitability. Furthermore the impact of the collapse of the Daewoo group was still being felt in the bond market, requiring further restructuring of some non-bank financial institutions. Problems also remained in other areas, notably life insurance.

To address these problems the government launched a second restructuring programme in September 2000. Additional expenditure of 50 trillion won was allocated to the task, about half of which had been spent by March 2001 (Table 5.5). Approximately 50 per cent of the remaining 25 trillion won was set aside to resolve the commercial banks' remaining problems (Table 5.6).

Thanks to the injection of public funds and massive rights offerings the BIS ratios of domestic banks continued to rise. At the end of 1999 the average

Table 5.5 Expenditure on financial sector restructuring (trillion won)

	First programme (to August 2000)	Second programme (as of March 2001)	Total
Expenditure by type of institution			
Banking sector	70.3	10.4	80.7
Investment trusts	12.2	3.7	15.9
Merchant banks	11.9	4.6	16.5
Insurance companies	10.5	2.0	12.5
Other[1]	4.7	4.4	9.1
Total	109.6	25.1	134.7
Sources of financing			
Government guaranteed borrowing	64.6	19.8	83.8
Recycled funds	18.6	8.6	27.2
Other public funds	27.0	−3.3	23.7
Total	109.6	25.1	134.7
Percentage of GDP in 2000	21.2	4.8	26.0
Net outlays			
Total minus recycled funds	91.0	16.5	107.5
Percentage of GDP in 2000	17.6	3.2	20.8

Note:
1. Mutual savings and loans, and credit cooperatives.

Source: Ministry of Finance and Economy.

Table 5.6 Outlays in the second stage of the finanical restructuring plan (trillion won)

	April–June 2001	July–December 2001
Recapitalisation of commercial banks and life insurance companies	4.5	7–8.0
Repayment of borrowed funds[1]	4.0	2–3.0
Payment to depositors at failed mutual savings and finance companies	1–2.0	1–2.0
Liquidation of Hanareum[2]	2.0	–
Restructuring of life insurance companies	1.0	–
Repayment of matured bonds[3]	0.4	0.7
Put-back option payment[4]	0.1	0.7
Total	13–14.0	11.4–14.4

Notes:
1. To financial institutions.
2. A bank for failed merchant banks.
3. Used to finance the first stage restructuring plan.
4. Paid to Newbridge Capital, which purchased Korea First Bank in 1999.

Source: Ministry of Finance and Economy.

BIS ratio of 17 commercial banks was 10.8 per cent, well above the BIS recommended level of 8 per cent. However at the end of 2000 the non-performing loans of all financial institutions amounted to 65 trillion won (10.4 per cent of total loans), virtually unchanged from the previous year (Table 5.7). Continued corporate restructuring and the implementation of stricter loan classification standards put upward pressure on the amount of substandard loans. Consequently the total failed to fall significantly, despite another 30 trillion won of purchases of non-performing loans by KAMCO and write-offs by banks. Since taking charge of the Non-Performing Asset Fund at the end of 1997 KAMCO had purchased a total of 95.2 trillion won of non-performing loans at a purchase price of 36.8 trillion won. This was financed by an initial 20.5 trillion won of publicly guaranteed borrowing and by recycled funds obtained from the sale of non-performing loans purchased from financial institutions. In 2001 KAMCO planned to purchase a total of 15.2 trillion won of non-performing loans at a price of 5.2 trillion won, about half of which would be from six commercial banks that were under restructuring plans. Such purchases were part of the goal to reduce non-performing loans to 4 per cent of total loans by the end of 2001. KAMCO's role as the agency responsible for resolving non-performing loans was scheduled to end in November 2002.

The KDIC also played a key role in recapitalising financial institutions and meeting the claims of failed institutions' depositors (Table 5.8). At the beginning of 2001 the blanket coverage of deposit insurance introduced in the wake of the crisis was replaced with a system in which coverage was limited to 50 million won (principal and interest) per deposit in insured financial institutions. This amount was more than double the average size of deposit accounts. The introduction of the partial coverage system was designed to enhance market discipline.

Despite the major restructuring of the commercial banking sector it continued to record large losses in 2000 as provisions for bad loans far exceeded operating profits (Table 5.9). Moreover there was a widening gap between a group of privately owned banks with capital adequacy ratios of over 10 per cent and a second group that were primarily government owned and had lower ratios. The strong group consisted of specialised banks and relatively new institutions that had not played a significant role in lending to the *chaebols*. Moreover this group had a significant degree of foreign participation. The weaker banks, in contrast, had been heavily exposed to the *chaebols*. One positive sign was the turnaround of Korea First Bank, which was sold to foreign investors in 1999, and of Seoul Bank, which was restructured prior to its planned sale to foreign investors. However this turnaround was not without cost. By early 2001 some 12.5 trillion won (2.5 per cent of GDP) of public money had been injected into Korea First Bank and a further 4.7 trillion won into Seoul Bank.

Table 5.7 Non-performing loans, December 1997 to December 2000 (trillion won)

	1997			1998			1999			2000		
	Total loans	NPLs	Ratio (%)	Total loans	NPLs	Ratio (%)	Total loans	NPLs	Ratio (%)	Total loans	NPLs	Ratio (%)
Banks	518.6	31.6	6.1	443.3	33.7	7.6	474.0	39.7	8.4	526.1	42.1	8.0
Commercial banks	375.8	22.7	6.0	300.5	22.2	7.4	328.3	27.4	8.3	361.4	32.0	8.9
Specialised and development	142.8	8.9	6.2	142.8	11.5	8.1	145.7	12.3	8.4	164.7	10.1	6.1
Non-bank financial institutions	128.7	12.0	9.3	133.1	26.5	19.9	116.2	27.0	23.2	95.3	22.5	23.6
Merchant banks	24.1	1.0	4.1	28.0	5.6	20.0	14.9	2.3	15.4	3.5	1.3	37.1
Insurance companies	51.7	4.8	9.3	38.8	3.4	8.8	41.8	5.8	13.9	44.5	3.8	8.5
Mutual savings and loans	28.1	3.3	11.7	22.0	5.3	24.1	17.8	5.8	32.6	15.7	5.8	36.9
Credit unions	12.7	1.3	10.2	11.2	2.5	22.3	10.2	2.2	21.6	10.3	1.3	12.6
Leasing companies	n.a.	n.a.	n.a.	25.8	7.8	30.2	20.4	7.4	36.3	13.7	5.9	43.1
Securities companies	12.1	1.6	13.2	7.3	1.9	26.0	10.0	3.4	34.0	7.6	4.0	52.6
Total	647.3	43.6	6.7	576.4	60.2	10.4	590.2	66.7	11.3	621.4	64.6	10.4

Note: Non-performing loans were partly reduced by purchases by KAMCO, which amounted to 44.1 trillion won in 1998, 11.9 trillion won in 1999 and 30.9 trillion won in 2000.

Source: Financial Supervisory Service.

Table 5.8 Expenditures by the Korea Deposit Insurance Corporation (trillion won)[1]

	Equity participation	**Contributions and insurance claim payments**	**Asset purchases**	**Other**	**Total**
Original 64 trillion won[2]	20.5	21.0	1.8	0.2	43.5
Banks	16.5	9.6	1.8	0	27.9
Five merged banks	1.2	9.6	0.2	0	11.0
Korea First and Seoul Bank	9.0	0	1.6	0	10.6
Other banks	6.3	0	0	0	6.3
Other financial institutions	4.0	11.4	0	0.2	15.6
Life insurance	3.9	1.4	0	0	5.3
Guaranty insurance	0.1	0	0	0	0.1
Merchant banks	0	5.8	0	0	5.8
Credit cooperatives	0	1.3	0	0	1.3
Mutual savings	0	2.9	0	0.2	3.1
Recycled funds	–	–	–	–	9.2
Used	3.0	4.4	3.1	0	10.4[3]
Total expenditures[4]	23.5	25.4	4.9	0.2	54.0

Notes:
1. Financed by government guaranteed borrowing as of November 2000.
2. Authorised in June 1998.
3. Including KAMCO's recycled funds that were borrowed and used by KDIC.
4. Original 64 trillion won of borrowing plus recylced funds.

Source: Ministry of Finance and Economy.

To deal with other weak banks, including two nation-wide banks (Hanvit and Peace) and two regional banks (Kwangju and Kyungnam), the government created a financial holding company that began operating in April 2000. Prior to the establishment of the holding company the non-performing loans of the banks in question were cleaned up and public funds were injected to boost their capital adequacy ratios to above 10 per cent. The holding company approach allowed the affiliated companies to maintain their clients and employees, which had not been possible with liquidation or the purchase and acquisition approach used in 1998. The government also hoped to maximise the synergy effects by reducing overlapping branches and encouraging joint investment in information technology and marketing. In April 2001 the government helped to engineer the merger of two strong banks, Kookmin and Housing, despite significant union opposition. The merged bank is currently the largest in Korea.

Measures to improve the governance structures of the remaining banks, securities companies, investment trust companies and merchant banks were also put in place. An outside director system and an audit committee system were introduced following amendment of the relevant legislation.

Table 5.9 Indicators of bank profitability, nationwide banks, 1999–2000 (billion won, per cent)

	Banks with high capital ratios[1]	Banks with lower capital ratios[2]	Seoul Bank and Korea First Bank	Total
1999				
Before tax profits[3]	1071.5	−3772.4	1161.6	−1539.3
After tax profits	866.9	−3582.9	−3237.7	−5953.7
Return on equity (%)	7.4	−35.4	−146.2	−24.8
Return on assets (%)	0.4	−2.2	−5.9	−1.4
Total loans	152946.5	124575.9	28025	305547.4
NPLs	8471.1	13342.5	4604.1	26417.7
NPL ratio (%)	5.5	10.7	16.4	8.7
Loan loss reserves	7127.1	10133	1613.5	18873.6
Reserves/NPLs (%)	84.1	76	35	71.4
Capital adequacy ratio (%)	12.2	9.1	11	10.8
Number of branches	1869	1544	627	4040
Operating expenses/ operating reserves (%)	80.5	46.2	181	53
2000				
Before tax profits[3]	1496.7	−4755.2	−597.2	−3855.7
After tax profits	1240.8	−3427.3	−213.4	−2399.9
Return on equity (%)	10.1	−42.3	−11.6	−10.8
Return on assets (%)	0.5	−2	−0.5	−0.5
Total loans	186047.7	125048.5	26831.3	337927.5
NPLs	7389.3	11697.5	3274.2	22361
NPL ratio (%)	4	9.4	12.2	6.6
Loan loss reserves	6350.2	9616.2	2530.5	18496.9
Reserves/NPLs (%)	85.9	82.2	77.3	82.7
Capital adequacy ratio (%)	10.8	9.8	12.1	10.5
Number of branches	1908	1439	630	3977
Operating expenses/ operating reserves (%)	91.4	44.8	58.3	53.7

Notes:
1. BIS capital adequacy ratio of more than 10 per cent. This group includes Shinhan Bank, Hana Bank, KorAm Bank, Kookmin Bank and Korea Housing and Commercial Bank (since 1997).
2. BIS capital adequacy ratio of less than 10 percent. This group includes Chohung Bank, Hanvit Bank, Korea Exchange Bank and Peace Bank.
3. Operating profits after provisioning. A simple sum method is used in this table.

Source: Financial Supervisory Commission.

Henceforth more than half (at least three persons) of the total board membership should consist of outside directors, and at least two thirds of the new audit committees should consist of outside directors. Internal controls and a compliance system were introduced to strengthen the soundness of financial institutions. Finally, the legal rights of minority shareholders were strengthened by lowering the holding thresholds for certain rights.

In the wake of the financial crisis, financial sector restructuring was primarily focused on the commercial and merchant banks, but later attention was increasingly turned to non-bank financial institutions, which accounted for many of the outstanding problems in the financial sector. For example non-performing loans accounted for almost a fourth of their lending in 2000 (Table 5.7). In many cases these institutions had been used as financial vehicles by the *chaebols*. In the life insurance sector, the government injected 10.8 trillion won of public money and reduced the number of companies by nine, either through closure or mergers with stronger companies. By the end of 2000 all but four of the remaining 23 companies had met the required solvency ratio of 100 per cent or more. Three companies, however, had more liabilities than assets and were offered for sale by public bidding. Only nine companies made profits during the fiscal year 2000/1, so there was a loss for the sector as a whole compared with a profit of 1.8 trillion won the previous year.

The weak bond market was a key factor in the credit crunch conditions experienced during 2000–1. The problems in the bond market were directly linked to the high credit risks in the corporate sector due to inadequate restructuring and the problems being experienced by the investment trust companies (ITCs), traditional investors in corporate bonds, following the collapse of the Daewoo group. The funds held in ITC trust accounts fell by nearly 50 per cent the year after the demise of Daewoo in mid 1999. Many of the ITCs, which had increased their exposure to the corporate sector in 1998 and 1999, were undercapitalised and remained vulnerable to turmoil in that sector.

The restructuring of the ITCs was postponed several times. For example the government declared Korea Investment Trust and Daehan Investment Trust insolvent and agreed to provide them with an injection of 8 trillion won, but only 3 trillion won had changed hands by early 2000. Confidence in the ITCs ebbed quickly and their investors withdrew, thereby putting the squeeze on the *chaebols*, the ITCs' biggest borrowers. Therefore the government decided to provide them with an additional 4.9 trillion won in public funds, although this was unlikely to cover the total amount of the two companies' liabilities. Only then did the government attempt to restructure the ITCs. First KAMCO purchased nearly 29 trillion won of bad debts from the ITCs. Next the regulatory provisions were improved by requiring the ITCs to have external audits and at least three independent directors. This was followed by a strengthening of the legal and governance framework for ITCs. Finally, the ITCs were made eligible to sell tax-deductible financial products from December 2000.

In the early stages the restructuring of the financial sector focused primarily on the clearance of depressed assets under government supervision.

However the increasing presence of foreign financial companies in Korea meant that capital market liberalisation and the promotion of FDI became important aspects of the restructuring process. Various measures were taken by the government to liberalise the capital market and promote FDI. (More discussion will be provided in section 5.3.5.) The ceiling on foreign investment in Korean equities was raised from 26 per cent to 55 per cent in December 1997, and was completely abolished in May 1998. Thus foreign financial institutions were able to establish subsidiary banks and security companies, and to set up joint-venture banks. Virtually all restrictions on foreign access to the bond markets had been lifted by 1 January 1998. Easing the rules on ownership was seen as one means of strengthening governance and permitting both foreign and domestic interests to acquire strategic stakes in Korean institutions. Hence foreign ownership of up to 100 per cent was allowed as of April 1998. However as foreigners reached the thresholds of 10 per cent, 25 per cent and 33 per cent of total equity they became subject to increasingly strong reviews by the FSC. Similar rules were also imposed on domestic investors seeking strategic positions in banks.

Evaluation of progress to date

It is uncertain whether the funds allocated to the second stage of the programme will be sufficient to complete the restructuring of the financial sector, but it is important to pay attention to limiting the ultimate cost to taxpayers. As of March 2001 the government had recouped 32.8 trillion won of the public funds injected, most of this amount being recycled into the financial system (Table 5.4). With total net expenditure of 107.5 trillion won by March 2001, the recovery rate was about 30 per cent. Given that the expenditure on financial sector restructuring will surpass total central government debt it is important to achieve a high recovery rate. In terms of recovering funds KAMCO has been successful thus far, with asset sales in 2000 being well above the target. By the end of 2000 it had recouped 21 trillion won on the sale of 45.7 trillion won of non-performing loans, for which it had originally paid 18.8 trillion won. Furthermore the innovative securitisation techniques used to sell these assets are contributing to the development of the financial system. The situation of the KDIC is more difficult since recouping the funds it has used to recapitalise financial institutions requires the successful turning around of those institutions. Allowing the KDIC to play a more active role as a shareholder in banks should help it to recoup public funds, although investigating corporations may be a more difficult task for this organisation.

At present the share prices of banks are depressed, suggesting that the recovery of public funds will require a delay in privatisation. However there are also significant costs to leaving a large portion of commercial bank ownership – almost two thirds of its total capital at present – in government hands. The government expects that the share prices of financial institutions will gradually increase owing to recapitalisation and the KDIC's power to act as a shareholder when turning around financial institutions. The authorities plan to privatise the commercial banks from the second half of 2002, depending on the degree of normalisation among the financial institutions and conditions in the stock market and economy. Active, bank-led corporate restructuring is the key to improving the prospects of both the financial sector and the corporate sector. As this appears to be stymied in the current circumstances it is crucial for the government to prioritise bank privatisation and the continued development of a market-oriented financial system.

Most of the problems in the financial sector are due to weaknesses in the corporate sector. Consequently financial sector instability will continue as long as the corporate sector remains weak. To promote the restructuring of the corporate sector, financial institutions should improve their credit risk assessments and lending practices and take an aggressive stance on asset quality. The non-bank financial sector remains a concern, and strict implementation of the new supervisory framework is necessary to limit the risk of future problems in the life insurance and investment trust sectors.

5.3.2 Corporate sector reform

The very high leverage of and overinvestment by Korean firms were crucial factors in the financial crisis. In particular the *chaebols* tended to borrow excessively through cross-payment guarantees among interlinked subsidiaries.[9] By the end of 1997 the top 30 *chaebols* had debt–equity ratios of 519 per cent, in sharp contrast with 154 per cent in the USA and 193 per cent in Japan (see Chapter 3, Table 3.10). Poor corporate practices and governance also contributed to the 1997 crisis in the form of inaccurate company financial information, non-transparent corporate decision making, the lack of a credible exit threat, insufficient financial institution monitoring, and inadequate legal rights and protective measures for minority shareholders (Joh, 1999). Hence the priorities in the reform of the corporate sector were to achieve a major reduction in corporate indebtedness, to bring corporate governance practices into line with international standards, and to attain corporate international competitiveness.

The first stage of the corporate reform programme

In the wake of the crisis the government adopted a three-pronged approach to reforming the corporate sector. First, the five largest *chaebols* (the Big Five) were to be reformed and restructured by improving their capital structure. The parameters within which the reform of the Big Five was to proceed were contained in an agreement reached in January 1998 between President-elect Kim Dae Jung and the leaders of the Big Five. The agreement contained five principle aims: (1) to improve the transparency of corporate management, (2) to bring a halt to cross-guarantees between affiliates, (3) to improve the *chaebols'* financial structure, (4) to concentrate on core competences and (5) to reinforce the responsibility of governing shareholders and management. On the basis of this, in early 1998 the Big Five and their creditors reached an agreement on debt reduction and other restructuring measures. The latter agreement included (1) the production of consolidated financial statements from fiscal year 1999, (2) compliance with international standards of accounting, (3) strengthening the voting rights of minority shareholders, (4) the inclusion of at least one outside director on the board of directors from 1998, (5) the establishment of an external committee of auditors, (6) the prohibition of cross-subsidiary debt guarantees from April 1998, and (7) the removal of all existing cross-debt guarantees by March 2000.

The government also required the Big Five to reduce their debt–equity ratios to 200 per cent by the end of 1999 and to improve their financial structure by means of asset sales, recapitalisation and foreign capital inducement. In addition they had to terminate the cross-guarantees between subsidiaries in different lines of business and to consolidate their business by exchanging non-core businesses with other *chaebols*. The latter process became known as 'Big Deals' that were aimed at enhancing the competitiveness of the *chaebols* by streamlining investment and improving efficiency in key areas such as semiconductors, petrochemicals, aerospace, railway vehicles, oil refining, power generation and vessel engines. Tax incentives were offered to the *chaebols* to reach an agreement on these measures, and deals on the semiconductor, oil refining, aerospace and railway vehicle industries were duly made and completed. However the Big Deals relating to the other industries eventually failed or were delayed.

Second, the sixth to sixty-fourth largest *chaebols* were made subject to restructuring through a debt work-out programme with their designated creditor bank based on the London approach. The London Approach evolved in the UK in the early 1990s when numerous business bankruptcies occurred. The approach involved creditor financial institutions and indebted firms voluntarily working under the close coordination of a government institution (in the UK case the Bank of England), and without recourse to the judicial system. Financial institutions signed the Corporate Restructuring Agreement, which provided for informal debt work-outs as an alternative to formal procedures under the insolvency law. The programmes involved debt-term extensions, deferred payments and/or the reduction of principal and interest. As of February 2000, 77 corporations were engaged in the programmes.

Under the programmes creditor banks were required to oversee the management of the firms concerned, as well as to reschedule their debts. Many of these banks, however, lacked management expertise so the government later established corporate restructuring vehicles (CRVs) – independent agencies specialising in corporate restructuring and the management of debt work-out firms.

Third, the restructuring of small and medium-sized enterprises (SMEs) was left to the creditor banks but was largely postponed. To prevent insolvency and preserve employment, these firms were given easy access to working capital. In Korea, unlike in the other crisis countries, SMEs account for a relatively small proportion of outstanding bank loans. While this may justify the delay in their restructuring a comprehensive programme to work out their debts is still urgently needed.

Outcomes of the first stage of the reforms. The measures outlined above brought mixed results. The positive developments will be discussed first.

The number of affiliates owned by the top 30 *chaebols* fell from 804 in April 1998 to 567 in January 2001. The average debt–equity ratio of the top four *chaebols*, excluding the dismantled Daewoo Group, fell to below 200 per cent by the end of 1999, down from 352 per cent in 1998 and over 500 per cent in 1997.[10] The average debt–equity ratio of the top 30 fell from 519 per cent to 219 per cent over the same period. All cross-debt guarantees were resolved by March 2000, as planned, and the *chaebols* began to publish consolidated financial statements. The legal proceedings for corporate rehabilitation and bankruptcy were simplified to facilitate market exit for non-viable firms, and to ensure better representation of creditor banks in the resolution process.

Various measures to enhance the corporate governance structure and improve transparency were also introduced: the legal rights of minority shareholders were strengthened by lowering the holding threshold of certain rights;[11] the role of boards of directors was strengthened; outside directors were appointed to form one quarter of the total board membership; and audit committees were set up, with outside directors forming at least two thirds of the membership. In addition, owners who played an active role in the management of corporations were registered as directors. Transparency was further enhanced by upgrading accounting standards and requiring *chaebols* to prepare combined financial statements. The bankruptcy procedure was improved by introducing time limits and giving greater weight to economic criteria.

In addition to the above, the new corporate governance framework was expanded to include firms listed on KOSDAQ,[12] the shadow voting requirement for mutual funds was removed,[13] the use of cumulative voting was facilitated, the merger and acquisition procedure was simplified,[14] and the requirements for holding companies were eased.

Despite these advances a number of shortcomings remained. For example economic power was still concentrated in the hands of the top five *chaebols*, and according to the Fair Trade Commission their total assets rose by 13.8 per cent in 1998. Furthermore their combined debts increased to 234 trillion won in 1998, up from 221 trillion won in 1997. Nonetheless their debt–equity ratios decreased because their mode of financing changed drastically in favour of direct financing through the stock market, while some *chaebols* attracted liquidity through trusts and mutual funds. Finally, the founding families of *chaebols*, rather than the market and shareholders, still tended to wield absolute power and the boards of directors often lacked power as decision making bodies.

The government repeatedly stressed that the structural reforms had been and would continue to be driven by market forces. However it is fair to say that the structural reform efforts were driven by government initiatives and the government intervened heavily in the restructuring process. For example it instigated the consolidation deals among the *chaebol* subsidiaries, informally selected bankrupt firms for debt work-out programmes, set a uniform reduction of debt–equity ratios regardless of the characteristics of the business, and implicitly placed a limit on *chaebols'* entry into new business (Samsung Economic Research Institute, 2000). In the future government intervention should be minimised and corporate sector reform should concentrate more on profit maximisation or cost minimisation than on fitting government standards.

The changing structure of the chaebols. After the crisis the structure of the *chaebols* underwent a number of important changes. Of the top 30 groups in 1997, only 18 remained on the list in 2001 (Table 5.10). Five new groups were previously part of Hyundai, the largest *chaebol* in 2000. As before the crisis, the top five *chaebols* still dominated, accounting for one third of the affiliated companies and almost two thirds of the assets of the top 30 groups. The financial crisis brought about a turning point in the business behaviour of the *chaebols*. The average number of affiliates held by the top 30 fell by a third between 1997 and 2000 as they had to sell assets to reduce their debts, and the average number of business lines declined from 19 to 15 over the same period. The average number of affiliates, though, increased in 2001, largely as a result of an increase in the number of information technology firms. However the new firms were relatively small, and the average amount of assets per firm fell by 10 per cent in 2001. Total assets declined between 1999 and 2001, reversing the large increases that occurred in the wake of the crisis.

To achieve the 200 per cent debt–equity target imposed by the government the *chaebols* issued large amounts of new equity. The debt–equity ratio of the top 30 was 519 per cent in 1997, falling to 219 per cent at the end of 1999 and 171 per cent at the end of 2000, excluding financial affiliates (Table 5.11). A large part of this reduction was due to an increase in equity, which rose by 125 per cent between 1997 and 2000. A 26 per cent decline in debt over the same period also helped. Reductions in

Table 5.10 The top 30 *chaebols*, 2001

	Number of affiliates 2000	Number of affiliates 2001	Total assets (trillion won)	Rank in 1997
1. Samsung	45	64	69.9	2
2. Hyundai	35	26	53.6	1
3. LG	43	43	52.0	3
4. SK	39	54	47.4	5
5. Hyundai Motors	–	16	36.1	Not on list
6. Hanjin	18	19	21.3	7
7. POSCO	–	15	21.2	Not on list
8. Lotte	28	31	16.7	10
9. Kumho	20	17	11.6	11
10. Hanwha	23	25	11.5	9
11. Doosan	16	18	11.2	14
12. Ssangyong	22	20	9.0	6
13. Hyundai Petrochemicals	3	2	7.2	Not on list
14. Hansol	19	19	7.8	16
15. Dongbu	19	19	5.8	22
16. Daelim	18	17	5.4	15
17. Tongyang	25	30	5.1	23
18. Hyosung	13	15	4.9	17
19. Cheil Chedang	18	30	4.8	Not on list
20. Kolon	17	25	4.6	20
21. Dongkuk	14	8	4.3	18
22. Hyundai Industrial Dev.	7	9	4.1	Not on list
23. Hanaro Communications	–	7	3.4	Not on list
24. Shin Sehgye	10	9	3.2	Not on list
25. Yeongpoong	21	24	2.9	Not on list
26. Hyundai Department Store	–	15	2.9	Not on list
27. Dongyang Hwahak	–	22	2.8	Not on list
28. Daewoo Motors	3	4	2.7	Not on list
29. Taekwang Sanob	–	15	2.6	Not on list
30. Kohap	6	6	2.5	21
Total of top 30	544[1]	624	437.9	
Total of top five	180	212	259.0	

Note:
1. Based on the rankings in 2000.

Source: Fair Trade Commission.

financial costs, or at least relative to 1998, were accompanied by lower labour costs. The number of workers at firms affiliated with the *chaebols* declined by 30 per cent between 1996 and 1999, compared with a 6 per cent fall at independent companies. Consequently labour costs fell from 12 per cent to 8 per cent of total costs over the same period. These cost reductions also improved profitability. The percentage of firms with interest coverage

Table 5.11 The debt to equity ratio of the top 30 *chaebols*, 1997–2000 (trillion won)

	1997	1998	1999	2000
Equity	68.9	96.9	129.6	154.8
Liabilities	357.4	367.0	283.4	265.1
Ratio	518.9	378.8	218.7	171.2
Percentage change				
Equity		40.7	33.8	19.5
Liabilities		2.7	–22.8	–6.5

Source: Ministry of Finance and Economy.

ratios[15] of less than one fell to 44 per cent for *chaebol* affiliated companies and 29 per cent for independent companies. Finally, the increase in equity in 1998 and 1999 boosted the number of the top 30 *chaebols* that were owned by their affiliated companies in 1999. Consequently the 'inside ownership ratio' rose above 50 per cent in 1999, despite the continued decline in the shares of the principal owners and their families. The reimposition in April 2000 of a rule prohibiting *chaebol*-affiliated firms from owning more than 25 per cent of another firm reversed the rise in shareholding by sister companies. That share was likely to decline further as firms tried to meet the 25 per cent limit by the March 2002 deadline.

As discussed earlier, in the wake of the crisis the government set up the Corporate Restructuring Agreement, under which 220 leading lenders agreed to participate in debt work-out programmes for troubled companies. Creditors preferred this approach because it provided a higher rate of debt recovery than legal procedures, which include bankruptcy, composition of the enterprise or its board of directors and reorganisation. Moreover legal procedures would result in an immediate increase in non-performing loans, threatening the viability of financial institutions struggling to meet their capital adequacy ratios. Managers also had an incentive to avoid legal proceedings as these would lead to their dismissal after the appointment of trustees. The lack of resort to legal procedures is illustrated by the fact that only four *chaebol*-affiliated companies were subject to court-administered procedures in 2000. As indicated in Table 5.12, of the 104 companies nominated for a work-out programme a third subsequently graduated and another third remained in the programme at the end of 2000. Of the remaining 34, 19 dropped out or were rejected, and 15 merged with other companies. Of the agreements reached by the time of writing, 20 had to be renegotiated as the firms concerned were unable to meet their restructuring commitments. Ten of the remaining companies were affiliated with the Daewoo group, which collapsed in 1999. The companies still in the programme had received a total of 71.5 trillion won of concessions by December 2000, 60 trillion won of which consisted of interest rate cuts or

Table 5.12 The corporate work-out programme, end 2000

	Nominated (A)	Total (B)	Excluded			Graduated (C)	Remaining (A–B–C)
			Dropped out	Merged	Rejected		
Daewoo companies	12	1	0	0	1	1	10
Affiliates of *chaebols* ranked 6–64	49	22	5	12	5	12	15
Medium-sized firms	43	11	3	3	5	23	9
Total	104	34	8	15	11	36	34

Source: Financial Supervisory Service.

exemptions. Debt to equity swaps and the conversion of bonds to equity accounted for less than 6 trillion won.

The second stage of the corporate restructuring programme

Despite improved profitability and the progress made in reducing companies debt–equity ratios and streamlining their operations, a substantial portion of the corporate sector remained financially troubled. In 1999 more than a fourth of externally audited firms failed to make sufficient profits to cover the interest payments on their debts let alone repay some of the principal, and this situation continued in 2000 despite buoyant growth. The situation seemed even more severe among *chaebol*-affiliated companies. The high degree of credit risk clearly undermined confidence in the Korean economy during the course of 2000. As the impact of the public funds injected in the first stage of the financial restructuring programme faded, financial institutions became increasingly cautious about lending. The tightening of loan classification standards also made banks more reluctant to lend. The resulting credit crunch conditions, combined with slower growth, exacerbated their balance sheet difficulties and made it clear that the strong post-crisis expansion could not resolve all the outstanding problems. Consequently the authorities launched the second stage of the restructuring programme. This consisted of enforced removal of non-viable companies and the introduction of bond recycling schemes to promote the survival of firms judged as viable. However, this came too late to prevent the economic slowdown at the end of 2000 (see Chapter 4, Figure 4.5).

In October 2000 the government instructed the banks to evaluate the prospects of financially distressed firms in an effort to identify which ones they should continue to support. This approach had been used in May 1998, when of the 313 companies examined 55 had been designated as non-viable. The selection of firms for the second evaluation process was based on three criteria: their loans were classifiable as precautionary or worse under the forward-looking loan classification scheme, their interest coverage ratio had been less than one for three consecutive years, or they were already being monitored by banks for default risks. A total of 287 firms were found to be eligible for evaluation under at least one of these criteria. However this total was considerably below the number of externally audited firms found to have interest coverage ratios of less than one for three consecutive years. Of the enterprises that were evaluated, 52 were classified as non-viable, of which 18 were liquidated, 11 were put under court receivership and 23 were disposed of through mergers and acquisitions. Almost half the companies (136) were judged to be 'normal'. The remainder were classified as having temporary (28) or structural (69) liquidity problems. The small number of firms judged as non-viable raised doubts about the government's commitment to ensuring the removal of non-viable firms.

Evaluation of the corporate restructuring

In 1999 5 per cent of firms had been unable even to meet their interest payments for three consecutive years. Such non-viable companies absorbed resources that could be allocated to more productive enterprises, and because they were protected from creditors they were able to dump products, thereby eroding the profit margins of viable companies and distorting competition both domestically and abroad. They were also detrimental to the health of the financial sector.

The restructuring of the Big Five and the debt work-outs of other large corporations had mixed results and the participating banks were accused of including firms that should have been immediately liquidated. Given their financial fragility the banks were reluctant to absorb losses and kept on their balance sheets many troubled firms that were unlikely to survive. They were also unable to devise a comprehensive work-out programme involving debt to equity swaps, debt write-downs and debt rescheduling. This raised concern about the fairness and effectiveness of using differential measures to support different firms in different industries. Disagreements about loan loss provisioning, disputes over asset valuation and managers' resistance to loss of control further complicated the process. Consequently many firms failed to meet their obligations to their banks. Some critics have also argued that the provision of preferential financial treatment to indebted firms could unnecessarily prolong the lives of failing firms, eat away at banks' assets and exacerbate the credit crunch on other firms.

It is not clear whether the excess capacity problems that plagued the *chaebols* were solved or not. Evidence is also mixed as to whether the Big Four[16] fulfilled their commitment to improve corporate governance and slim down their operations to a few core businesses. Likewise the effectiveness of the inter-*chaebol* deals remain unclear. The firms involved in these deals remained in financial distress because there was no debt reduction or injection of new capital. Without lay-offs and plant closures the excess capacity problem continued, and reducing the number of firms reduced competition and facilitated collusive behaviour.

Furthermore the commercial banks faced major losses from the debt work-out programmes. For instance the restructuring of Daewoo, which was Korea's second largest *chaebol* until domestic creditors decided on a debt-rescheduling programme for its subsidiaries, resulted in bank losses of an estimated $10.4 billion. The requirement that the Big Five reduce their debt–equity ratios to less than 200 per cent by the end of 1999 also led to debt write-downs and debt to equity swaps that cut the earnings of major commercial banks. These costs made it difficult for the banks to build up the capital and loan-loss provisions needed to absorb the losses from further corporate restructuring.

These problems suggest that the bank-led work-out programmes were not as effective as hoped, and that further improvements in the bankruptcy procedures are needed. The work-out programmes focused on temporary debt relief rather than on asset sales and operational restructuring. A second problem was that the strategy adopted by creditors appeared to be aimed more at limiting their immediate losses than at addressing larger problems in the longer term. While the quick sale of assets would have presumably resulted in immediate losses for the creditors, delaying their sale appears to have led to a decline in their value. The weakness of the bank-led restructuring may reflect the fact that one third of the commercial banks are owned by the government. Therefore the early privatisation of the banks and the development of a more market-oriented financial system should be a priority. The use of corporate restructuring vehicles (CRVs) may be an effective way of turning around indebted companies. Legislation authorising the creation of CRVs until 2006 was passed in October 2000 and KAMCO and some commercial banks are in the process of developing such vehicles. In addition, strengthening the legal bankruptcy procedures would help financial institutions take the lead in corporate restructuring. Improving the ability of the judicial system to deal with bankruptcies should also be a priority.

5.3.3 Labour market reform

The rigid labour market was a key factor in the weakened international competitiveness of Korean firms and therefore in the financial crisis. According to Fitch ICBA (1999), with the advent of democratisation in 1987 and the subsequent liberalisation of trade unions, nominal wages increased by 15 per cent per annum until 1996 while productivity increased by only 11 per cent. However, tight employment conditions and strong trade union power prevented reform of the labour market: an excessive degree of job protection prevented lay-offs and encouraged overmanning, working hours were inflexible and there were few limits on strike action. Therefore a major goal of the reform programme was to increase flexibility in the labour market.

The reforms started with the opening of channels of communication between workers and management. Key to this unprecedented facilitation of consultation and cooperation was the establishment in January 1998 of the Tripartite Commission, composed of representatives from labour, management and the government. In February 1998 the Tripartite Social Accord was signed, covering not only labour issues but also a wide range of socioeconomic matters, including freedom of association, management transparency, business restructuring, labour market policy, reform of the social security system, wage stabilisation, labour–management cooperation and labour market flexibility.

The protection of workers' rights

To protect workers' rights, all workplaces are now subject to laws on the minimum wage, unemployment insurance and industrial accident insurance. Regulations on working conditions have also been implemented. The minimum wage law, which was formerly applicable only to workplaces with more than five employees, was extended to all workplaces from November 2000. It protects not only full-time workers but also temporary, daily and part-time workers. The disabled and trainees may be excluded if their employers obtain the approval of the Ministry of Labour. In addition various occupational groups have been allowed to organise unions, including teachers.

Labour market flexibility

Two measures have been introduced to improve labour market flexibility. First, the Tripartite Social Accord resulted in the revision of the Labour Standards Act (LSA) to legalise lay-offs for 'managerial reasons'. Lay-offs can only be conducted as a last resort and four preconditions have to be met. First, there must be valid managerial reason. Second, all means of avoiding lay-offs should first be exhausted, such as limiting overtime work, putting a freeze on new recruitment and reduce the staffing level via voluntary redundancy or natural wastage. Third, the selection of workers to be laid off should conform to a reasonable and fair standard. Finally agreement to the lay-offs should be reached with union representatives. Managers are also required to submit a report when lay-offs exceed a certain quantity. When economic conditions permit and managers want to employ new personnel they are required to make every effort to reinstate dismissed workers. In spite of these very stringent preconditions the revised LSA has facilitated lay-offs in the interest of financial and corporate reform.

Legislation allowing the establishment of manpower agencies took effect in July 1998. These agencies provide personnel for 26 work types and 118 job classifications, including computer professionals, interpreters, secretaries and tour guides. Such workers are temporarily assigned to companies, and when economic conditions allow the original employer rehires the temporary workers. The employment period is one year, although it can be extended to a maximum of two years.

Countering unemployment

Dealing with the problems that result from unemployment, an inevitable by-product of corporate reform, has emerged as a key task for the government. Numerous policies and programmes have been introduced to ease the social pain of restructuring and address unemployment more actively. These include the expansion of unemployment benefits, retraining programmes and support in job hunting. However these measures have provided support to only a fraction of those who lost their jobs as a result of the financial crisis (Lee and Lee, 2000). Social safety nets have been reinforced and expanded with the implementation of the National Basic Livelihood Security Law, which increased the number of recipients of subsistence benefits from 0.5 million in 1999 to 1.5 million in 2001.

Fostering management transparency and labour–management cooperation

In the past the improvement of labour–management relations was hindered by the opaqueness of company operations. As transparency provides the basis for mutual trust and can result in enhanced productivity, measures to induce transparency are not only a necessary part of corporate sector restructuring but can also help to establish a more confident environment in the labour market. Indeed efforts to improve transparency have contributed greatly to the stabilisation of labour–management relations. To secure management transparency in the corporate sector the Tripartite Commission recommended, and the National Assembly subsequently approved, the use of combined financial statements, the recruitment of outside directors and a ban on cross-debt guarantees. Supplementary policies to further transparency and accountability in the corporate sector are to be implemented. These include the introduction of class-action lawsuits, to be phased in from 2002, enhanced monitoring by institutional investors and peer reviews of accounting practices.

The government has also worked to create a more cooperative labour–management culture in which disputes are actively managed and profits are shared equitably. Labour–management relations have now improved to the point where amicable resolutions have become possible, as shown in the resolution of disputes at Korea Telecom, the Housing & Commercial Bank and Kookmin Bank. In some major companies, such as the Seoul Metropolitan Subway Corporation and LG Electronics, no-strike agreements have been reached between labour and management.

5.3.4 Public sector reform

Public sector reform was an important part of the economic reform programme initiated in 1998. In the interest of better government, several key objectives were set: reducing the size of the government to facilitate the efficient allocation of resources and encourage creativity, entrepreneurship and initiative in the private sector; delivering government services with minimum use of taxpayers' money; and enhancing public sector efficiency by introducing competition and performance measurement and improving feedback. Prior to the financial crisis the public sector was criticised for its poor productivity, inflexibility and inefficiency. In response to this criticism, and with the added impetus for reform provided by the crisis, in early

1998 the government established the Planning and Budget Commission (PBC)[17] which would report directly to the president. The PBC was mandated to formulate and oversee public sector reform, and to this end was given wide jurisdiction over administrative and budgetary issues in the public sector, including state-owned enterprises (SOEs).

The public sector reform programme encompasses all public sector entities, including the central government, local governments, SOEs and other government-affiliated organisations. The last category includes state-owned and state-funded research laboratories, public corporations, hospitals and so on. Only political and judicial groups are excluded from the drive.

The reforms have progressed in phases. The first phase was aimed at paring down waste and inefficiency by means of comprehensive restructuring, and by rationalising the structure and personnel of public organisations. It also aimed to instil an atmosphere of change and reform in the civil service. A firm foundation having been laid by the governmental reorganisation in May 1999, attention shifted to building a new system based on competition and creativity. The ultimate aim is to achieve a public sector that is customer-oriented and capable of continual innovation.

The public sector reforms can be classified under four headings: rationalisation, innovations in public management, improving the management of public finance, and privatisation. Each of these is briefly discussed below.

Rationalisation

With the accession of the new administration under President Kim Dae Jung came a growing recognition that the government was in need of serious restructuring – similar to that required of the private sector – and that it was necessary to establish a new system of national governance and a new paradigm for government. Accordingly the central government reorganised itself on two occasions, in February 1998 and May 1999, and in the process shed 16 offices, 74 bureaus and 136 departments. As a result the number of government employees fell by 11 per cent by the end of 2000. Another downsizing plan involved reducing the number of civil service employees by 16 per cent (about 26 000 persons) by 2001. Local governments also streamlined their organisations, and by October 1998, 12 per cent of total jobs had been eliminated. Streamlining also took place in the quasi-governmental sector, including public institutions and various associations. Some 23 government training institutions were consolidated into 10 in June 1998 and the 320 government committees were reduced to 175 in November 1998.

Between November 1998 and February 1999 a joint task force, consisting of private sector management consultants and experts from government ministries, conducted a review of the functions of the entire central government and some local governments. After careful analysis the team came up with recommendations for eliminating or reducing unnecessary or redundant functions, and for the intra- and interdepartmental adjustment of personnel and responsibilities. It also suggested alternative service delivery measures such as outsourcing or decentralising central government functions and transforming existing organisations into executive agencies. The second government reorganisation, which came into effect in May 1999, reflected the advice given by the review team, including the phased reduction of local government personnel by 19 per cent, or about 26 000 persons.

Innovations in public management

The drive to change the workings of public management focused mainly on introducing the principles of competition and performance. With this in mind, in January 1999 an executive agency system was adopted. In the second governmental reorganisation in May 1999, 10 organisations were designated to take part in a pilot programme for the new system, which took effect in January 2000.

In a move described by the government as perhaps the most significant qualitative change to the civil service in decades, 130 senior government positions were opened to outside applicants. This amounted to 20 per cent of all central government positions at the director-general level or higher. The basis of the system was laid in May 1999 in amendments to the laws on government organisation and civil service management. In the event, however, most of the positions were filled by inside government officials, suggesting only a superficial change to the system. Meanwhile 88 government functions were selected for outsourcing in two reviews that took place in 1998 and 1999.

Improving the management of public finance

Government funds, commonly criticised for loose management, were subjected to an overhaul. The 75 separate funds that existed in 1999 were consolidated into 55, and those in the 'other funds' category were reduced from 38 to 16. A formal review process was introduced to ensure that the funds were continually subjected to monitoring and evaluation. Furthermore a process to deliberate on fund policy was introduced in order to better coordinate the management of government funds with public finance in general. In addition to government funds, the government special account system, which had come under similar criticism for lack of transparency and efficiency, was revised. In the area of fiscal management an incentive system was introduced to help improve efficiency. The new system allowed for incentives of up to 20 million won to be paid to individuals who contributed to budget savings or revenue increases.

An intensive effort was made to instil performance-oriented thinking into the system and practice of public financial management. Beginning with the budget for fiscal year 2000 the government introduced performance-based budgeting at 16 pilot organisations, and scheduled a larger number of organisations for performance-based budgets in 2001. In addition a study is under way of a proposal to implement double-entry accounting in all central and local government departments by 2003, with the ultimate goal of fiscal transparency. Both the Kangnam District of Seoul and the city of Puchon in Kyonggi Province have commissioned research into pilot projects for this purpose.

Other projects to improve public management include feasibility studies of ways to increase efficiency in public construction projects. In addition various measures have been adopted to improve efficiency in budget compilation and administration, including explicit limits on the total budget of long-term projects and a budget ceiling system that allows individual ministries and agencies more flexibility in their budgets within a specified limit.

Privatisation

State-owned enterprises (SOEs) are an important component of the public sector. Hence as part of the overall reform of the public sector the privatisation and restructuring of public enterprises was initiated in 1998. The objectives of privatisation are to enhance economic efficiency, to reduce the extent of direct government involvement in economic activities and to generate resources to support the structural adjustment programmes. The guiding criterion for privatisation is that if an SOE is engaged primarily in commercial activities and there is no justifiable reason for it to remain under state control it should be privatised. There are two important principles in the privatisation process: the process must be transparent and fair, and it must be open to all investors, both domestic and foreign, although the ceiling on aggregate foreign ownership remains.

There are two types of SOE in Korea: state-capitalised enterprises (SCEs) and state-invested enterprises (SIEs). SCEs are subject to the Basic Law Regarding the Management of State-Capitalised Enterprises (the SCE Management Act), and the government's equity ownership of these enterprises is in excess of 50 per cent of the outstanding shares. Currently there are 13 SCEs.[18] SIEs have no statutory definition but are generally understood to be SOEs that are not subject to the SCE Management Act but are under state control by virtue of the government's status as their largest shareholder. The Government's equity ownership in SIEs varies widely between enterprises. Currently there are 13 SIEs,[19] and all but the Korea Appraisal Board and two media corporations (Korea Daily News and the Korea Broadcasting System) are included in the privatisation plan. Only one SCE, the Korea Electric Power Corp., is included in the plan, although some subsidiaries of the SCEs have been earmarked for privatisation.

After a comprehensive review by the PBC[20] and consultation with line ministries the first phase of the privatisation plan was announced on 3 July 1998. Out of the 26 non-financial SOEs examined 11 were made subject to privatisation as no justifiable reasons could be found to keep them under state control. Five of these, plus their 21 subsidiaries, would be privatised immediately and six would be privatised by 2002. The second phase was announced on 4 August 1998 and involved the privatisation of SOE subsidiaries not covered in the first phase, plus the restructuring of 19 non-financial SOEs. Of the 55 subsidiaries of the latter, 40 were to be privatised, six were to be merged with their respective parents and eight were made subject to comprehensive restructuring, involving managerial reform and consolidation.

The restructuring of parent SOEs involved the divestment of assets unrelated to their core business activities, or merger or consolidation to avoid duplication. The corporate governance structure of SOEs was also to be reformed in order to allow greater management autonomy over such matters as personnel and organisation and to enhance management accountability. Emphasis was placed on the appointment of impartial members to a 'CEO Recommendation Committee' to ensure the selection of capable CEOs. In addition, the authority of the board of directors was to be strengthened, and a performance-based incentive system would be adopted. To enhance corporate transparency the SOEs would be required to make public the results of their activities, including performance indices, and to prepare financial statements using internationally accepted accounting principles.

Institutional arrangements were also made for the continuing privatisation effort. The privatisation Steering Committee, which was and still is charged with overseeing the entire programme and making important decisions, was created in 1998, shortly after the announcement of the first phase of the plan. The committee consists of a government minister, vice-ministers, high-level government officials, civilian experts and others. It is chaired by the head of the Ministry of Planning and Budget (MPB) and the vice-minister of the Ministry of Finance and the Economy serves as vice-chair.

The line ministries assume the government's shareholder's rights and are responsible for overseeing the management of the SOEs. The role of the MPB is to oversee and coordinate the overall privatisation and restructuring programme. On matters relating to privatisation and the restructuring of SOEs the line ministries are required to submit details of their plans and their progress to the MPB.

The elimination of excessive regulations has been another important task in the process of public sector reform. In 1998 the Regulation Reform Committee (RRC) abolished approximately 49 per cent of the 11 125 government regulations on private sector matters. It is fair to say, however, that many of the public sector reform tasks and their implementation have hardly been satisfactory. Many critics argue that the government may have satisfactorily led the structural reform of other sectors but it has not followed through with its own public sector restructuring. There has also been considerable antagonism towards the privatisation of SOEs among workers and unions.

5.3.5 Capital market and foreign exchange liberalisation

Financial liberalisation and market opening have been accelerated to induce long-term foreign capital inflows and enhance external credibility. The markets for government and corporate bonds were opened up in December 1997, short-term money market instruments such as Commercial papers were opened up in May 1998, and the ceiling on foreign stock market investment was abolished. In the same month, hostile takeovers by foreigners were allowed and the business areas open to them were widened. Controls on foreign acquisition of real estate, such as its use, size and other qualifications, were eased or abolished in July 1998.

In June 1998 the government announced a plan to liberalise all foreign exchange transactions in two stages. In the new foreign exchange system emphasis would be placed on *ex post facto* management through reports and prudential supervision rather than on prior regulation. The first stage of liberalisation – which took effect on 1 April 1999 with the replacement of the old Foreign Exchange Control Act with the new Foreign Exchange Transactions Act – included the deregulation of most foreign exchange transactions by enterprises and financial institutions. Current account transactions, except for a few types of international current account transactions, by business firms and banks (but not individuals) were fully liberalised on 1 April 1999.

With regard to the liberalisation of capital account transactions, the legal regulatory framework was changed from a positive list system to a negative list system. In order to enhance transparency, all capital account transactions would be liberalised unless specifically prohibited by the negative list. In addition, to reduce inefficiencies stemming from the selective licensing of foreign exchange banks, all financial institutions that could prove themselves able to maintain an effective *expost* transaction management system would be allowed to participate in foreign exchange business.[21]

The second stage of liberalisation took effect on 1 January 2001, when restrictions on foreign exchange transactions, including current account payments by individuals and domestic deposits by non-residents, were lifted. Related measures included the liberalisation of residents' foreign exchange transactions, including elimination of the ceilings on overseas travel expenses and foreign currency purchases and abolition of the restrictions on overseas deposits and trusts; the liberalisation of non-residents foreign exchange transactions, including elimination of the restrictions on domestic deposits and trusts with maturities of less than one year; and the streamlining of the securities investment process.

With an eye to international capital movements and the domestic and international market environment, the government retained the following restrictions on capital transactions: limits on Korean won funding by non-residents, and restrictions on overseas short-term borrowing by financially unsound corporations.[22]

Table 5.13 Foreign portfolio investment trend, 1995–2000 (billion dollars)

	1995	1996	1997	1998	1999	2000
Inflow	10.22	12.57	13.20	16.48	41.74	60.06
Outflow	7.77	8.00	12.12	11.70	36.25	48.45
Net Inflow	2.45	4.57	1.08	4.78	5.50	11.61
Total	17.99	20.57	25.32	28.18	77.99	108.51

Source: Bank of Korea.

Table 5.14 Ratio of foreign investment outstanding to market capitalisation, December 1996 to December 2000 (per cent)

	1996	1997	1998	1999	2000
Korea Stock Exchange	13.0	14.6	18.6	21.9	30.1
KOSDAQ	–	4.5	3.4	7.5	6.9
Bond Market	0.04	0.1	0.3	0.3	0.2

Source: Bank of Korea.

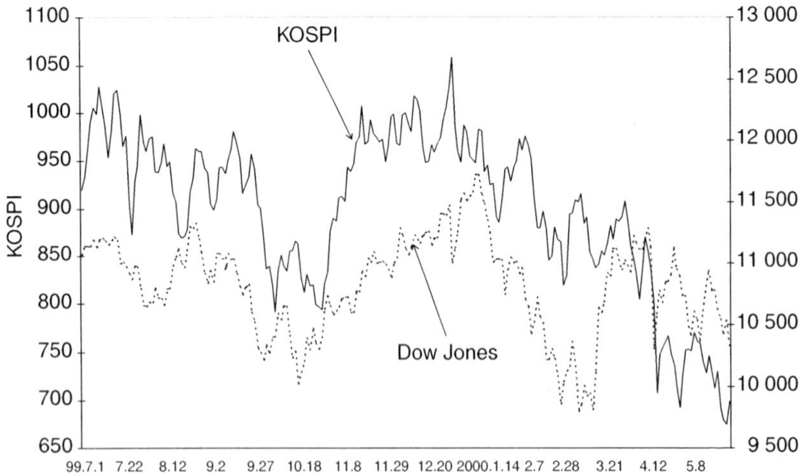

Figure 5.2 Movement of KOSPI and Dow Jones indices

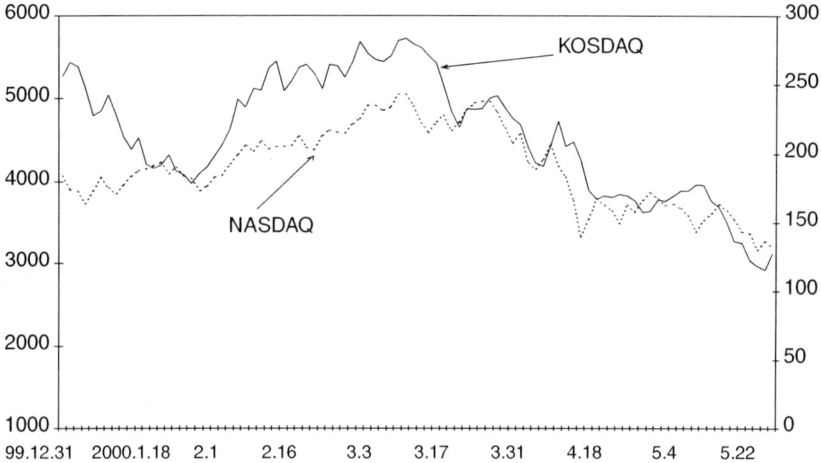

Figure 5.3 Movement of the KOSDAQ and NASDAQ indices

Following the liberalisation of the capital markets and renewed confidence in the Korean financial markets, foreign portfolio investment substantially increased. The net inflow of foreign portfolio investment, which had been a mere $1 billion in 1997 when the crisis broke out, increased to $5 billion in 1998, $5.5 billion in 1999 and to $11.6 billion in 2000 (Table 5.13). Accordingly the ratio of foreign investment to market capitalisation increased substantially. For the Korean Stock Exchange it rose from 13 per cent in 1996 to 30 per cent in 2000. As a result the movement of foreign portfolio investment now has a considerable influence on the Korean stock market (Table 5.14). In particular, movement between the Korean market and the US market has increased substantially (Figures 5.2 and 5.3).

5.4 Reforms, economic progress and future challenges

Table 5.15 summarises the major macroeconomic indicators for Korea over the period 1997–2001. Real GDP, which recorded a negative growth rate of 6.7 per cent in 1998, thereafter became positive, reaching 8.8 per cent in 2000. Inflation remained very low and unemployment fell, although the latter remained above the precrisis level. With regard to public finances, a fiscal deficit was recorded in 1998 and 1999, equivalent to 4.3 per cent and 3.3 per cent of GDP respectively. However in 2000 the budget had moved into a small surplus of 1.3 per cent of GDP. The current account continuously recorded a sizeable surplus from 1998. Total external liabilities fell to $117.7 billion in 2001 from $159.2 billion in 1997. Indeed Korea became a net external creditor in 1999. At the end of 2001 Korea's usable foreign

Table 5.15 Major economic indicators, 1997–2001

	1997	1998	1999	2000	2001
Real Economy					
Real GDP growth rate (%)	5.0	–6.7	10.9	8.8	3.0
Inflation rate of CPI (%, year average)	4.4	7.5	0.8	2.3	4.1
Core inflation (%, year average)	3.4	5.9	0.3	1.8	3.6
Unemployment rate (%, year average)	2.6	6.8	6.3	4.1	3.7
Public finances (% of GDP)					
Consolidated government budget balance[1]	–1.5	–4.2	–2.7	1.3	1.3
Balance of payments					
Current account (US$ billion)	–8.2	40.4	24.5	12.2	8.6
Current account (% of GDP)	–1.5	12.7	6.0	2.4	na[2]
Total External liabilities (US$ billion, end of year)	159.2	148.7	137.1	131.7	117.7
Long–term Liabilities (US$ billion, end of year)	95.7	118.0	97.8	83.7	78.5
Short–term Liabilities (US$ billion, end of year)	63.6	30.7	39.2	47.9	39.1
Short–term Debt/Total Debt (%, end of year)	39.9	20.6	28.6	36.4	33.2
Total External Credit (US$ billion, end of year)	105.2	128.5	145.4	164.7	162.8
Net External Credit (US$ billion, end of year)	–54.1	–20.2	8.3	33.1	45.2
Foreign Exchange Reserves (US$ billion, end of year)	8.8	48.5	74.1	96.2	102.8
Short–term Debt/FX Reserves (%, end of year)	722.7	63.3	52.9	49.8	38.0
Money and Credit					
M3 growth rate (% change, end of year)	13.8	12.5	8.0	7.1	11.6
Overnight call rate (%, end of year)	31.3	6.5	4.7	6.0	4.0
3-year corporate bond yield (%, end of year)	29.0	8.0	9.6	8.1	6.4
Exchange Rate					
Won–US$ nominal exchange rate (year average)	951.3	1401.8	1188.0	1131.0	1290.0
Nominal effective exchange rate (1995 = 100)	92.4	64.5	73.1	78.4	na[2]
Real effective exchange rate (1995=100)	97.3	72.3	82.1	88.8	na[2]

Notes:

1. Data prior to 2000 exclude the civil service pension fund, in equivalent terms, the balance in 1999 was –3.8 per cent.
2. na – not available.

Sources: The Bank of Korea, Ministry of Planning and Budget.

exchange reserves reached $102.8 billion, up from just $8.8 billion in 1997, a remarkable transformation. The exchange rate and interest rates remained below where they stood before the crisis erupted. Even though these indicators tended to become more volatile in early 2001, by mid year the economy had overcome the worst of the crisis and the possibility of a repetition of 1997's external liquidity crisis had been significantly reduced.

However, unstable elements and conditions are increasingly appearing both inside and outside the country. Among the destabilising factors within Korea are the structural reform process and foreign investors' loss of confidence in the Korean economy. Maintaining the momentum of the reforms is crucial to the restoration of this confidence, but (bearing in mind that the 1997 financial crisis erupted during the lame-duck period running up to the presidential elections) some Korea watchers are concerned that the incumbent Kim Dae Jung government is paying less attention to the reform efforts in the run-up to the presidential election in December 2002.

The large current account surpluses in 1998, 1999, 2000 and 2001 helped the commercial banks and the *chaebols* to repay, or refinance, some of their short-term foreign debts, and for the government to amass huge foreign exchange reserves. However the slowing of US economic growth since late 2000 means that Korean exports to that country have been experiencing difficulties, and consequently the current account surpluses are shrinking rapidly. In view of all the above uncertainties there is even greater need to ensure that the structural reforms are pursued in a rigorous manner.

The social consequences of the financial crisis and the subsequent reforms also warrant closer inspection. The crisis had tumultuous and painful repercussions on all sections of Korean society, but low-income households and marginal workers such as women, the young, the less educated and first-time job seekers were the hardest hit. The social protection system was unable to cope adequately with the social consequences of the crisis, and as a result income distribution became less equitable (Lee and Lee, 2000). Consequently a special effort to strengthen the social protection system is greatly needed (this is discussed in detail in Chapter 8).

There remain many internal and external obstacles to the full recovery of the economy, and if these are not properly overcome the Korean people are likely to continue to suffer. On the other hand, if the structural reforms are successful the crisis could turn out to be a blessing in disguise and may pave the way for another economic miracle in the twenty-first century (Lee, 1999a). This will require strenuous efforts to safeguard macroeconomic stability, maintain the momentum of the reforms, and increase efficiency and productivity. Korea has to establish a true market economy – an economy led by the private sector and conforming to the basic principles of transparency, accountability and fair competition, guided by prudential supervision (Lee *et al.*, 2001).

5.5 Summary and conclusions

The financial and economic crisis that hit Korea in 1997 took many by surprise. The country's strong economic fundamentals, including high economic growth, rapid export growth, low unemployment and sustainable current account deficits, masked fundamental weaknesses in the country's corporate and financial sectors that were to combine in 1997 to unravel domestic and international confidence in the economy. Since then the Kim Dae Jung government has taken concerted action to return the economy to high and sustainable economic growth. This has involved the use of monetary and fiscal policies to stabilise the financial market by restoring investor confidence, restructuring the Achilles heel of the economy (the financial and corporate sectors) and maintaining domestic demand. However these policies would have been fruitless on their own and fundamental structural reforms of the economy were needed. This chapter has focused on the reform of five key areas: the financial sector, the corporate sector, the labour market, the public sector, and the capital and foreign exchange markets. While considerable progress has been made in each of these areas, there is still much to be done and it is essential that the authorities maintain the reform momentum.

Korea's recovery from the crisis has been truly remarkable, but there is no room for complacency. Since the second half of 2000 economic growth has slowed and confidence in the economy has retreated. This has been compounded by a number of developments in 2001, most importantly the events of 11 September. Internal and external factors indicate that the economy will face a bumpy ride in the near future, so maintaining macroeconomic stability and completing the structural reforms must remain at the centre of government policy if sustainable economic growth is to be achieved in the medium to long term.

6
The Boom in Information and Communication Technology: A New Economy Emerging?

6.1 Introduction

As discussed in Chapter 1 the world is experiencing a revolution in which information and knowledge have become the principal drivers of competitiveness. Rapid advances in information and communications technology (ICT) have brought fundamental changes to modes of business, government and lifestyles. Indeed, access to ICT-related tools and skills has become crucial to economic development worldwide. Therefore in order to become more competitive in world markets and return to sustainable growth Korea needs to move away from the old economic paradigm and make the transition to a knowledge-based economy.

This chapter provides a picture of Korea's degree of computerisation and its ICT industries, and discusses the challenges that the emergence of the new 'information economy' – if it exists – may pose to Korea. Specifically, Section 2 provides an overview of the ICT boom and some interesting theories on why Koreans have taken so readily to the Internet. Section 3 investigates whether the Korean economy is being transformed into a knowledge economy by conducting a comparison with other OECD member countries. Based on a study by the Bank of Korea (2000a), Section 3 also examines the part played by ICT industries in the nation's recent record of rapid growth and low inflation. Section 4 discusses future challenges and prospects. A summary and conclusions are provided in Section 5.

6.2 The ICT boom

Table 6.1 summarises the trend of various ICT-related indicators for Korea during the period 1994–2000. For the purpose of comparison, indicators for a number of key countries are presented in Table 6.2. The number of personal computers (PCs) in Korea increased from 4.5 million (9.9 per cent of the population) in 1994 to 10.3 million (22 per cent of the population) in 1999 and 13.0 million (27.8 per cent of the population) in 2000. Thus

Table 6.1 Information indicators, Korea, 1994–2000

	1994	1995	1996	1997	1998	1999	2000
Personal computers (thousands)	4459	5349	6304	6931	8269	10300	13000
Personal computers (per 100 inhabitants)	9.9	11.9	13.8	15.1	17.8	22.0	27.8
Internet users (thousands)	138	366	731	1634	3103	10860	19040
Internet users (% of population)	0.3	0.8	1.6	3.5	6.7	23.2	40.5
Mobile phone subscribers (per 100 inhabitants)	2.1	3.6	7.0	15.0	30.2	50.0	58.1
Main telephone lines (per 100 inhabitants)	39.3	41.2	43.0	44.4	43.3	43.8	47.6

Sources: Korea Network Information Centre (http://stat.nic.or.kr); National Computerisation Agency and Ministry of Information and Communication (2000); International Telecommunications Union (http://www.itu.int).

Table 6.2 Information indicators, cross-country comparison, 1999

	Personal computers (per 100 inhabitants)	Internet users (per 100 inhabitants)	Mobile phone subscribers (per 100 inhabitants)	Main telephone lines (per 100 inhabitants)
Australia	47.1	31.7	34.3	52.0
China	1.2	0.7	3.4	8.6
Finland	36.0	32.3	65.1	55.2
France	22.1	9.6	36.4	57.9
Germany	29.7	19.4	28.6	58.8
Hong Kong	29.1	25.2	63.6	57.6
Japan	28.7	14.5	44.9	55.8
Korea	22.0	23.2	50.0	43.8
Singapore	52.7	29.5	41.9	48.2
Taiwan	18.1	20.5	52.2	54.5
United Kingdom	30.6	21.3	45.7	56.7
United States	51.1	39.8	31.2	66.4
Asia Average	2.5	1.4	4.5	8.3
Europe Average	14.6	8.8	22.4	38.5
World Average	6.8	4.4	8.2	15.2

Sources: As for Table 6.1; International Communications Union (http://www.itu.int).

Korea is not as 'personal-computerised' as major developed countries such as the USA (52.7 per cent), Australia (47.1 per cent), Finland (36.0 per cent), the UK (30.6 per cent), Germany (28.7 per cent) and Japan (28.7 per cent). Korea also lags well behind its Asian competitor, Singapore, where 52.7 per cent of the population have personal computers.

On the other hand Korea has a high ratio of Internet users to total population. At the end of 2000 the number of Internet users reached about 19 million, equivalent to 44.7 per cent of the population over the age of 7 and 40.5 per cent of the total population. This represented a jump of about 75 per cent from the 10.9 million in 1999 and of over 500 per cent from the 3.1 million in 1998. Among the Asian countries Korea is second only to Singapore, where 42 per cent are online, and way ahead of Hong Kong, Taiwan and China. The figure of 40.5 per cent for Korea in 2000 exceeded the 39.8 per cent for the USA in 1999, which was then the highest in the world.

The recent Internet boom in Korea is due in part to the rapidly spreading network of so-called 'PC rooms' – Korean-style Internet cafes that have sprouted like mushrooms since 1998.[1] In 1998 there were a handful of such cafes; in 2000 there were more than 20 000. For less than $1 an hour Internet cafes offer the use of multimedia PCs and high-speed lease lines. The national love affair with the Internet is demonstrated by the fact that by June 2000, 69 per cent of all stock trading was being done online. According to a survey by NetValue, an Internet usage measurement company, in January 2001[2] Korea was the world leader in Internet banking, with 49.7 per cent of all home Internet users visiting either a banking or an investment website. The total value of electronic commerce reached 7.1 trillion won in 2000 (National Computerisation Agency and Ministry of Information and Communication, 2001). Although not yet substantial in absolute size, it has been growing at an annual rate of over 100 per cent.[3]

Mobile phone use has burgeoned in Korea. In 2000, 58.1 per cent of the population owned mobile phones, compared with 2.1 per cent in 1994. In 1999, 50.0 per cent of Koreans were already mobile phone users, exceeding most advanced countries but lagging behind Finland (65.1 per cent), Hong Kong (63.6 per cent) and Taiwan (52.2 per cent). Land-line telephone connections have also steadily increased. In 1994 there were 39.3 telephone lines per 100 residents but by 2000 there were 47.6, almost the level in advanced countries.

Korea not only has a high ratio of Internet users to total population, but Koreans are also the most frequent users of the Internet. According to a NetValue survey Koreans spend an average of 18.1 hours a month on the web, which ranks them number one in the world, followed by Hong Kong with 12.1 hours. Korea also comes top in audio and video usage on the Internet, with 65.7 per cent of all Internet users using this facility, more than twice the percentage for Spain, which comes next with 30.6 per cent.

Clearly, then, Koreans' embrace of the Internet has been remarkably rapid and wholehearted. As *Time* magazine (11 December 2000) puts it, 'overnight, South Korea has become one of the world's most connected countries – and Koreans are doing just about everything on the Internet'. Some interesting theories have been offered to explain this phenomenon. Bremner (2000), for example, suggests the following.

> *Gadget-happy Korea:* Koreans, as a rule, are very impatient. The fast pace of life online strummed some impatient chord of the national character, and Koreans seized the Net as a tool to make their lives easier, more convenient and, sometimes, a lot more interesting. If South Koreans can bank, shop, or make disastrous stock trades online, they will. Nor are they reluctant to snap up the latest thing, no matter how untested in the marketplace. A variation on this theme is that Koreans finally have an opportunity to expend pent-up energy, enthusiasm, and individuality. They've lived through the Korean War, military-led and repressive governments, and the borrow-and-spend boom years that saw the government channel their savings into building up major export industries. But now the barriers to foreign investment have crumbled and enshrined ways of thinking no longer hold. *Chaebol* executives are jumping ship for start-ups. And consumers are lapping up technology that makes their lives easier.
>
> *Competition:* South Korea started introducing competition, albeit mostly domestic, into its telecom sector decades ago. And successive governments have made sure that phone charges are not stratospheric. Internet-connection charges are about one-third of what they are in Japan. And by keeping regulations to a minimum, Koreans enjoy the same kind of quick access to the newest broadband technologies that Netizens in Finland have.
>
> *Survival instincts:* South Korea simply has no other choice than to hop on the new economy express. The humiliation of an IMF bailout dispelled any doubts that the South Korean post-war economic model had run its course. A quasi-command-and-control economy made sense when South Korea was playing catch-up in industrialisation, but it is death to a knowledge-based economy. With pricey workers and few natural resources, Korea has figured out it cannot continue to rely on exports of ships and low-end memory chips to juice the economy. Which is why Korea, with the single-minded aggressiveness that made it a name in a slew of export industries, has rallied around the Internet.

Lee Jae Woong (2000), CEO of Daum Communications Corp (Korea's largest portal and e-mail service provider) adds the following:

> *The Korean alphabet:* Unlike in China and Japan where the *Kanji* alphabet is used, which is very troublesome when it comes to typing, Korea uses *Hangul*, the Korean alphabet. *Hangul*, which was invented

by King Sejong in the 15th century, makes it easy for Koreans to use computers.

Strong education belief: Korean parents believe so strongly in education that they would do whatever they think is necessary for their children's education. They have unconditionally invested in PCs and high-speed access to the Web for the home, hoping that their children will not lag behind in the information age.

Small size of the country: Korea is a small country with a population density of 476/km^2 (in 2000), which is one the of highest in the world. Its population is concentrated in Seoul and other metropolitan areas. Some 20 million out of 46 million Korean people live in Seoul and its suburbs. More than half of its population live in high-rise apartment buildings. All these factors have led to a low cost in the provision of infrastructure for access to the Internet.

6.3 Is a new economy emerging?

6.3.1 An OECD comparison

A study by the OECD (1999b) measured the size of the ICT sector (including ICT services and ICT manufacturing) in member countries. Table 6.3 shows the relative importance of the ICT sector to the total business sector in each of the OECD countries, which are ranked as high, medium or low in terms of ICT intensity. As can be seen, Korea towards the late 1990s had a high rating for three of the four measures but only a low rating for employment. There were only four other OECD members with high ratings for three or more of the measures: Sweden, the UK, the USA and Finland. With regard to ICT sector employment as a share of total business sector employment, Korea's share, at 2.5 per cent, was the third lowest after Turkey and New Zealand. But the Korean ICT sector's share of value added was 10.7 per cent, the largest for any country,[4] its share of R&D was 40.9 per cent, the fifth largest following Finland, Ireland, Greece and Canada; and its share of total trade was 20.2 per cent, the third largest among the OECD countries after Ireland and Hungary.

The best indicators of Internet infrastructure development are metrics based on Internet hosts. Table 6.4 shows the number of Internet hosts per 1000 inhabitants in the OECD countries. In January 2000 Korea had 18.8 Internet hosts per 1000 inhabitants and ranked twenty second among the OECD countries. Thus Korea was still way behind most of the OECD countries in terms of Internet hosts,[5] but it is worth noting that the number grew very rapidly. Between July 1995 and January 2000 Korea added an additional 18.1 Internet hosts per 1000 inhabitants, representing a 2585.7 per cent increase a rate exceeded only by Turkey and Mexico.

Table 6.3 ICT sector intensity rating, OECD countries, 1997/98

	Employment (1997)		Value added (1997)		R&D (1997)		Trade of goods and services (1998)	
	Share of ICT in total business sector	Ranking	Share of ICT in total business sector	Ranking	Share of ICT in total business sector	Ranking	Share of ICT in total business sector	Ranking
Australia	2.6	Low	4.1	Low	26.8	Medium	8.9	Medium
Austria	4.9	High	6.8	Medium	–	–	6.6	Low
Belgium	4.3	Medium	5.8	Medium	20.1	Low	7.1	Low
Canada	4.6	Medium	6.5	Medium	43.7	High	9.8	Medium
Czech Republic	3.3	Low	4.7	Low	4.6	Low	8.0	Medium
Denmark	5.1	High	–	–	21.1	Medium	10.4	Medium
Finland	5.6	High	8.3	High	51.0	High	18.1	High
France	4.0	Medium	5.3	Low	26.4	Medium	10.2	Medium
Germany	3.1	Low	6.1	Medium	20.1	Low	9.8	Medium
Greece	–	–	–	–	46.9	High	7.6	Medium
Hungary	5.7	High	9.2	High	11.3	Low	20.6	High
Iceland	4.2	Medium	–	–	21.8	Medium	4.9	Low
Ireland	4.6	Medium	–	–	47.7	High	33.1	High
Italy	3.5	Medium	5.8	Medium	26.5	Medium	6.3	Low
Japan	3.4	Low	5.8	Medium	40.4	High	19.2	High
Korea	**2.5**	**Low**	**10.7**	**High**	**40.9**	**High**	**20.2**	**High**
Mexico	–	–	–	–	0.2	Low	19.5	High
Netherlands	3.8	Medium	5.1	Low	19.6	Low	15.6	High
New Zealand	2.1	Low	–	–	17.7	Low	7.4	Medium
Norway	5.3	High	6.4	Medium	29.2	High	5.6	Low
Poland	–	–	–	–	7.6	Low	7.2	Low

(continued)

Table 6.3 ICT sector intensity rating, OECD countries, 1997/98 (*continued*)

	Employment (1997)		Value added (1997)		R&D (1997)		Trade of goods and services (1998)	
	Share of ICT in total business sector	**Ranking**	**Share of ICT in total business sector**	**Ranking**	**Share of ICT in total business sector**	**Ranking**	**Share of ICT in total business sector**	**Ranking**
Portugal	2.7	Low	5.6	Low	23.5	Medium	7.5	Low
Spain	–	–	–	–	21.4	Medium	7.0	Low
Sweden	6.3	High	9.3	High	27.9	High	14.6	Medium
Switzerland	6.0	High	–	–	–	–	7.3	Low
Turkey	0.5	Low	–	–	21.7	Medium	7.1	Low
United Kingdom	4.8	High	8.4	High	21.8	Medium	14.9	High
United States	3.9	Medium	8.7	High	38.0	High	15.9	High
OECD average	3.6		7.4		34.6		12.8	

Source: OECD (1999b), Table 5.

Table 6.4 Internet hosts per 1000 inhabitants, OECD countries, July 1995 to January 2000

	1995	1996	1997	1998	1999	2000	% Change
Finland	22.5	55.3	67.1	104.0	122.7	148.1	558.2
United States	14.0	26.2	37.2	78.1	118.0	141.5	910.7
Iceland	25.6	40.5	52.6	77.1	108.2	137.0	435.2
Norway	16.1	29.4	50.1	77.0	92.8	120.3	647.2
Sweden	14.6	26.3	39.7	62.1	96.0	114.8	686.3
Canada	14.0	25.2	38.7	73.4	93.6	111.1	693.6
Denmark	9.0	18.8	32.0	51.1	73.4	92.7	922.2
New Zealand	12.3	21.7	42.5	49.6	59.2	88.1	612.2
Netherlands	9.9	16.3	25.5	42.0	56.9	84.8	756.6
Australia	12.2	23.3	40.6	45.5	60.2	77.3	533.6
Switzerland	10.6	17.9	25.6	41.3	59.6	76.1	617.9
United Kingdom	6.0	12.1	18.1	28.2	43.7	60.3	905.0
Austria	5.6	9.9	12.4	20.2	35.5	50.0	792.9
Belgium	2.8	5.3	10.0	19.1	36.8	49.2	1657.1
Luxembourg	4.9	9.5	12.8	23.6	38.1	43.5	787.8
Ireland	3.3	7.1	10.8	16.6	28.8	36.4	1003.0
Germany	4.8	7.9	12.4	18.4	25.6	34.0	608.3
France	2.5	4.4	6.6	11.4	22.7	29.8	1092.0
Japan	1.4	4.2	8.0	11.8	18.1	25.8	1742.9
Spain	1.5	2.6	4.6	9.9	16.2	22.8	1420.0
Italy	1.1	2.6	4.6	8.0	12.6	18.9	1618.2
Korea	**0.7**	**1.5**	**3.5**	**5.4**	**8.5**	**18.8**	**2585.7**
Hungary	1.2	2.6	3.5	7.7	10.3	14.2	1083.3
Portugal	1.0	2.0	2.2	5.4	8.1	12.8	1180.0
Czech Republic	1.5	3.2	4.9	6.7	9.4	12.8	753.3
Greece	0.6	1.4	2.1	4.4	8.1	9.6	1500.0
Poland	0.4	1.0	1.2	2.6	4.4	6.0	1400.0
Turkey	0.1	0.3	0.6	1.0	2.6	5.4	5300.0
Mexico	0.1	0.3	0.4	1.1	2.7	5.0	4900.0
OECD Average	5.9	11.2	16.8	31.4	47.1	59.3	905.1

Source: OECD (2000c).

Table 6.5, which shows secure socket layer (SSL) servers per one million inhabitants, enables us to compare the relative development of electronic commerce in the OECD countries.[6] In March 2000 Korea had only 3.3 SSL servers per one million inhabitants. However the rate of increase between September 1997 and March 2000 was 725 per cent, a little over the OECD average. Nonetheless Korea is way behind the other OECD countries in terms of electronic commerce infrastructure.

Table 6.6 shows that in 2000 there were only 1.8 websites per 1000 inhabitants in Korea, well below the OECD average of 9.5. The USA was the clear leader with 27.

Table 6.5 Secure servers per one million inhabitants, OECD countries, September 1997 to March 2000

	1997	1998	1999	2000	% Change
Iceland	36.6	47.1	104.1	193.9	429.8
United States	27.6	60.8	116.0	170.4	517.4
Australia	13.6	36.6	69.8	119.1	775.7
New Zealand	15.4	26.6	59.3	92.7	501.9
Switzerland	8.0	24.1	54.6	91.5	1043.8
Canada	18.1	33.5	58.0	87.1	381.2
Luxembourg	7.2	28.4	61.0	86.8	1105.6
Sweden	6.0	20.7	45.7	71.0	1083.3
United Kingdom	6.0	14.0	29.5	55.2	820.0
Finland	3.9	15.7	34.8	54.4	1294.9
Norway	5.2	14.5	29.3	49.3	848.1
Ireland	4.6	16.6	26.2	47.8	939.1
Austria	3.2	13.0	29.5	42.1	1215.6
Denmark	2.1	10.1	21.2	39.8	1795.2
Germany	1.8	6.8	19.8	34.5	1816.7
Netherlands	4.8	9.4	19.4	29.4	512.5
Belgium	2.1	5.1	15.7	23.6	1023.8
France	1.1	4.3	10.7	18.0	1536.4
Spain	3.0	6.7	10.9	15.6	420.0
Japan	1.6	4.2	9.2	15.4	862.5
Czech Republic	0.6	2.5	8.6	13.0	2066.7
Italy	1.5	3.4	7.5	10.8	620.0
Portugal	1.6	3.1	6.0	9.0	462.5
Greece	0.5	1.4	4.5	6.5	1200.0
Hungary	0.7	1.9	2.6	4.9	600.0
Korea	**0.4**	**0.9**	**2.3**	**3.3**	**725.0**
Poland	0.2	0.7	1.6	3.1	1450.0
Turkey	0.1	0.2	0.8	1.5	1400.0
Mexico	0.2	0.3	0.6	1.3	550.3
OECD average	8.9	20.1	39.6	60.1	575.3

Source: OECD (2000c).

To summarise, based on the ICT sector's share of value added, R&D expenditure and trade in the total business sector, in 2000 Korea ranked very well compared with other OECD member countries. Based on Internet infrastructure, however, it ranked poorly.

The cost of access to the Internet is a key factor in the relative development of the ICT sector. Table 6.7 shows the cost of an Internet access basket in 2000. As can be seen, the cost of Internet access in Korea was among the lowest in the world. In US dollar terms Korea ranked second, only slightly behind Turkey, and in terms of PPP[7] it ranked fifth, behind Finland, France, the USA and Italy.

Table 6.6 Websites per 1000 inhabitants, OECD countries, 2000

United States	27.0	Belgium	4.1
United Kingdom	15.2	Czech Republic	3.2
Switzerland	13.1	Ireland	1.9
Denmark	12.1	**Korea**	**1.8**
Luxembourg	11.1	Italy	1.4
Iceland	10.0	Hungary	1.3
Germany	9.7	Poland	1.2
Netherlands	9.1	France	1.1
Sweden	8.5	Greece	1.1
New Zealand	8.1	Portugal	1.0
Austria	7.9	Spain	0.7
Canada	7.5	Japan	0.6
Australia	6.5	Mexico	0.2
Norway	6.4	Turkey	0.2
Finland	5.8	OECD average	9.5

Source: OECD (2000c).

6.3.2 Economic performance of the ICT industries

As we have seen, the use of information technology has advanced at a tremendous rate in Korea. This, combined with the recent phenomena of low inflation and rapid growth, has encouraged some economic forecasters and Korean government officials to assert that the Korean economy is being transformed into a new economy (Jun, 2000). This section discusses the economic performance of the ICT industries and their impact on growth and inflation.

Table 6.8 compares the growth rate of value added in the Korean ICT sector with that of real GDP during the 1990s. The ICT sector grew at more than three times the rate of the overall economy, and this trend is likely to continue. During the period 1991–99 the average annual growth rate of real GDP was 5.9 per cent compared with the ICT sector's 23.9 per cent. It is worth noting that the ICT sector recorded a positive growth rate of 20.7 per cent in 1998 at the height of the economic crisis, while the overall economy recorded a negative growth rate of 6.7 per cent in terms of real GDP. The growth rate of value added in the ICT sector surged to 41.2 per cent in the first half of 2000. This outstanding performance by the ICT sector contributed significantly to the growth of the economy as a whole. Specifically, it contributed 38.3 per cent and 45.9 per cent to the increase of real GDP in 1999 and the first half of 2000 respectively.

The ICT sector has also led the other domestic sectors in terms of investment and exports. For example in 1999 ICT exports amounted to \$40 billion, imports amounted to \$26.5 billion. Thus the sector's trade surplus was \$13.4 billion, over half of the country's total trade surplus of

Table 6.7 Internet access basket for 30 hours at peak times using discounted PSTN rates, including VAT, OECD countries, 2000

	PSTN fixed charge		PSTN usage charge		ISP charge		Total	
	US$	PPP	US$	PPP	US$	PPP	US$	PPP
Finland	13.22	11.40	17.98	15.50	8.07	6.95	39.26	33.84
France	11.64	11.19	0.00	0.00	23.72	22.81	35.36	34.00
United States	14.29	14.29	3.50	3.50	16.45	16.45	34.23	34.23
Italy	12.43	13.97	18.52	20.81	0.00	0.00	30.96	34.79
Korea	**2.42**	**3.90**	**15.70**	**25.32**	**3.77**	**6.09**	**21.89**	**35.31**
Canada	17.11	20.61	0.00	0.00	12.63	15.22	29.74	35.83
Mexico	17.01	23.62	0.00	0.00	8.88	12.34	25.89	35.96
Australia	8.55	9.71	2.78	3.16	21.60	24.55	32.92	37.41
Turkey	2.11	3.83	6.58	11.96	12.28	22.33	20.96	38.12
Japan	18.45	10.61	34.07	19.58	21.77	12.51	74.29	42.70
New Zealand	17.73	22.73	0.00	0.00	17.07	21.89	34.80	44.61
Iceland	7.30	5.57	39.72	30.32	12.32	9.41	59.35	45.30
Greece	7.95	9.82	12.44	15.36	17.28	21.34	37.68	46.52
Germany	12.42	11.94	27.02	25.98	9.96	9.58	49.40	47.50
Sweden	12.07	10.14	41.84	35.16	2.76	2.32	56.67	47.62
Norway	19.17	14.52	37.71	28.57	11.82	8.95	68.70	52.05
Spain	11.55	14.08	38.95	47.51	0.00	0.00	50.50	61.58
OECD average	13.63	15.84	30.27	32.94	11.63	13.78	55.53	62.57
Netherlands	15.37	15.84	46.10	47.53	0.00	0.00	61.47	63.37
Ireland	15.40	16.56	30.94	33.26	15.04	16.17	61.37	65.99
Denmark	15.81	12.35	69.09	53.98	0.00	0.00	84.91	66.33
Switzerland	15.36	11.72	72.98	55.71	0.00	0.00	88.34	67.44
United Kingdom	19.12	16.48	65.94	56.84	0.00	0.00	85.06	73.32
Austria	17.07	16.41	67.86	65.25	0.00	0.00	84.93	81.66
Luxembourg	13.39	13.39	0.00	0.00	70.24	70.24	83.64	83.64
Portugal	12.79	17.53	34.96	47.89	18.93	25.94	66.69	91.35
Poland	5.88	10.89	47.65	88.25	0.00	0.00	53.54	99.14
Belgium	15.85	16.18	87.19	88.97	0.00	0.00	103.05	105.15
Czech Republic	4.82	11.22	45.14	104.98	12.35	28.73	62.32	144.93
Hungary	39.12	88.91	13.20	30.01	20.19	45.90	72.52	164.81

Note: PSTN fixed charges include monthly rental fee and additional monthly charges related to discount plans, if applicable. Includes 30 one-hour calls. In France and Luxembourg, ISP and PSTN usage charges are bundled and included under the ISP.

Source: OECD (2000c).

$23.9 billion that year. In 2000 the ICT trade surplus was $15.6 billion while the total trade surplus was $11.8 billion. Table 6.9 summarises these trends.

When it comes to the new economy scholars seem to agree that the ICT sector will play an important role in enhancing productivity growth in other industries, resulting in a sustainably high growth rate with low interest rates.

Table 6.8 Growth rate of the ICT sector, Korea, 1991–2000 (per cent)

	1991	1994	1997	1998	1999	2000 (1st half)	Average
Real GDP growth rate	9.2	8.3	5.0	−6.7	10.7	11.1	5.9
ICT sector growth rate	10.7	26.4	30.5	20.7	41.1	41.2	23.9
Rate of ICT sector contribution to real GDP growth	3.6	12.1	37.6	−23.8[1]	38.3	45.9	–
Share of ICT sector in GDP	3.7	4.7	5.6	6.3	7.6	–	–

Note:
1. Since real GDP fell, the minus sign means that the contribution of the ICT sector to GDP growth was positive in 1998.

Source: Bank of Korea (2000a).

Table 6.9 Export and import trend in the ICT sector, 1991–2000 ($ billion)

	1991	1994	1997	1998	1999	2000
Exports in ICT sector (A)	10.9	20.2	31.3	30.5	40.0	51.1
Total exports (B)	71.9	96.0	136.2	132.3	143.7	172.3
ICT export ratio (A/B, %)	15.1	21.1	23.0	27.8	31.0	29.7
Imports in ICT sector (C)	8.6	12.1	21.9	18.2	26.5	35.5
Total imports (D)	81.5	102.3	144.6	93.3	119.8	160.5
ICT import ratio (C/D, %)	10.6	11.8	15.1	19.6	22.1	22.1
ICT trade balance (A−C)	2.3	8.2	9.4	12.3	13.4	15.6
Total trade balance (B−D)	−9.7	−6.3	−8.5	39.0	23.9	11.8

Source: Korea Association of Information and Telecommunication (http://www.kait.or.kr).

Table 6.10 Growth rate of total factor productivity, Korea, 1976–99 (per cent)

	1976–99	1998	1999
All industries	0.7	−13.8	10.0
Intensive in ICT	–	−15.0	8.6
Non-intensive in ICT	0.1	−18.1	4.9
ICT sector	10.5	14.6	32.2

Source: Bank of Korea (2000a).

Table 6.10 shows the trend in total factor productivity growth. As can be seen, during the period 1976–99 ICT total factor productivity growth far outstripped that of the other industries. Table 6.11 shows the trend in price changes. While the producer price index rose by an average current rate of

Table 6.11 Price changes Korea, 1995–99 (per cent)

	1995	1996	1997	1998	1999	Average
Producer price index	4.7	3.2	3.9	12.2	−2.1	4.4
Price of ICT products	−2.6	−1.8	−2.6	6.7	−5.4	−2.9
Contribution of ICT price changes to PPI	−0.4	−0.3	−0.4	1.0	−0.8	–

Source: Han (2000).

4.4 per cent over the period 1995–99 the price of ICT products recorded a negative average annual rate of 2.9 per cent. Thus the falling price of ICT products helped to lower inflation.

But this is not sufficient evidence to state that the Korean economy has become an ICT-led new economy. That is, while the statistics show that the ICT sector contributed to the average growth of productivity in industry as a whole and helped to stabilise the average price level, there is no evidence to suggest that the ICT sector contributed to the productivity growth of non-ICT industries.

6.4 Government policy and beyond

This section looks at the policy measures implemented by the Korean government in relation to ICT and considers possible policy directions in the building of the new economy. Issues relating to the digital divide are also discussed.[8]

6.4.1 Policy

During the past few years the Korean government has put ICT building blocks in place by laying high-speed lines and deregulating the ICT industries. Aggregate foreign ownership restrictions have been increased to 49 per cent and foreigners are now permitted to be principal shareholders. This has required the enactment or revision of many laws (Table 6.12), starting with the enactment of the Basic Act on Information Technology Promotion in 1995.

In March 1999 the government launched 'Cyber Korea', an ambitious plan to make Korea one of the most advanced ICT nations in the world by 2002. The targets include the following (MIC, 1999):

- The establishment of an advanced, broadband telecommunications network to provide high-speed Internet services by 2002.
- The creation of a 'digital government' by digitalising the administrative services, establishing Intranet services among government agencies, and providing user-centred services.

Table 6.12 Acts relating to the ICT sector

Legislation	Major provisions
Framework Act on Telecommunications (enacted in December 1983, revised in January 2000)	Basic guidelines on telecommunications
Telecommunications Business Act (enacted in December 1983, revised in January 2000)	Licensing criteria and reporting procedures for telecom service providers; telecom service providers' competition safeguards; rights of telecom service users; construction and maintenance of telecom facilities
Software Development Promotion Act (enacted in December 1987, revised in January 2000)	Basic guidelines on software program development and promotion; information management; operation of the Software Promotion Committee
Computer Program Protection Act (enacted in December 1986, revised in January 2000)	Registration and operation of programs; establishment of Evaluation and Coordination Committee; scope, content, limitations and effective period of intellectual property rights
Basic Act on Information Technology Promotion (enacted in August 1995, revised in January 1999)	Basic plan for ICT promotion; establishment and operations of the ICT Promotion Committee; operation of the ICT Promotion Fund
Act on the Promotion of the Information and Communications Network (enacted in May 1986, revised in December 2000)	Basic guidelines on utilisation of information and communications networks and their operation; basic plan for the utilisation and operation of information and communications networks
Basic Act on Electronic Commerce (enacted in February 1999)	Regulations on the legal validity and concept of electronic documents
Digital Signature Act (enacted in February 1999)	Basic guidelines on digital signatures; promotion of the use of digital documents
Act on the Management of Knowledge Information Resources (enacted in January 2000)	Basic guidelines on the management and use of information resources
Act on Solving the Digital Divide (enacted in January 2001)	Establishment of plans for solving the digital divide; establishment of the Digital Divide Solution Committee
Act on the Protection of ICT Infrastructures (enacted in January 2001)	Protection of major ICT infrastructures; assigning major ICT infrastructures and analysing their defects

Sources: Ministry of Information and Communication; National Computerisation Agency and Ministry of Information and Communication (2001).

- The creation of one million new jobs in the ICT sector by 2002.
- Reducing the government's work process time by up to 30 per cent by providing e-mail accounts to all public servants, introducing digital authorisation and digitising more than 80 per cent of the governmental document circulation.
- Designating 'competitive telecommunications products and services' as key products and providing financial assistance for the development of the relevant technologies.

In fact Korea began the construction of the Korea Information Infrastructure (KII)[9] in 1993. The completion year was set at 2010 and the first stage was completed in 1997. The second stage, involving the establishment of an optical transmission network (155 Mbps–40 Gbps backbone network) and an ATM network, was completed in 2000, one year earlier than planned. The optical transmission network links 144 cities, counties and towns across the nation and offers high-speed Internet access. By March 2001 there were over five million high-speed Internet subscribers. The third stage, extension of the high-speed network, is now scheduled for completion in 2005, five years earlier than planned. The government also plans to promote the next generation of Internet technology by creating an environment to facilitate the use of a 20 Mbps service with mobile communication devices.

As Table 6.13 shows, investment in ICT infrastructure in Korea more than doubled during the 1990s, and as a percentage of GDP it far outstripped similar investment in other countries. It is worth noting that in Korea 25 per cent of total investment came from the public sector in the second half of the decade, down from 48 per cent in the first half, while the public sector's share in investment was zero in three of the countries in Table 6.13 and very low in the others. In short the Korean government has played an important part, directly and indirectly, in the establishment of Korea's ICT infrastructure.

Table 6.13 Investment in Information infrastructure, 1991–99

	Investment/GDP (%)		**Public investment (% of total)**	
	Average 1991–95	**Average 1996–99**	**Average 1991–95**	**Average 1996–99**
Korea	0.80	1.85	48	25
Hong Kong	0.58	0.98	0	0
Japan	0.14	0.34	0	0
Malaysia	1.12	1.04	6	5
Singapore	0.35	0.57	38	4
United Kingdom	0.23	0.35	2	2
United States	0.58	0.52	0	0

Source: OECD and World Bank (2000), Table 4.1.

Table 6.14 Summary of the general plan for the promotion of electronic commerce

Main objective	Main contents	Detailed contents
Consolidate Acts and policies to increase the reliability of cyber market	• Ensure e-commerce reliability	• Affirm identity of e-commerce user; prevent forgery of electronic documents; prevent abuse/misuse of personal data; protect e-commerce system from hackers
	• Strengthen consumer protection	• Strengthen refund system; clarify the responsibilities between consumer and supplier; clarify the duties and rights of parties concerned with e-payments; consolidate international e-commerce related acts
	• Improve e-commerce business conditions	• Prepare tax support policy, abolish non-proper Acts for e-commerce
	• Early completion of Information Super Highway	• Construct a high-speed network (1.5–2 Mbps) nationwide
Expand the e-commerce infrastructure	• Promote technology development and standardisation	• Develop core technology through cooperation between public and private sectors; promote ISO standardisation
	• Train e-commerce experts	• Offer more e-commerce-related courses in universities; institute national certificate system
	• Construct e-commerce material basis	• Strengthen connection between delivery network and trade, customs and finance networks; support computerisation of delivery companies
Promote the use of e-commerce in the public sector	• National defence sector	• Complete CALS/EC; complete EDI system (currently under test); spread to 3000 companies
	• Construction sector	• Construct e-supply system of bid contracts; operate e-commerce conferencing in construction sector
	• Government-run companies	• Promote change from simple product purchasing to construction bids; reflect promotion results to management evaluation; consolidate relevant Acts; appoint experts for spreading e-supply in government companies

(*continued*)

Table 6.14 Summary of the general plan for the promotion of electronic commerce (*continued*)

Main objective	Main contents	Detailed contents
	• Government	• Complete computerisation of supply business; increase use of cybermall in government purchases (from 500 to 5000 items); support computerisation of self-supply business in public organisations; establish government supply electronification environment
Spread industrial e-commerce	• Expand model project	• Complete e-commerce model projects in 9 main industrial sectors; induce civil investment by means of tax deductions and increased government support
	• Compose e-CEO council	• Continuous promotion of B2B e-commerce
Establish the basis for cyber trade	• Amend Cyber Trade Support Act	• Solve errors according to Cyber Trade Map; computerise trade customs business
	• Establish a unified buyer development system (Silk Road 21)	• Provide one-click service; strengthen e-commerce cooperation with advanced countries

Source: National Computerisation Agency and Ministry of Information and Communication (2001).

Even though electronic commerce has been growing at an annual rate of over 100 per cent it is not yet substantial in absolute size. In an effort to boost e-commerce the government drew up a plan to consolidate the relevant Acts and policies to increase the reliability of the cyber market, expand the e-commerce infrastructure, promote the use of e-commerce in the public and industrial sectors, and establish the basis for cyber trade (Table 6.14). These issues are addressed in the Basic Act on Electronic Commerce (enacted in February 1999) and the Digital Signature Act (enacted in February 1999).

From 1998 the government also promoted the development of venture businesses – small firms characterised by high risk but potentially high returns – by ensuring the availability of finance, technology, manpower and physical facilities. It also provided tax incentives to facilitate the start-up of new venture businesses (OECD, 2000a). In 1997 there were about

3600 such businesses, rising to more than 5000 in 1999, 8860 in 2000 and 10 963 in 2001. Almost two fifths of all venture businesses focus on computer or telecommunications equipment, thus contributing to the boom in the ICT sector (ibid.)

6.4.2 Future challenges

This section discusses some of the problems facing the ICT sector and suggests policy measures that could enhance the already rapid growth of the sector.

First, in order to help reduce costs and promote the diffusion of ICT the government should further liberalise the ICT industry and open up the sector to even more foreign investment. The OECD and World Bank (2000) point out that the Ministry of Information and Communication (MIC) still tries to orchestrate much of the sector's development. They also raise the question of the return on public investment, and argue that in the absence of reform the return on investment (both public and private) in information infrastructure will remain lower than it should be. The high share of public investment in information infrastructure may reflect a lack of competition in the sector, so steps need to be taken to eliminate the restrictions on foreign investment. Other than this the government should restrict its activities to the addressing of market failures.

Second, in order to boost ICT and e-commerce the government should construct a regulatory and legal framework that is in harmony with international standards. In particular, intellectual property right laws and cyber laws covering privacy, security and digital transactions are needed to encourage the diffusion and use of information and knowledge technologies. Immediate attention should be paid to intellectual property rights as Korea ranked forty-first out of 47 countries in terms of patent and copyright protection in the 1999 World Competitiveness Index, produced annually by the International Institute for Management Development.

Third, the government should use the Internet to force change in the economy. Internet usage could help increase the transparency of government and improve the quality and effectiveness of public services. It could also improve the efficiency and transparency of businesses, give consumers greater power and transform the country's traditional cosy and opaque business relations. For example B2B e-commerce would break the links between *chaebols* and their suppliers, and thus help to loosen the stranglehold the *chaebols* have on the economy (*Economist*, 2000d).

Fourth, the government needs to improve the venture capital market and encourage the establishment of small and medium-sized enterprises (SMEs) as they are important sources of new ideas and innovations and are not afraid to explore new frontiers. In the ICT sector the demand patterns are unclear, the risks are large and the technology has not been entirely worked out. In such emerging areas small firms have an advantage over large established firms because they tend to be more flexible and better at harnessing creative talent and providing the right incentives. To improve the venture capital market the restrictions on capital funds need to be reduced and regulatory oversight and information disclosure strengthened.

Fifth, as recommended by the OECD and World Bank (2000) and Pilat (2000), the education system needs to be reformed as human capital is crucial to the new economy. In particular there is an urgent need for qualified personnel for the ICT sector, where there is expected to be a shortfall of approximately 1 400 000 workers until 2005.

Finally, Korea needs a more competitive environment in which incentives are provided for the creation and efficient use of information and knowledge technology.[10]

6.4.3 Addressing the digital divide

Due to rapid technological change and because people differ in their preparedness for change, the new economy is bringing not only opportunities but also the risk of increasing social inequality between those who have access to ICT and those who do not. Thus attention has to be paid to making ICT available to the socially and economically vulnerable – the poor, women and the uneducated.

According to a survey conducted in March 2000 a digital divide is strongly evident in Korea, as in the rest of the world (National Computerisation Agency and Ministry of Information and Communication, 2000). Nearly 90 per cent of Internet users are in their thirties or younger. Some 52.2 per cent of college graduates use the Internet, compared with 16.2 per cent of high school graduates and just 1.0 per cent of middle school graduates. About 70 per cent of students use the Internet, compared with 1.4 per cent of farmers and fishermen. The proportion of female Internet users is 37.4 per cent, while that of male Internet users is 62.6 per cent. In short the middle aged and elderly, the less educated, non-office workers and females are being left behind in ICT terms. It is also notable that the usage rate among people with incomes above 4 million won per month is more than four times that among people earning less than 1 million won.

To offset this growing digital divide the government has introduced policies to foster the availability of information services. For example it has provided free PCs and five years of free high-speed Internet access to 50 000 students from poor families, connected more than 10 000 schools to the Internet and provided computers free of charge to 200 000 classrooms. It has also provided subsidised or free Internet training for groups such as housewives, juvenile delinquents and the disabled. To provide rural dwellers with access to the Internet the government has installed satellite Internet cafes and information education centres (which serve as both computer training centres and Internet cafes) in post offices in small cities and farming/fishing villages. Twenty-five information education centres were set up in 1999 and it was planned to open a further 25 per year thereafter. The government also plans to establish 3000 residents' information access centres and 1000 Internet cafes by 2002.

While the ICT revolution is threatening to increase inequalty it also holds out the prospect of reducing poverty by integrating rural and poor urban communities into economic life, and thus improving their income levels (OECD and World Bank, 2000). Public information centres could provide training for rural and poor urban adults in basic computing skills, and support for farmers. The Internet could also be used to monitor the poor and evaluate the extent to which such programmes affect their lives. Furthermore the ICT revolution has brought more flexible working arrangements that enable housewives to work from their homes. In fact the Internet may prove to be a godsend for women in Korea, as noted by Veale (2000).

Despite the progress made so far, efforts to alleviate the digital divide need to be strengthened. As the OECD–World Bank (2000) report indicates, special efforts are needed to increase the opportunities for retraining and to extend access to ICT to poor urban and rural communities and the disabled.

6.5 Summary and conclusions

Since the 1960s the economic growth of Korea has been driven by several industries. In the 1970s growth was driven by labour-intensive light industries such as textiles and clothing. During the 1980s the capital-intensive heavy and chemical industries took the lead, and in the 1990s high-tech assembly industries such as the electronics and car industries rose to the fore.

ICT offers the potential for further innovation of the economy as it has reduced communications costs and provides virtually free access to a huge amount of information. It has broken down geographical borders and allowed remote countries to tap into the global business centres. In the latter respect Korea is likely to benefit more from ICT than many other countries in the world, enabling it to catch up with developed countries such as Japan.

This chapter has summarised the current status of Korea's computerisation and described its impact on the overall economy. While the recent Internet boom among Koreans and the development of ICT industries has been enormous with the ICT sector becoming a major driving force of the economy, ICT remains limited in certain areas. Compared with international standards PC use is quite limited, and the spread of Internet hosts and secure servers for electronic commerce is low. Furthermore Korea has yet to exploit the full benefits of ICT such as improved productivity growth without undue pressure on prices. The full economic impact of ICT cannot yet be precisely evaluated, but it is expected to give a new momentum to the economy and become the main engine of growth over the next couple of decades.

However a couple of caveats have to be added. First, the rise of ICT does not mean that Korea can avoid developing an efficient financial market, reforming the *chaebols*, reforming the labour market and relaxing government regulations. Indeed ICT has made it even more important to do all these things.

Secondly, ICT is not a panacea for growth. In fact the recent recession in the USA seems to have been caused by excess investment in the ICT industries. For instance the NASDAQ price index in the USA, which rose beyond 5000 in 1999, fell to less than 2000 in March 2001. The KOSDAQ has followed a similar trend. KOSDAQ, which was created in July 1996, made a very dramatic increase until 1999, and this made a large contribution to the boom in ICT venture business. However the KOSDAQ price index, which recorded 256 at the end of 1999, had dropped to 52 by the end of 2000. As in the USA there seems to have been overinvestment in ICT industries and this might have built up the so-called ICT bubbles that contributed to the recent recession in Korea. Thus digitalisation may bring dangers to the Korean economy, and this warrants special attention in the course of the transition to the new economy. Nonetheless the ICT revolution offers more opportunities than threats.

7
Economic Integration with North Korea: A New Economic Territory

7.1 Introduction

In the first year of the new millennium the summit meeting between President Kim Dae Jung of South Korea and Chairman Kim Jong Il of North Korea marked an important turning point in inter-Korean relations and offered the possibility of peace, reconciliation and cooperation between the two Koreas in economic and many other areas.

The current state of the North Korean economy is briefly reviewed in Section 2, while Section 3 discusses the prospect of major economic reform and the opening of the North Korean economy. Section 4 considers the current state of inter-Korean relations, and Section 5 discusses how gradual economic integration between the two Koreas could ultimately lead to the unification of the Korean peninsula. Final remarks are made in Section 6.

7.2 Overview of the North Korean economy

Oh and Hassig (2000) note that, under communism, North Korea is as independent as Yugoslavia, as closed as Albania, as harsh a dictatorship as Romania and as loyal to socialism as Cuba. This captures the gist of North Korea, which since 1946 has been a highly centralised and planned command economy. Virtually all natural resources are owned by the state and resource allocation is completely controlled by the central planning board. But the North Korean economy is operated differently from that of the former Soviet Union in that it is based on the ideology of self-reliance or *juche*, with as little reliance on external sources of capital, investment and technology as possible.

The North Korean economy surpassed that of South Korea until the early 1970s in terms of per capita income. However this was not because of the command economy system and the *juche* ideology but largely because of substantial assistance from the Soviet Union and China. The first serious economic problems emerged in the late 1960s when the Sino-Soviet dispute resulted in diminished aid to North Korea. To cope with this challenge North Korea began to borrow capital from the West. However it was unable to pay off its initial loans, largely because of its ineffective economic structure, the oil price increase and the worldwide recession in the 1970s. Furthermore its emphasis on heavy industry and arms production damaged the economy by exacerbating structural bottlenecks and inefficiencies. Subsequent defaults on the foreign loans severely reduced its international credit rating. Consequently the economy had become even further isolated from the West by the end of the 1970s.

In 1984 North Korea promulgated a Joint Venture Law to attract foreign capital and technological investment, but the response from the West was negligible because of North Korea's poor international financial standing and domestic economic conditions. By 1993 144 foreign joint ventures had been established, but 133 of these were by pro-Pyongyang Koreans living in Japan. Accordingly the economy continued to stagnate in the 1980s.

Furthermore the collapse of the communist bloc from the late 1980s caused a sharp decline in North Korea's trade volume. The Soviet Union had been a major supplier of strategic resources to North Korea (including petroleum, most intermediate capital goods, and equipment used in the heavy and chemical industries) and trade had been conducted on a barter basis. But the Russian Federation required the North to pay in hard currency at world market prices, and this prompted a sharp reduction in trade. Furthermore public transfers to North Korea from the former Soviet bloc were curtailed from 1989. To make matters worse, North Korea has been subject to major crop failures due to heavy rains and flooding each year since 1995.

As shown in Table 7.1, in the 1990s North Korea had nine consecutive years of negative economic growth. There were shortages of raw materials, energy, food and foreign exchange, and there were numerous reports that the majority of the North Korean people were having to obtain many of their basic necessities from farmers' markets. Thus the functioning of the central distribution system was debilitated and replaced largely by private markets.

Somewhat surprisingly, however, the economy is reported to have grown by 5.2 per cent in 1999 and 1.3 per cent in 2000 (Bank of Korea, 2000a, 2001b). According to the Bank of Korea (BOK) this growth was partly driven by foreign aid and increased food production in 1999, and by construction and mining projects in 2000. But this assertion was greeted with considerable scepticism by specialists working outside the South Korean government. Eberstadt (2000), for example, argues that the BOK used high-end estimates of North Korean agricultural output to calculate its figures, and if it had used other estimates it would have concluded there had been no economic growth at all in North Korea in 1999.

Table 7.1 Trends in major economic indicators, North Korea, 1990-2000

Year	Nominal GNI (US$ billion)	Real GDP growth rate (%)	Per capita GNI (US$)	Exports (US$ billion)	Imports (US$ billion)	Trade balance (US$ billion)	Total trade (US$ billion)	Total trade/ GNI (%)	Foreign debt (US$ billion)	Foreign debt/ GNI (%)
1990	23.1	−3.7	1,142	1.96	2.76	−0.8	4.72	20.4	7.86	34
1991	22.9	−3.5	1,115	1.01	1.71	−0.7	2.72	11.9	9.28	40.5
1992	21.1	−6	1,013	1.03	1.64	−0.61	2.67	12.6	9.72	46
1993	20.5	−4.2	969	1.02	1.62	−0.6	2.66	12.9	10.32	50.3
1994	21.2	−2.1	992	0.84	1.27	−0.43	2.11	10	10.66	53.3
1995	22.3	−4.1	1,034	0.74	1.31	−0.57	2.05	9.20	11.83	53
1996	21.4	−3.6	989	0.73	1.25	−0.52	1.98	9.3	12	56.1
1997	17.7	−6.3	811	0.91	1.27	−0.36	2.18	12.3	11.9	67.2
1998	12.6	−1.1	573	0.56	0.88	−0.32	1.44	11.4	12.1	96.8
1999	15.8	6.2	714	0.52	0.96	−0.44	1.48	9.4	12.3	77.8
2000	16.8	1.3	757	0.56	1.41	−0.85	1.97	11.7	12.46	74.2
S. Korea 2000	455.2	10.7	8581.0	145.2	116.8	28.4	262.0	65.5	136.5	33.9

Note:
GNI stands for Gross National Income.

Sources: (1) Bank of Korea, *Estimation Results of North Korean GDP, 1999*, Seoul, 2000 (in Korean).
(2) Bank of Korea, *Estimation Results of North Korean GDP, 2000*, Seoul, 2001 (in Korean).

In 2000 North Korea's gross national income (GNI) and per capita GNI were one-twenty-seventh and one-thirteenth of those of South Korea, respectively. North Korea's foreign trade had contracted sharply during the previous 10 years (Table 7.1), falling from $4.72 billion in 1990 to $1.44 billion in 1998. However it did show signs of recovery in 1999 and 2000, increasing to $1.48 billion in 1999 and $1.97 billion in 2000, due largely to an increase in imports in both years. North Korea also experienced chronic trade deficits from 1990, which served to increase its external debt. The latter is estimated to have rise from $7.86 billion (34 per cent of GNI) in 1990 to $12.46 billion (74.2 per cent of GNI) in 2000. China and Japan replaced Russia and other former socialist countries as North Korea's largest trading partners in 2000, accounting for 50 per cent of total trade, or 24.8 per cent and 23.5 per cent respectively.

7.2.1 Sectoral trends

Energy crisis

Energy supply in North Korea deteriorated dramatically in the 1990s. Among the energy sources, coal supplied 70 per cent, electric power 16 per cent, petroleum 10 per cent and other fuels 4 per cent. Difficulties in extracting the increasingly inaccessible and low-quality coal reserves resulted in production falling from 33.2 million tonnes in 1990 to 18.6 million tonnes in 1998 (Table 7.2). However production is estimated to have risen to 21.0 million tonnes in 1999 and 22.5 million tonnes in 2000.

Electricity generation was adversely affected by the decreased production of coal, with total amount of electricity generated falling from 27.7 billion kWh in 1990 to 17.0 billion in 1998. While it increased in 1999 and 2000, yielding 18.6 kWh and 19.4 kWh respectively, the power grid was said to have suffered extraordinarily large transmission losses (Noland, 2000b). To overcome this problem, in 1994 North Korea signed an agreement with the USA in which North Korea agreed to freeze its nuclear weapons development programme in return for the establishment of a multinational consortium (the Korea Energy Development Organisation, KEDO) to build two light water nuclear reactors in North Korea. But the completion of these reactors, which was originally scheduled for 2003, may not take place until after 2006 (Hong, 2001).

To make matters worse North Korea's lack of foreign exchange forced it reduce its crude oil imports from 2.52 million tonnes in 1990 to 0.32 million tonnes in 1999, just 13 per cent of the 1990 level. This not only exacerbated the energy supply shortage but also caused a reduction in agricultural fertiliser production, which was generated by crude petroleum. Production fell from 1.2 million tonnes in 1990 to 0.5 million tonnes in 2000, and this played a significant part in the North Korean food crisis.

Table 7.2 Trends in microeconomic indicators, North Korea, 1990–2000

Year	Coal production (million tonnes)	Electricity production (billion kWh)	Import of crude petroleum (million tonnes)	Grain production (million tonnes)	Import of grain (million tonnes)	Iron production (million tonnes)	Steel production (million tonnes)	Cement production (million tonnes)	Fertiliser production (million tonnes)
1990	33.2	27.7	2.52	4.02		8.4	3.4	6.1	1.2
1991	31.1	26.3	1.89	4.43	1.29	8.2	3.2	5.2	1.1
1992	29.2	24.7	1.52	4.27	0.83	5.7	1.8	4.7	1
1993	27.1	22.1	1.36	3.88	1.09	4.8	1.9	4	1.2
1994	25.4	23.1	0.91	4.13	0.49	4.6	1.7	4.3	1
1995	23.7	23	1.1	3.45	0.96	4.2	1.5	4.2	0.9
1996	21	21.3	0.94	3.69	1.05	3.4	1.2	3.8	0.7
1997	20.6	19.3	1.11	3.49	1.63	2.9	1	3.3	0.6
1998	18.6	17	0.61	3.89	1.11	2.9	0.9	3.2	0.5
1999	21	18.6	0.32	4.22	1.07	3.8	1.2	4.1	0.8
2000	22.5	19.4	0.39	3.59	1.23	3.8	1.1	4.6	0.5
S. Korea 2000	4.2	266.4	120.8	5.91	na	0.2	43.1	51.3	3.7

Sources: (1) Bank of Korea, *Estimation Results of North Korean GDP, 1999*, Seoul, 2000 (in Korean).
(2) Bank of Korea, *Estimation Results of North Korean GDP, 2000*, Seoul, 2001 (in Korean).
(3) Ministry of Unification, *The South and North Korean Economy since 1945*, (weekly report) vol. 500, August 2000, pp. 53–68 (in Korean).
(4) Korea Trade-Investment Promotion Agency (KOTRA), *North Korea's Foreign Trade, 2001*, Seoul, 2001 (in Korean).

Food crisis

According to estimates by the Bank of Korea (2000b), grain production in North Korea fell from more than 4 million metric tonnes in the early 1990s to 3.45 million metric tonnes in 1995, at which point North Korea requested food assistance from international organisations. An official North Korean report showed that food production in the harvest year 1995/96 was 3.76 million metric tonnes while the aggregate demand was 7.64 million metric tonnes, leaving a food shortage of almost 4 million metric tonnes. This figure, however, seems a little exaggerated. For example the South Korean government estimated that the North Korean food demand in 1997 was 5.7 million metric tonnes, about 2 million metric tonnes less than stated in the North Korean report, while the United Nations estimated that 4.8 million metric tonnes of grain was needed to feed North Korea's 22 million people.

Grain production is estimated to have risen to 4.22 million metric tonnes by 1999 but to have declined again to 3.59 million metric tonnes in 2000. The requirement gap was narrowed, but not closed, by grain imports and international assistance, and as a result millions of people suffered starvation and malnutrition. By the North's own estimate, more than 0.2 million people died of starvation or hunger-related diseases in the late 1990s. A nutritional survey by the United Nations in 1998 found that 63 per cent of North Korean children's growth had been stunted by long-term undernourishment.

The North Korean authorities blamed the domestic shortage on the floods of 1995 and 1996, and the drought and tidal waves of 1997 (Cho and Zang, 1999), but it is fair to say that the chronic fall in crop production, and hence the food shortage, was largely due to North Korea's misguided economic policies, inefficient production and irrigation methods and the shortage of fertilisers.

Shortage of primary and intermediate inputs

As shown in Table 7.2, the production of primary and intermediate inputs such as iron, steel and cement fell from 1990, and this, along with the shortage of energy, contributed to the low capacity utilisation of manufactures in North Korea. For example iron production, which stood at 8.4 million tonnes in 1990, fell to 2.9 million tonnes in 1998. This of course had a direct impact on steel production, which fell from 3.4 million tonnes in 1990 to 0.9 million tonnes in 1998. Meanwhile the production of cement fell from 6.1 million tonnes to 3.2 million tonnes over the same period. All these primary and intermediate inputs are estimated to have increased a little in 1999 and remained stable in 2000.

Contraction of mining and manufacturing

Owing to North Korea's pursuit of socialist industrialisation from the 1950s the share of mining and manufacturing in total production rose to

Table 7.3 Changing patterns of industrial structure of North Korea, 1960–2000 (%)

	1960	1970	1987	1990	1997	1998	1999	2000
Agriculture, forestry, and fishing	28.9	21.5	20.0	26.8	28.9	29.6	31.4	30.4
Mining and Manufacturing	41.3	57.3	60.0	42.8	25.5	25.6	25.6	25.4
SOC and Services	29.8	21.2	20.0	30.4	45.6	44.9	43.0	44.2

Source: Korea Trade-Investment Promotion Agency (KOTRA) Internet Website (http://www.kotra.or.kr).

Table 7.4 Industrial structure of the Two Koreas, 2000 (%)

	North Korea	South Korea
Agriculture, forestry, and fishing	30.4	4.6
Mining and quarrying	7.7	0.3
Manufacturing	17.7	31.5
light manufacturing	(6.5)	(7.2)
heavy and chemical manufacturing	(11.2)	(24.3)
Electricity, gas, and water	4.8	2.8
Construction	6.9	8.2
Services	32.5	52.6
government services	(22.6)	(9.9)
other services	(9.8)	(42.7)
GDP	100	100

Source: Bank of Korea, *Estimation Results of North Korean GDP, 2000*, Seoul, 2001.

60 per cent in 1987. With the collapse of the socialist bloc, however, this share dropped consistently thereafter, reaching 25.4 per cent in 2000. This decrease can be attributed to the shortage of energy and raw materials, and to North Korea's lack of infrastructure and the consequent transportation difficulties. The share of agriculture and fishing in total production, on the other hand, rose from 20 per cent in 1987 to 30.4 per cent in 2000. This is in sharp contrast with the situation in South Korea, where agriculture and fishing are considerably less important than heavy industries and the private service sector (Tables 7.3 and 7.4).

7.2.2 Consequences and policy responses

As discussed in the previous section the North Korean economy nearly collapsed because of economic mismanagement, the loss of major subsidies after the break-up of the Soviet Union, and a series of natural disasters. In particular the shortage of food, energy and raw materials resulted in the breakdown of the traditional food distribution system, and the government implicitly permitted private transactions in farmers' markets by largely ignoring illegal private cultivation. By the late 1990s ordinary urban households were purchasing 70 per cent of their food from farmers' markets in rural areas, and about 50 per cent of the population shopped daily in farmers' markets and black markets (Cho and Zang, 1999).

The paralysis of the official distribution system and the resultant rise of private markets has caused a weakening of the social system in North Korea. For instance at one time North Korean citizens could not travel to another province without official approval. However the migration of workers to relatively affluent regions has become commonplace as the authorities can no longer prevent people from travelling to search for ways of making a living. About one million refugees are believed to have fled across the Tumen River into China (*Economist*, 2000a).

Crimes such as smuggling, embezzlement and theft have become increasingly common. For example, with the help of ethnic Koreans living in north-eastern China and the managers of state-governed shops, smugglers bring many Chinese commodities into North Korea to sell in the black market (Cho and Zang, 1999).

With regard to policy responses, unlike China, which has pursued economic reform for a considerable time, North Korea held on tightly to its planned economy after the collapse of the Soviet bloc. However this was probably due less to its belief in the superiority of the socialist planned economy and more to its concern that reforms might threaten the stability of the regime. Nonetheless its economic problems from the early 1990s forced it to adopted a limited number of reform initiatives. The period 1994–96 was a time of economic adjustment, with priority being placed on agriculture, light industry and foreign trade. The economy was opened up just enough not to affect its systemic organisation. The government introduced a new foreign investment law and related regulations, created a free economic and trade zone in the Rajin–Sunbong area, and participated in the Tumen River Area Development Program (TRADP), which was initiated in 1991 by the United Nations Development Program (UNDP) and whose members are North Korea, South Korea, China, Russia and Mongolia.

The Rajin–Sonbong free economic and trade zone covers 621 square kilometres along the north-eastern coast and is very isolated from the rest of the country. In June 1997 an independent cost accounting system was introduced to the enterprises in the area, followed by a floating exchange rate system and foreign investors are not required entry visas. Despite these efforts little interest has been shown by Western investors because of the inadequacy of the infrastructure, the absence of market mechanisms and the country's rigid political system.

It has recently been reported that the government is considering opening Wonsan and Nampo as bonded processing areas. Unlike the Rajin–Sunbong area, Wonsan and Nampo are located fairly near to the demilitarised zone between North and South Korea. The port of Wonsan faces the East Sea and is a reasonable travelling distance from South Korea's Sokcho, Tonghae, Pohang and Pusan. Nampo faces the Yellow Sea and lies north from Inchon in South Korea. Daewoo, a South Korean *chaebol*, has set up a joint company in Nampo, and Wonsan is very close to Mt Kumgang, where Hyundai operates tours for South Koreans.

North Korea enacted a new law on processing trade in April 2001 in the hope of luring more foreign investment. The law covers the expansion of free-trade zones, the adoption of trade guarantees and simplification of the administrative procedures for trade-related affairs such as taxation and dispute arbitration (*Wall Street Journal*, 25 April 2001). The new law has broadened the types of North Korean firm that can form partnerships with foreign firms, and set up a legal mechanism by which foreign firms can seek financial compensation if their contracts in the country are violated.

It has been reported that in an effort to solve the chronic shortage of food, North Korea is set to expand the farmers' contract system nationwide following a successful pilot test (*Chosun Ilbo*, 2001b). This system, which is similar to that in China allows farmers to use part of their produce for their own consumption or to sell it at a farmers' market instead of to the state at a fixed price.

7.3 The future direction of North Korea

7.3.1 From a rogue nation to what?

Kim Jong Il became North Korea's *de facto* leader when his father, Kim Il-Sung, died in 1994, but he did not assume his father's position of secretary-general of the ruling party until 1998 and he has yet to be made state president. Among the reasons suggested for the long delay in his succession were his poor health and the existence of internal power struggles. But these speculations were proved wrong when he and South Korea's Kim Dae Jung held their historic summit meeting in Pyongyang in June 2000.

The most convincing reason, perhaps, is that he needed time to establish solid domestic and foreign policies in connection with his desire to resuscitate the ailing economy, and to improve relations with South Korea and Western countries without jeopardising the North's political existence. But did the summit herald a fundamental strategic reorientation on the part of Kim Jong Il? Sceptics argue that he is not genuinely interested in reforming his regime, but is simply pretending in order to reap substantial rewards for his country. More neutral observers argue that North Korea's intentions are still not known. But for the following reasons we believe he has finally made up his mind.

As Noland (2000c) points out, in the 1990s North Korean officials described reform as 'honey-coated poison' and economic opening up as 'a Trojan horse' to destabilise socialism. But the language used during Kim

Jong Il's visit to Beijing in May 2000 was very different. During that visit he commented on Chinese reformer Deng Xiao Peng's 'great achievements in opening up the country' and announced that North Korea supported China's reform policy. These comments suggested a new receptiveness to economic reform on the part of the North Koreans, and opened up the possibility of China adopting the role of mentor in this regard (ibid.).

A month after his visit to China, Kim met Kim Dae Jung in Pyongyang. It seems obvious that the latter's visit to Pyongyang and the consequent joint declaration not only created a new paradigm of reconciliation and cooperation between the two Koreas, but also signalled a fundamental change in North Korea's policy towards economic reform and openness.

Early in January 2001 Kim Jong Il called for 'new ways of thinking' about the economy, as reported by *Rodong Shinmun*, the newspaper of the Central Committee of the Korean Workers Party. In the same month he visited Shanghai, the beacon of China's economic reform and development, where he toured joint venture enterprises involving General Motors and a Japanese semiconductor manufacturer, as well as the stock exchange and the new Pudong commercial development zone. According to numerous reports, Kim was genuinely impressed with the enormous changes that had taken place since his first visit to Shanghai in 1983. In the words of a Chinese Foreign Ministry spokesman, 'Mr. Kim stressed that the big changes that have taken place in China, and Shanghai in particular, since China began its reform and opening-up have proved that the policies pursued by the Chinese Communist Party and people are correct' (*New York Times*, 21 January 2001). These remarks were considered significant because he had criticised China for 'revisionism' when he had visited Shanghai in 1983. It was also reported that during his talks with Chinese President Jiang Zemin he pledged faithfully to implement the inter-Korean summit pact and nurture the rapprochement with South Korea.

While it would be premature to conclude that North Korea is irreversibly committed to reform, it has taken tentative steps towards greater openness. For instance in September 2000 Foreign Minister Paek Nam Sun sent letters aimed at establishing rapprochement with EU member states that lacked diplomatic ties with the North and during the course of that year North Korea established or renewed bilateral relations with Australia, Italy, Kuwait, the Philippines, New Zealand and the UK. In the first quarter of 2001 diplomatic ties were established with the Netherlands, Belgium, Canada, Spain, Germany and Brazil, so North Korea's positive attitude towards improved relations with Western nations had obviously persuaded the EU member countries to form ties with Pyongyang. Multilaterally, North Korea joined the ASEAN Regional Forum (ARF) in June 2000, and formally applied to join the Asian Development Bank (ADB) in August 2000.

Why did Kim Jong Il change strategic direction and what sort of policies will he adopt? He seems to have realised that the limited and controlled open-door policy pursued by North Korea was a failure, and that economic recovery depended on liberalisation and structural reform. But this would require abandonment of the principle of *juche* and put the socialist political system at risk. Therefore he had to find a way of reconciling two contradictory policy goals – economic reforms and opening the door to economic collaboration with capitalist states on the one hand, and maintaining tight political control of the North Korean people on the other. He seems to have found the answer in China, and is most likely to implement the Chinese model of reform.

The next question is, how will this affect inter-Korean relations and the South Korean economy? North Korea is expected to continue to show a more cooperative attitude towards South Korea, which could provide South Korea with a new economic territory in a climate of détente. This issue will be discussed in more detail in Section 7.5.

7.3.2 Money matters!

Even if North Korea adopts the Chinese model of economic reform, success is not guaranteed. Determining factors will be the capabilities of the North Korean elite, the financial resources available and the international environment. But it is money that will matter most. According to Noland (2000b), North Korea's external financing needs will be around $1 billion a year. Where will this money come from? There are many possibilities, but the largest amount would come from resolution of North Korea's claim for compensation for the Japanese colonial occupation.

When South Korea and Japan normalised their diplomatic relations in 1965 the Japanese government paid South Korea $800 million in compensation for its colonial and wartime activities, $300 million in the form of grants, $200 million in development assistance loans, and $300 million in commercial credits. The North Korean government expects a similar amount. Noland (ibid.) has adjusted the South Korean payment to allow for population differences, accrued interest, inflation and appreciation of the yen since 1965 and obtained a figure in excess of $20 billion. On the other hand Suh (2000) predicts a payment of $5–10 billion, and Kim (2000) considers that Japan will probably want to pay the reparation in goods, so does not expect much of the reparation to take the form of cash. Noland (2000b) also points out that additional compensation will be demanded for the Korean 'comfort women' who were pressed into sexual slavery during the Second World War. North Korea has insisted that $10 billion will be the minimum acceptable amount, but whatever the final sum this money, if properly deployed, could go a long way towards restoring North Korea's creditworthiness and financing its economic development.

Additional funding could be obtained from international financial organisations. North Korea has periodically expressed interest in joining the International Monetary Fund (IMF), the World Bank and the Asian

Development Bank (ADB), and formally applied for ADB membership in August 2000. Under normal circumstances membership of these organisations implies access to significant development loans. Noland (ibid.), based on the case of Vietnam and scaling down the multilateral development banks' lending programme for the smaller size of the North Korean population, obtains a loan figure of $150–250 million per annum.[1] He also argues that more money might be available if the USA, Japan, South Korea and others set up a special fund for North Korea at the World Bank or ADB, and under some circumstances North Korea might be able to access multilateral development bank loans even if it is not a member. Technical advice and assistance from these organisations would also be important – perhaps more so than their lending activities, which would ultimately only complement the input by private investors.[2]

South Korea has been and will continue to be a significant provider of funds and other necessities. For example, between November 1998 and December 2000 Hyundai, paid North Korea a total of $342 million (equivalent to over 60 per cent of North Korea's exports for one year) for its exclusive Mt Kumgang tourism project. In addition the South Korean government has provided fertiliser and grain to the North. South Korean firms are also likely be the biggest source of 'foreign' investment in North Korea, which will be vital to the North's recovery from economic stagnation.

Private investors from Japan, the EU countries and the USA are also potential sources of funds. North Korea's hasty resumption of diplomatic ties with these countries indicates how desperately it needs foreign investment, but because of its failure to pay back its existing foreign debt of over $12 billion, foreign banks and multinationals remain very cautious.

7.3.3 The USA matters too

The Korean peninsula is flanked by the Eastern superpowers – China, Japan and the Russian Federation – but in terms of North Korea's future development the USA is likely to be the most important of the superpowers as it is the biggest shareholder in the IMF and the World Bank and loan provision depends on it dropping North Korea from its list of terrorism-sponsoring states.

North Korea seems to have recognised this reality. For instance it dealt solely with the USA on the question of its nuclear weapons development programme and in 1994 agreed to freeze this programme. As discussed earlier in the chapter, this resulted in the establishment of the multinational Korea Energy Development Organisation (KEDO). It should be noted, however, that South Korea has borne the greatest cost of KEDO, contributing $3.22 billion or 70 per cent of the total cost. The USA's contribution has been restricted to 0.5 million tonnes of heavy oil per year.

Under President Bill Clinton the USA began to show a more lenient attitude towards North Korea. In 2000 for example, it removed most of its sanctions against the country (but did not remove it from the list of terrorism-sponsoring states). In the same year, during special envoy Jo Myong Rok's visit to Washington and US Secretary of State Madeleine Albright's subsequent visit to Pyongyang, the two countries talked of the possibility of ending their mutual hostility and normalising relations. President Clinton seriously considered visiting North Korea before he left office in January 2001. Had he done so, this would have represented a major breakthrough in relations between two Cold War foes who had been enemies for half a century.

Unlike the Clinton administration, however, when the Bush administration took office in January 2001 it made clear its distrust of North Korean leader Kim Jong Il and demanded 'reciprocity and verification'. The Bush administration has thus far promoted only limited engagement with North Korea, so it may take some time to establish formal diplomatic ties.

7.3.4 South Korea matters as well

The relationship between the North and the South will, of course, have the biggest impact on the future course of developments in both parts of the peninsula. In other words, South Korea matters the most! The following two sections are devoted to this issue.

7.4 The current state of relations between the two Koreas

7.4.1 Overall relations

As is well known, a furious war broke out between the two Koreas in June 1950 and ultimately caused millions of casualties. Although an armistice was reached in July 1953, this was never followed by a peace treaty so the two Koreas are still technically at war. Indeed up until a few years ago the relationship between North and South could be described as one of violent confrontation. For instance the North was accused of killing 17 South Koreans in 1983, including several cabinet ministers, in Yangon, the capital of Myanmar, and of blowing up a South Korean airliner in 1987.

However relations began to show signs of change when South and North agreed simultaneously, but separately, to join the United Nations in September 1991. Then in December they signed the landmark Agreement on Reconciliation, Non-Aggression, Exchange and Cooperation, which provided for the integrated and balanced development of the two economies through trade, the joint development of resources, and cooperation in the fields of science and technology. This was envisioned by some as an interim arrangement prior to formal unification, and not as a relationship between independent states. However North Korea wanted to keep economic exchanges and cooperation to the private, non-governmental level because full-scale economic cooperation with South Korea might result in the collapse of its regime. For its part, South Korea was concerned that North Korea would take advantage of the situation and try to alienate the civilian sector from the South Korean government, and hence it wanted to limit private economic relations with North Korea.

After Kim Dae Jung assumed the presidency in 1998, however, South Korea began to pursue the so-called 'sunshine policy' towards North Korea. This seems to have won a warm welcome from North Korea, as in June 2000 an inter-Korean summit was held for the first time in the 55 years of national division. The summit appeared to mark a dramatic turning-point from animosity and confrontation to reconciliation and cooperation. At the summit the leaders of the two Koreas reaffirmed the principles set out in the South–North Joint Communiqué of 1972 and the 1991 agreement, and agreed to put them into practice.

Since the summit there have been several rounds of ministerial talks between the two Koreas as well as working-level discussions. Topics include inter-Korean exchanges and cooperation in various fields, most notably on the humanitarian issue of separated families and institutional arrangements for the expansion of economic cooperation, such as double taxation and investment guarantees. During the first two rounds of ministerial talks the two Koreas agreed to connect the Kyungui Railway between Seoul and Shinuiju (a northern city near the border between North Korea and China), and the highway between the Southern and Northern border cities of Munsan and Kaesong. In subsequent meetings it was decided to create a Joint Committee for Promoting Inter-Korean Economic Co-operation, through which such issues as the supply of electricity and construction of the Kaesong industrial complex would be discussed. Other issues included flood prevention facilities along the Imjin River and allowing South Korean fishing boats to operate off the east coast of North Korea.

7.4.2 Inter-Korean trade

Trade between the two Koreas began in 1989 with exchanges to the value of \$18.7 million. Trade grew steadily thereafter to reach \$308.3 million in 1997 (Table 7.5). It is worth noting that this growth continued even when the suspected nuclear threat from North Korea was at its peak in 1994. However the financial crisis in South Korea in 1997 caused a significant setback for inter-Korean trade, resulting in a decline to \$221.9 million in 1998, when the South's imports from the North fell by more than 50 per cent. Thereafter trade increased continuously, reaching \$425.1 million in 2000.

In 2000, agricultural products accounted for the largest proportion (26 per cent) of South Korea's imports from North Korea, followed by textiles (20 per cent), steel and metal products (4 per cent) and home appliances and other electronic products (3 per cent). Goods exported to

Table 7.5 Commodity exchanges between the two Koreas, 1989–2000, US$ thousand

Year	From N. to S.	From S. to N.	Total trade	Net trade	POC trade	POC/Total (%)
1989	18,655	69	18,724	−18,586	0	0
1990	12,278	1,188	13,466	−11,090	0	0
1991	105,722	5,547	111,269	−100,175	0	0
1992	162,863	10,563	173,426	−152,300	839	0.5
1993	178,298	8,425	186,723	−169,873	7,008	3.8
1994	176,298	18,248	194,546	−158,050	25,663	13.2
1995	222,855	64,436	287,291	−158,419	45,892	16
1996	182,400	69,639	252,039	−112,761	74,402	29.5
1997	193,069	115,270	308,339	−77,799	79,069	25.6
1998	92,264	129,679	221,943	37,415	70,988	32
1999	121,604	211,832	333,436	90,228	99,620	29.9
2000	152,370	272,770	425,140	120,400	129,190	30.4
Cumulative Sum	1,618,676	907666	2,526,342	−711,010	532,671	

Note:
POC trade stands for Processing on Commission Trade.

Source: Korea Trade Association (KOTRA) Website (www.kotra.or.kr).

the North included fertilises, medicines and chemical products (35 per cent of the total), textiles (16 per cent), machinery (12 per cent) and electronic goods (10 per cent).

Inter-Korean trade in the form of processing on commission (POC)[3] began in 1992 to the tune of $839 000 and expanded rapidly thereafter, much faster than the growth of overall inter-Korean trade and reaching $129.2 million in 2000. POC trade in textiles, machinery and transportation equipment is very suitable for both Koreas as it takes advantage of the complementarities between them, combining North Korea's relatively well-educated but inexpensive labour force and South Korea's capital and technology. Non-commercial transfers of humanitarian aid and materials for the light water reactor began in 1995 and grew steadily thereafter, facilitated by the Mt Kumgang tour business, the importation of crude oil into North Korea by KEDO and the progress of the light-water reactor project. In 2000 non-commercial transfers amounted to $144.4 million, or 65.6 per cent of total imports from the South.

Finally, it is worth noting that in 2000, with a total trade of $425 million, South Korea was North Korea's third largest trading partner, following China ($488 million) and Japan ($464 million).

7.4.3 The South's investment in the North

In November 1994 the South Korean government announced its 'Measures for the Revitalisation of Inter-Korean Economic Co-operation' and allowed South Korean firms to invest in North Korea. The Measures were revised in April 1998, as summarised in Table 7.6. Under the terms of the new measures there is no restriction on the size of investment or the areas of business, except for strategic and heavy industries.

Between 1992 and June 2001 the status of 'cooperation partner' was granted to 41 firms, 18 of which have since established 'cooperation projects' in North Korea. The first of these was a joint venture by Daewoo in North Korea's Nampo industrial complex, which was approved in 1995 and produces garments and bags.

The Mt Kumgang tourism project is one of the major cooperation projects. Under the terms of the contract between Hyundai and the North Korean authorities, Hyundai would have the exclusive right to conduct tours in the area of Mt Kumgang, which many Koreans perceive as the most beautiful mountain in the Korean peninsula. In return Hyundai was to pay North Korea a total of $942 million between November 1998 and February 2005. By the end of December 2000 Hyundai had paid out $342 million, but because of difficulties associated with the project it notified its North Korean counterpart that from January 2001 it wanted to reduce its monthly payments by half to $6 million (*Chosun Ilbo*, 18 January 2001a). In June 2001 the Korea National Tourism Organisation (KNTO), a government-invested public company, announced that it would establish a new corporate entity

Table 7.6 Measures for revitalisation of inter-Korean economic cooperation

Items	Previous (November 1994–March 1998)	Revised (since April 1998)
Level of economic cooperation	Government-led economic cooperation	Self-regulatory economic cooperation under the responsibility of business enterprises
Visit to North Korea by businessmen	Selective permit	Permit upon preparation of invitation papers from North Korea
Effective period of visit to North Korea by businessmen	1 year following approval and single visit only	3 years following approval and multiple visit
Period of handling permission for visit to North Korea	Contact: 20 days Visit: 30 days	Contact: 15 days Visit: 20 days
Allowed amount in carrying out of production equipment	Less than US$ 1 million	No limit
Size of investment in North Korea	US$1–5 million	No limit
Investment Items	Light industry, service sectors	All sectors excluding national defence and strategic industries
Limited items of North-South trade	205 limited items of overall approval	Gradual expansion of overall approval

Source: Cho, Myung Chul and Hyoungsoo Zang, *The Present and Future Prospects of the North Korean Economy*, Working Paper 99–07, Seoul: Korea Institute for International Economic Policy, 1999.

with Hyundai Asan to assume charge of tourism in North Korea, including in the Mt Kumgang area. In the same month North Korea agreed to open a land route and designate the Mt Kumgang area as a special tourism zone in an effort to revitalise the sagging project.

More recently, cooperation has extended to the ICT sector. For instance South Korea's Samsung Electronics and North Korea's Chosun Computer Centre established a joint venture in Pyongyang in 2000 to develop computer software programmes. In 2001 a South Korean corporation, Hanabiz, and the Pyongyang Informatics Centre of North Korea established a similar joint venture in Dandong, a Chinese city near the border between China and North Korea. Pohang University of Science and Technology and the Pyongyang Informatics Centre have agreed to promote inter-Korean exchanges in the fields of science and technology, and North and South Korea have agreed jointly to set up an information and technology university in Pyongyang. The university will consist of three departments: ICT technology, biotechnology and commercial-economy.

The two Koreas also signed four agreements in December 2000 providing an institutional mechanism for inter-Korean economic cooperation, including investment protection, avoidance of double taxation, account settlement and business dispute arbitration. South Korean investment is expected to speed up with the transfer to the North of production facilities by large and small businesses.

7.4.4 Cross-border visits

In 2000, 7280 South Koreans visited North Korea (excluding visitors to Mt Kumgang), up from 146 in 1996, 1015 in 1997, 3317 in 1998 and 5599 in 1999. In addition to this, 371 637 South Korean tourists travelled to Mt Kumgang between November 1998, when the tour programme was launched, and the end of 2000. A further 800 South Koreans work at the KEDO nuclear reactor site in North Korea, along with 100 North Koreans.

The number of North Korean visitors to the South has also increased. There were no North Korean visitors to the South between 1994 and 1998, but after the inauguration of the Kim Dae Jung administration 62 travelled South in 1999 rising to 706 in 2000. Just before and after the inter-Korean summit in 2000 a number of North Korean cultural groups, including the Pyongyang student art troupe, the Pyongyang circus troupe and the North Korean National Symphony Orchestra, performed in the South. North Koreans also visited the South for various inter-Korean meetings, including inter-Korean ministerial talks, defence ministers' meetings and working-level economic discussions.

After the summit the two sides in a Red Cross talk signed an agreement on cross-border visits by family members separated by the 1950–53 war, plus the establishment of a permanent meeting centre. Two family reunions were held in 2000, during which two hundred separated families from each side visited Seoul or Pyongyang to meet their relatives for the first time in half a century.

7.5 Inter-Korean economic integration

7.5.1 Unilateral benevolence versus common prosperity

Inter-Korean cooperation is regarded by many as little more than Southern assistance to the North. For example Ahn (2000) argues that 'Seoul provides the economic co-operation and in return Pyongyang provides assurance on ease of tension and renunciation of nuclear and missile development programmes'. Similarly the *Economist* (2000c) reports that 'Nobody ever doubted that the price for peace between the Koreas would involve a steady supply of food aid, along with enormous sums of money to repair North Korea's clapped-out infrastructure.'

Of course, given the historical enmity and distrust between North and South some sort of benevolence on the part of the South may be necessary to build up confidence and trust, but the South also stands to gain major benefits. First, inter-Korean economic exchanges and cooperation will help to alleviate both the continuing tension between the two Koreas and the consequent country risk perceived by foreign investors. Thus exchanges and cooperation between North and South may convey positive externalities to South Korea, and the social rate of return from these may well exceed the private rate of return. Of course economic cooperation alone cannot ensure reconciliation and peace, but it can increase mutual trust and may eventually lead to peaceful coexistence.

Second, at present South Korea is effectively an island as North Korea stands between it and the rest of mainland Asia. However the planned reconnection of the Seoul–Shineuiju railway will allow South Korean firms to transport goods at lower cost by land to Northern Asia, and the proposed establishment of a connection between a North–South trans-Korean railway and the Trans-Siberian Railway would enable goods to be transported to Europe and the Middle Eastern countries.[4] Furthermore the network could be extended to Japan by building a rail tunnel under the Korea Strait to connect Pusan and Shimonoseke.[5]

Third, investment opportunities for South Korean firms in the North will help revive South Korea's own ailing economy. South Korean businesses will be able to enjoy cost reductions by reallocating overinvested facilities in the North. Labour-intensive light manufactures such as textiles and clothing offer mutual benefits as the labour and natural resources of North Korea and the capital and techniques of South Korea are highly complementary. A survey of 2000 SMEs conducted in 2001 revealed that 77.1 per cent of SMEs in South Korea had plans to press ahead with investment in the North (*Chosun Ilbo*, 2001c). The cheap labour in North Korea was cited as the main reason for such investment by 59.4 per cent of the respondents, 20.9 per cent stated that the investment would provide them with increased market share when the two Koreas were unified, and 16 per cent said the investment would help secure raw materials. In fact a revived North Korean economy will have higher purchasing power and hence will offer a good market with 22 million customers for South Korean products.

Finally, the gradual phasing-in of economic cooperation between the two Koreas would reduce the eventual cost of reunification of the peninsula, while the abrupt collapse of North Korea and sudden reunification would place a great financial burden on South Korea. According to the Korea Development Institute the cost of sudden unification would range from $200 billion to more than $500 billion over a ten-year period. Noland *et al.* (1999) estimate that the cost of unification, defined as the capital investment needed to raise North Korean per capita income to 60 per cent of that of South Korea, would be in the order of $200–400 billion, while Hong (2000) considers that about 19 trillion won per annum would be required. Hence there is general agreement that the financial burden on South Korea would be huge. If North Korea's transition to a more open economy occurs gradually and with minimal political fallout the cost of unification may well be less than currently estimated. The most fruitful scenario for both Koreas would be to undergo closer economic integration to enhance overall efficiency in the peninsula. The next section explains why and how.

7.5.2 What kind of economic integration?

There are many forms of economic integration, such as free trade areas, customs unions, common markets and economic unions. It is highly likely that inter-Korean economic integration will take the simplest form (a free trade area) in the initial stage, and later move towards more complicated forms.[6]

The first step would be to create a legal framework for exchanges between the two countries. As stated in Section 7.4.3, the two Koreas have signed agreements on investment protection, avoidance of double taxation, account settlement and business dispute arbitration. These are the minimum requirements for inter-Korean cooperation and will be completed when a permanent peace mechanism is established.

The second formal step would be to set up a free trade area (FTA) in the peninsula, whereby the two Koreas would trade freely with each other but maintain their own trade policies with respect to other countries. This would be equivalent to the North American Free Trade Agreement (NAFTA) and the ASEAN Free Trade Agreement (AFTA).

The third step would be to form a customs union, in which North and South would adopt a common trade policy with respect to third parties while maintaining free trade between themselves.[7] The European Economic Community (EEC) in 1968 was an example of this. An even deeper form of integration, such as economic union, could follow. A common market, similar to the European Community (EC), the precursor of the European Union (EU), would permit the free movement of factors of production as well as goods throughout the peninsula. Free capital movement might be allowed first, while partially restricting labour movement. Monetary union would be the next step, as has recently occurred between some EU member states with the adoption of a single currency. The final stage would be political union or confederation. This would require the two Koreas to adopt common labour and social welfare policies and surrender their claims to sovereignty. Of course this is far beyond the bounds of possibility at the moment.

In the meantime a gradual, staged process of economic integration would promote stability in the peninsula. As evidenced by developments in the

EU, NAFTA and ASEAN, economic integration would enable North and South to exploit immense profit opportunities through economic complementarities and economies of scale. Of course the two Koreas are different from the member states of the EU, NAFTA and even ASEAN. Some might point out that the economic, social and political systems of the two countries differ radically, and that only half a century ago they were engaged in bloody battle against each other and are still technically at war. But remember that when the EEC was established in 1958 only 13 years had passed since the end of World War II, in which two of the six founder members had waged war on the others, and that armed conflicts had been rife on the European continent for hundreds of years. Furthermore member countries had different languages and cultures. In contrast the two Koreas have only been divided for a little over 50 years and share the same language and culture! But the fact that they have radically different economic, social and political systems is a strong reason for them to pursue a gradual process of economic integration, and in so doing gradually converge their economic, social and political practices.[8]

In sum, gradual economic integration will pave the way to the peaceful reunification of the peninsula, and in the process the efficiency of resource allocation will be enhanced in both economies.

7.5.3 Korean economic integration and North-East Asia[9]

Although the pace and process of inter-Korean economic integration will be primarily determined by the two Koreas, the cooperation of neighbouring countries in North-East Asia will be essential. As a matter of fact there has been increasing interest in economic cooperation among the North-East Asian countries, so the idea of Korean economic integration needs to be extended to include regional cooperation.[10] This would also provide the two Koreas with added opportunities for mutual contact and allow them to build up confidence in each other. Lee (1995) discusses some of the many cooperation possibilities between South and North Korea in North-East Asia. For example they could run joint ventures in natural-resource and labour-intensive fields such as timber, natural gas, agro-fishery and construction in the Russian Far East, where South Korea would provide capital and management skill and North Korea would supply the labour.

North-East Asian economic cooperation might also induce North Korea to open its economy more widely. Under a multilateral framework North Korea would gain increasing economic advantages by cooperating with other countries including South Korea. This might persuade it that a comprehensive open-door policy would be the right way to restore its economy.

Finally, by participating in bilateral and multilateral projects in North-East Asia, North Korea would become familiar with economic competition and learn the principles of the market economy. In other words cooperation would have educational effects. An existing example of this is the TRADP project (see Section 7.2.2), which prompted North Korea to establish the free trade zone in the Rajin–Sonbong area. If this experiment proves successful North Korea is likely to establish similar zones in other parts of the country thus introducing a market system in industry and narrowing the gap between the economic systems of South and North.

7.5.4 Obstacles to Korean economic integration

A number of obstacles have to be overcome before Korean economic integration and reunification of the peninsula can take place, including the unstable business environment, the lack of information on business in North Korea and North Korea's poor infrastructure.

A major obstacle is political–military distrust. The demilitarised zone (DMZ) between the Koreas is the world's most heavily armed border, with around one million soldiers deployed on either side of the 4 km wide strip. Despite several rounds of talks since the June 2000 summit the two Koreas have failed to introduce any concrete military measures to reduce tension on the peninsula. The North Korean army, with 1.1 million soldiers on active duty, is the world's fifth largest army and is overwhelmingly deployed in an offensive position.

Another major obstacle is cost. South Korea has been ridiculed for its history of 'check-book diplomacy' (Noland, 2000c). A notable example of this is the large sum it paid to normalise relations with the former USSR. Furthermore the Kim Dae Jung administration has been criticised for giving 0.3 million tonnes of fertiliser and pledging 0.6 million tonnes of grain to the North in exchange for North Korea's attendance at the summit in June 2000 and the brief reunion of separated families in August 2000. President Kim Dae Jung seems willing to underwrite the economic rehabilitation of the North and many observers have speculated about what he may have promised the North in order to secure reconciliation and cooperation.

7.6 Summary and conclusions

It has been argued that, given the right circumstances, gradual economic integration could ultimately lead to the reunification of the Korean peninsula. Whether economic integration along the lines examined in this chapter will proceed will depend in large part on the intentions of Kim Jong Il and his officials. To put it another way, a necessary precondition for economic integration will be willingness on the part of the North Korean elite to countenance major economic reform and openness.

We believe that Kim Jong Il realises that North Korea cannot progress without fundamental changes to its policies of *juche* and state control. We also believe that the events of 2000 heralded a fundamental strategic reorientation by North Korea, and that it is taking preparatory steps towards greater openness and economic reform. This will have a substantial effect on inter-Korean relations and the South Korean economy.

South Korea will need to continue to engage with North Korea, especially with regard to economic exchanges and cooperation. Of course economic cooperation alone cannot guarantee reconciliation, but it can increase mutual trust and lead to peaceful coexistence.

Of immediate need are the establishment of a permanent peace mechanism on the Korean peninsula and implementation of the agreements on investment protection, avoidance of double taxation, account settlement and business dispute arbitration. Thereafter economic exchanges should be based on the principles of the market economy, and economic issues should be separated from political ones. While some sort of government intervention will be needed, as Noland (2000b) notes it would be better to introduce broad tax incentives for investment in the North rather than for the state to use its influence over the financial system to encourage such investment on an *ad hoc* basis. Indeed the use of private South Korean firms as tools of South Korean foreign policy would complicate business–government relations and make the creation of a more liberal and transparent economic system in the South all the more difficult.

Another merit of separating economic issues from political problems is that business transactions would be removed from the dispute over the future structure of a unified Korea. The South favours a confederal system while the North would prefer a loosely federal system, in which Northern and Southern diplomacy and defence would remain for a fixed period in the hands of the respective state governments, although it has to be said that such a federal system would be very similar to a strong confederal system.

Finally, it should be emphasised that while the long-term objective is convergence of the two economic structures through a gradual process of economic integration, a fixed timetable is neither necessary nor desirable. But once goods and factors of production (labour and capital) are moving freely across the borders the two Koreas will have reached a stage of *de facto* unification and political unification can begin.

As the *Economist* (2000b) notes, 'The two Koreas face a huge task in restoring – rather, reinventing – relations.' This presents both opportunities and risks, but one should not avoid opportunities simply because they are accompanied by risks.

Part IV

8
Future Challenges and Prospects

8.1 Introduction

As discussed in Chapters 2 and 3, from the 1970s Korea enjoyed one of the fastest rates of economic growth in the world, and in December 1996 it became a proud member of the OECD. As many observers pointed out, this was a miracle – a miracle that could not have been anticipated in the 1960s. In 1997, however, Korea experienced its worst crisis since the Korean War. While this financial crisis was triggered by the currency crisis in Thailand in July 1997, more fundamental causes were the intrinsic weaknesses that had accumulated in the Korean economy during the realisation of the government's economic development strategy.

Korea is now at a crossroads and has to change its course of direction if it wants to revive its economic miracle. The three key areas were pointed out in chapters 5, 6 and 7: (1) the revival of the 'old' economy by successfully completing the structural reforms in the financial, corporate and public sectors and the labour market, (2) the successful implementation of a 'new' economy, and (3) expanding Korea's 'new' economic territory, by successfully pursuing economic integration with North Korea. This chapter discusses what else needs to be done to maintain sustainable growth and improve the quality of life of the Korean people in the twenty first century. We identify three pillars that must be addressed: education, social welfare and the promotion of competition. Section 2 deals with issues relating to the Korean education system, social issues are discussed in Section 3, and Section 4 looks at the question of increasing competition by further opening up the economy to trade and foreign investment. Finally, Section 5 discusses the short-and long-term prospects for the Korean economy.

8.2 Education

Koreans have long placed great importance on education, and commonly recognised that Korea's well-educated people were the primary source of the country's rapid economic growth during the era of industrialisation. Today Korea boasts one of the highest literacy rates in the world. In 2000, 84 per cent of general high-school graduates and 42 per cent of vocational high-school graduates entered a university or college. At the tertiary level Korea ranks very high among the OECD countries, with 23 per cent of the population aged 25–34 having attained at least a tertiary education by 1998, as shown in Table 8.1. Only the Netherlands, Norway and the USA

Table 8.1 Percentage of the population with at least tertiary education, by age group, 1998

	At least tertiary type A[1]				
	25–64	25–34	35–44	45–54	55–64
Australia	17	19	18	16	10
Austria[2]	6	7	8	5	4
Belgium	12	16	13	10	6
Canada	19	23	18	18	13
Czech Republic	10	10	12	10	8
Denmark	5	7	5	5	3
Finland[2]	13	14	15	13	8
France	11	15	10	10	6
Germany	14	14	16	15	10
Greece[2]	11	15	14	10	6
Hungary	13	14	14	14	10
Iceland	16	19	18	15	9
Ireland	11	16	11	7	5
Italy[3]	9	9	11	9	5
Japan	18	23	23	15	9
Korea	17	23	19	11	8
Mexico	12	15	14	10	5
Netherlands[3]	24	27	26	23	17
New Zealand	13	16	13	12	7
Norway[2]	24	27	25	22	17
Poland[3]	11	12	10	11	10
Portugal	7	8	7	5	4
Spain	14	21	16	11	6
Sweden	13	10	14	15	11
Switzerland	14	16	15	13	11
Turkey[3]	6	7	7	6	3
United Kingdom	15	17	17	15	11
United States	27	27	26	29	22
Country mean	14	16	15	13	9

Notes:
1. Includes advanced research programmes.
2. Year of reference 1997.
3. Includes tertiary-type B.

Source: OECD (2000e).

had higher percentages. The mathematical achievement of Korean students is exceptional. As shown in Table 8.2, in 1995 Korean eighth grade students ranked first among the OECD countries in terms of mean mathematical achievement. Thus as the OECD and World Bank (2000) note, 'Korea has attained remarkable achievements in education over the past three decades, and the quality of its basic education has been internationally acclaimed.'

One of the main reasons for the strength of the Korean education system is high investment. As can be seen in Table 8.3, total expenditure on education was equivalent to 7.4 per cent of GDP in 2000, the highest among the OECD countries. Expenditure on education as a percentage of public expenditure was 16.7 per cent in 1995, the highest of the sample of countries shown in Table 8.3. It should be noted, however, that educational expenditure in Korea comes mainly from the private sector. For instance public expenditure

Table 8.2 Mean mathematical achievement of students in eighth grade, 1995

	8th grade
Australia[1]	530
Austria[1]	539
Belgium (Flemish community)[2]	565
Belgium (French community)[1]	526
Canada	527
Czech Republic	564
Denmark[1]	502
France	538
Germany[1]	509
Greece[2]	484
Hungary	537
Iceland	487
Ireland	527
Japan	605
Korea	607
Netherlands[1]	541
New Zealand	508
Norway	503
Portugal	454
Spain	487
Sweden	519
Switzerland[2]	545
England[2]	506
Scotland[1]	498
United States[2]	500
Country mean	524

Notes:
1. Countries did not meet TIMSS sampling requirements, 8th grade.
2. Countries met TIMSS sampling requirements only partially, 8th grade.

Source: OECD (2000e).

Table 8.3 Educational expenditure as a percentage of GDP for all levels of education by source of funds, 1995

	Total educational expenditure (public and private sources) as a percentage of GDP	**Public educational expenditure as a percentage of total public expenditure**
Australia	5.6	13.2
Canada	6.5	13.0
Czech Republic	5.2	12.3
Finland	6.3	12.1
France	6.3	11.1
Germany	5.7	9.8
Hungary	5.2	15.2
Iceland	5.7	14.3
Ireland	5.0	13.8
Italy	4.8	9.1
Japan	4.8	10.1
Korea	7.4	16.7
Netherlands	4.7	10.2
Switzerland	6.0	14.9
United States	6.9	16.0

Source: OECD (2000e).

on tertiary education as a percentage of GDP was only 0.5 per cent in 1997, one of the lowest among the OECD countries, whereas the private contribution amounted to 1.95 per cent, the highest among the OECD countries (Table 8.4). Similarly, in 1998 the ratio of students to teaching staff in Korea was one of the highest among the OECD countries (Table 8.5).

Despite the high degree of educational attainment, Korean education has many intrinsic defects. It has been suggested, for example, that the great enthusiasm for education among Koreans, which is not so common in other countries, is not because of the knowledge and values they can acquire at school, but because they want to get into top-rank universities as *hakyeon*, or *alma mater* linkage, is highly important in business life. Thus students are so obsessed with getting into a reputable university that virtually all secondary schools are geared towards preparing their students to pass the university entrance exams. It is also worthy to note that learning has traditionally been by rote, with little emphasis on individual thinking and creativity. Hence the current education system has been criticised for producing students who may excel in subjects involving straightforward calculations but are unidimensional in their thinking and unable to do tasks requiring analytical reasoning and creativeness. This is in part due to the fact that the government over-regulates the school curriculum and the university entrance mechanism, resulting in homogeneous education throughout the country. A survey conducted by the Korea Educational Development Institute in June 2000

Table 8.4 Educational expenditure as a percentage of GDP for tertiary education, by source of funds, 1995

	Direct public expenditure on educational institutions	Private payments to educational institutions, excluding public subsidies to households and other private entities	Total expenditure (public and private) on educational institutions
OECD countries			
Australia	1.0	0.53	1.7
Austria	1.3	0.17	1.5
Belgium (Fl.)	0.8	0.10	0.9
Canada	1.2	0.35	2.0
Czech Republic	0.7	0.11	0.8
Denmark	1.1	0.01	1.2
France	1.0	0.14	1.2
Germany	1.0	0.08	1.1
Greece	1.0	0.18	1.2
Hungary	0.8	0.22	1.0
Iceland	0.7	0.04	0.7
Ireland	1.0	0.29	1.4
Italy	0.6	0.15	0.8
Japan	0.5	0.58	1.1
Korea	0.5	1.95	2.5
Mexico	0.8	0.27	1.1
Netherlands	1.1	0.03	1.2
Norway	1.3	0.09	1.4
Portugal	1.0	0.02	1.0
Spain	0.9	0.27	1.2
Sweden	1.6	0.16	1.7
United Kingdom	0.7	0.12	1.0
United States[1]	1.4	1.29	2.7

Note:
1. Includes post-secondary, non-tertiary data.

Source: OECD (2000e).

Table 8.5 Ratio of students to teaching staff by level of education, 1998 (calculations based on full-time equivalents)

	Preschool education	Primary education	Lower secondary education	Upper secondary education	All secondary education
Austria	18.6	12.7	9.3	9.7	9.5
Canada	16.2	21.0	21.0	23.1	22.1
Czech Republic	15.9	19.2	18.1	13.0	15.4
Germany	23.2	21.6	16.3	13.6	15.5
Greece	15.9	13.6	11.4	11.6	11.5
Hungary	12.1	11.0	11.1	10.5	10.8
Japan	19.3	21.4	17.3	14.4	15.7
Korea	23.6	31.0	22.5	23.1	22.8
New Zealand	5.6	24.7	25.9	16.8	21.0
Switzerland[1]	18.7	16.3	12.1	17.6	14.0
United Kingdom	21.5	22.0	16.7	16.7	16.7
United States	18.0	16.5	17.1	14.7	15.9

Note:
1. Public institutions only.

Source: OECD (2000e).

found that 57 per cent of students did not believe that the school curriculum was worth learning (*Korea Herald*, 5 January 2001).

Once students are admitted to a university or a college they no longer have to study hard because graduate certificates, students' main reason for entering university, are awarded to most final-year students. According to Lee (2001), university is treated as a four-year holiday rather than a time for personal growth and introspection. Indeed Korean firms complain that they have to retrain the graduates that enter their workforce. For example a study by the Korea Research Institute for Education and Training revealed that about 30 per cent of personnel managers and 58 per cent of college students regard college education as an inadequate breeding ground for the level of talent required by business (*Korea Herald*, 20 December 2000). Korean universities have also been criticised for carrying out very little research (OECD and World Bank, 2000). This explains why foreign students make up just 0.1 per cent of all students, the lowest percentage among the OECD countries (Table 8.6).

Table 8.6 Foreign students as a percentage of all students (foreign and national), tertiary education, 1998

Australia	12.6
Austria	11.5
Belgium	4.0
Canada[1]	3.8
Czech Republic	1.9
Denmark	6.0
Finland	1.7
France	7.3
Germany	8.2
Hungary	2.6
Iceland	2.4
Ireland	4.8
Italy	1.2
Japan	0.9
Korea	0.1
Luxembourg	30.5
New Zealand	3.7
Norway	3.2
Poland	0.5
Spain	1.7
Sweden	4.5
Switzerland	15.9
Turkey	1.3
United Kingdom	10.8
United States	3.2

Notes:
1. Tertiary-type A and advanced research programmes only.

Source: OECD (2000e).

As discussed in Chapter 6, in order to compete in the global economy Korea will have to embrace the new information economy, and this will require educated workers who can create and use knowledge and information effectively. But the current education system does not produce such people. Furthermore the production of new knowledge and information and its adaptation to a particular economic setting is generally associated with a high level of research, which does not currently exist. Hence the entire education system requires a major overhaul. Attention to foreign languages and culture will also be needed if Korea is to become part of the global community.

8.3 Welfare reform

8.3.1 Unemployment, income inequality and pensions

As discussed in Chapter 4, unemployment rose sharply in the wake of the financial crisis (see Table 4.5), with marginal workers such as women, the young, the less educated and first-time jobseekers being hit the hardest. While unemployment declined in 1999 and 2000, it was still higher than before the crisis, and when the economy entered a deep recession in late 2001 the jobless rate was expected to rise again.

The fall in employment was accompanied by an increase in income inequality. The lowest quintile's income share dropped from 8.3 per cent in 1997 to 7.3 per cent in 1999, while the highest quintile's share rose from 37.2 per cent to 40.2 per cent (Table 8.7). As a consequence the income ratio between the top and the bottom quintiles grew from 4.5 to 5.49 over the same period. Meanwhile the Gini coefficient, which had remained stable at about 28–29 per cent, increased to 32.0 per cent in 1999. There was some sign of improvement in 2000, but considering the slowdown of economic growth in 2001 the situation remains worrisome.

In tandem with this the percentage of the population living in poverty rose drastically. Estimates differ according to whether they are based on income or expenditure, but all report a two- to threefold increase between mid 1997 and mid 1998 (OECD, 2000a).

Table 8.7 Quintile income shares and Gini coefficient, 1989–2000 (per cent)

	1989	1990	1991	1992	1993	1994	1995	1996	1997	1998	1999	2000
Bottom 20% (a)	8.2	8.4	8.5	8.5	8.6	8.5	8.5	8.2	8.3	7.4	7.3	7.5
Middle 60% (b)	52.3	52.9	53.4	53.9	53.9	53.9	54.0	53.9	54.5	52.8	52.5	52.4
Top 20% (c)	39.6	38.8	38.0	37.6	37.4	37.6	37.5	37.9	37.2	39.8	40.2	40.1
(c)/(a)	4.85	4.64	4.46	4.42	4.35	4.42	4.42	4.63	4.49	5.41	5.49	5.32
Gini coefficient	30.4	29.4	28.7	28.3	28.1	28.4	28.3	29.1	28.3	31.5	32.0	31.7

Source: National Statistical Office (http://www.nso.go.kr).

While the financial crisis and the subsequent structural reforms can be blamed for the rise in the deterioration in income equality the rise in the incidence of poverty occurred because the system of social protection was unable to deal adequately with the consequences of the crisis. Prior to 1997 Korea's social welfare strategy focused on the financial benefits offered by macroeconomic stability through steady economic growth. Other social welfare provisions were seen as primarily the responsibility of the family and non-governmental organisations, so social expenditure by the government was the smallest in the OECD area, at 5 per cent of GDP in 1997 (OECD, 2000d). Even now the government's top priority is to bring about sustainable economic recovery so that the number of those in need of relief can be reduced through their steady reabsorption into newly created, high-income jobs. But the continuing effects of the crisis on employment, income redistribution and poverty cannot be entirely overcome by this means and there is great need of a support system for disadvantaged people who are unable to find work, particularly the marginal groups listed at the start of this section. Furthermore, in order to promote labour market flexibility the government must provide credible insurance against loss of employment and income. Thus an adequate social safety net is needed not only for reasons of equity but also for the efficient functioning of the labour market.

In the wake of the crisis the government did introduce policies and programmes to assist the unemployed, including emergency employment-creation schemes such as public works programmes, labour redeployment schemes and temporary income replacement schemes, but these were somewhat informal and temporary arrangements. More recently the government recognised the limitations of the existing system and began to develop a so-called 'productive welfare system', in which growth and welfare would be blended harmoniously.

The benefits structure and unemployment insurance coverage have improved. In 1997 the unemployment insurance scheme was limited to employees of firms with 30 or more workers, or an estimated 33 per cent of all employees, but coverage was extended to all firms in October 1998. Furthermore the duration of benefit payments was increased from 1–7 months to 3–8 months, and the minimum payment was raised from 50 per cent to 70 per cent of the minimum wage. In addition the Livelihood Protection Programme, which provided living expenses, medical care and help with the cost of education to about 1.4 million people (3.1 per cent of the population) in 1997, was extended to 1.5 million people (3.2 per cent of the population) in 1998 and 1.9 million (4.2 per cent of the population) in 1999.

Based on its concept of 'productive welfare' the government enacted the National Basic Security Livelihood Law in August 1999, to take effect in October 2000. Under the new law, social assistance is available to all those who fulfil the eligibility requirements. Benefit payments are set to bring each recipient's total income to the minimum cost of living level, and beneficiaries who are able to work are obliged to search for jobs or to accept training placements, public works jobs or any other jobs found by the welfare office.

The state retirement pension is also relatively insignificant in Korea. While public pension expenditure in other OECD countries averaged 8 per cent of GDP as early as 1995, in Korea it amounted to less than 0.3 per cent of GDP in 1999. This low expenditure is partly due to the fact that there are comparatively few elderly persons in Korea, where the proportion of persons over the age of 65 is the lowest in the OECD area, except for Mexico and Turkey (OECD, 2000a). In addition, 10 years is the minimum contribution period for the National Pension Scheme (NPS), which was not introduced until 1988, so the number of persons eligible for the pension will rise as the scheme matures. For example the number of persons over 65 is predicted to triple from 3.3 million (7.1 per cent of the population) to 10.2 million (19.3 per cent of the population) by 2030. Over the same period expenditure under the NPS is projected to increase by 13 per cent per annum in real terms.

In order to ensure the continuing financial viability of the NPS certain measures have been adopted, including lowering the payment and raising the retirement age. But the contribution rate will have to double from the current 9 per cent of wages to 18 per cent to maintain the balance under the current scheme, and this is likely to have adverse effects on national growth. The OECD and World Bank (2000) recommend that Korea introduce measures to improve the long-term viability of the NPS. In particular they suggest that firms be required to provide their employees with occupational pension schemes. They also recommend that, in order to promote equity, the NPS contribution rates be equalised across sources of income and the contributions deducted from taxable income. But as the increased outlays on social welfare will necessitate higher tax revenues in the medium term, measures to contain spending are also needed.

8.3.2 Employment biases against women

Korea ranks twenty-fourth out of 29 countries using the UN Gender Related Development Index and seventy-eighth out of 102 using the Gender Empowerment Measure (OECD and World Bank, 2000). Korean women are discriminated against and lag behind men in higher education, recruitment and wage levels. The average school leaving age is 16.4 years for men, which is above the OECD average, while that for women is 14.7 years, below the OECD average. Many women leave work immediately after marrying or having children because discrimination against women in the workforce is widespread and the support facilities for working women are limited. As a result the women's labour force participation rate was only 48.3 per cent in 2000, while that for men was 60.7 per cent. Furthermore women's wages are lower than men's. In 2000 the average monthly wage of female workers was 954 292 won, compared with 1 473 799 won for male workers. Thus the average female wage was only about 65 per cent of the average male wage.

Not only firms but also government agencies employ very few women in professional and managerial positions. For example women make up only 3 per cent of national and local government employees. As discussed in the previous section women were significantly affected by the crisis. They tended to be laid off before their male counterparts, and the contracts of those who were rehired tended to be short term. In absolute numbers more men than women lost their jobs due to the crisis, but a larger proportion of the female labour force was negatively affected by the crisis than was the case for the male labour force.

The scope of the Equal Employment Opportunity Act of 1987 has been broadened three times, the last time being in 1999, when the Anti-Discrimination Bill was introduced. In addition a Ministry of Women was established in 2001. Despite these measures women continue to be discriminated against. Not only is it morally indefensible for this to persist, but it is also economically inefficient as it is resulting in the misallocation of human resources that are vital to Korea's competitiveness and sustained growth. Therefore Korea should take steps to enhance the position of women in the workforce and hence the nation's productivity and growth.

8.4 Promoting competition

8.4.1 Opening up to trade

There is no doubt that international trade has been and will remain an engine of economic growth for Korea. There are three points to be made in this connection. First, the Korean economy has become increasingly dependent on trade, which accounted for 91.1 per cent of GDP in 2000, up from 73.0 per cent in 1997. Second, just 10 product categories – including semiconductors, other electronic goods, textiles, computers, cars, petrochemicals and related products, steel and ships – make up more than 80 per cent of Korea's exports. Therefore if any of these products experience international turbulence in terms of price and/or demand the country faces considerable difficulties. For example when the demand for and price of semiconductors, which account for nearly 15 per cent of total exports, fell in 2000–1, Korea's export revenue declined significantly and this no doubt contributed to the economic downturn in 2001.

Third, Korean exports are overdependent on the US and Japanese markets with these two countries respectively accounting for 22 per cent and 12 per cent of total exports in 2000 (Table 8.8). In particular exports of ICT equipment, such as semiconductors and computers, are vulnerable to

Table 8.8 Korean exports by destination, 1997–2000 (per cent)

	USA	Japan	European Union	Southeast Asia[1]	China	Middle East	Other
1997	15.9	10.8	12.4	27.0	10.1	3.8	20.2
1998	17.2	9.2	13.7	22.5	9.0	5.0	23.3
1999	20.5	11.0	14.1	23.0	9.5	4.5	17.3
2000	21.8	11.9	13.6	22.5	10.7	4.4	15.0
Percentage change[2]	6.0	1.0	1.2	−4.4	0.6	0.6	−5.2

Notes:
1. The 10 ASEAN countries plus Taiwan and Hong Kong.
2. Between 1997 and 2000.

Source: Bank of Korea.

slowdowns in the US economy, as occurred in 2001. Thus Korea needs to reduce its trade-dependency ratio and diversify its export markets and products. Another challenge is to open up the country to foreign trade and to promote competition in the domestic market. Korea has introduced significant trade liberalisation measures in recent years. In 1984–88 and 1989–94 it implemented two tariff reform programmes and the average tariff rate fell from 18 per cent in 1988 to 8 per cent in 1998. In addition significant progress has been made in dismantling non-tariff barriers. In 1994 there were 220 quotas, but these have gradually been reduced and eliminated in 2001 except for that on rice. The Import Diversification Programme (IDP), which had restricted certain imports from Japan since 1978 in an effort to reduce the bilateral trade imbalance, was completely eliminated in 1999.

Korea is promoting further trade liberalisation by a number of means (OECD, 2000a): it has supported a new round of multilateral trade negotiations covering a wide range of topics; it has been involved in the Early Voluntary Sectoral Liberalisation negotiations under APEC; and it has negotiated a bilateral free trade agreement with Chile and discussed the possibility of forming one with Japan.

Korea is one of the few WTO member countries that has not formed preferential trade arrangements (PTAs). However, in light of the new wave of regionalism in East Asia after the Asian financial crisis it has seriously considered forming PTAs with a number of countries. For example at the ASEAN+3 summit in November 1999, Japan, Korea and China agreed jointly to investigate the feasibility of forming a North-East Asian Free Trade Area. These countries are already the other's largest trading partners: for China, Japan is its largest trading partner and Korea the third; for Japan, China (including Taiwan) ranks second and Korea third; for Korea, Japan and China are the second and the third major trading partners respectively.

8.4.2 Opening up to foreign investment

After the crisis the government acknowledged that foreign investment would have to be a central part of Korea's restructuring and recovery programme. The immediate reasons for attracting FDI were to put Korean companies on a sound financial footing and to assist with economic restructuring. Other objectives included technology transfer, the attainment of management techniques to meet global standards, and access to foreign supply chains. In addition the presence of foreign companies would foster more open corporate governance practices and a more competitive atmosphere among domestic firms. It would discipline industrial behaviour and provide a more level playing field for new entrants, and thus usher in a new industrial era consistent with the development of a market economy.

Before the crisis there had been strong public feelings against foreign investment, but the majority of Koreans are now more receptive to the idea. Korea duly undertook a major liberalisation of its foreign investment regime through the New Foreign Investment Promotion Act (1998, revised in 1999). By May 2000, out of a total of 1148 classified sectors, only four (inshore fishing, coastal fishing, radio broadcasting and television broadcasting) remained closed to FDI, while 17 remained partially restricted. In addition the government provided various tax reduction/exemption incentives to 436 types of advanced-technology business, 97 types of service business to support domestic industry, and businesses located in a foreign investment zone.

A grievance often cited by foreign investors in the past was that there were too many contact points and administrative procedures, which often led to red tape and delay. To remedy this, in April 1998, the government set up the Korea Investment Service Centre (KISC) at the Korea Trade-Investment Promotion Agency to support foreign investors through all stages of investment, from consultation to approval, and its services would be free of charge.

As a result FDI in Korea steadily increased, rising from $3.2 billion in 1996 to a record $15.7 billion in 2000 (Table 8.9). It is worth noting that much of the increase was linked to the sale of major assets to foreign investors during the process of corporate restructuring. By nationality of

Table 8.9 Trends in foreign direct investment, 1996–2000 ($ billion)

	1996	1997	1998	1999	2000
FDI in Korea	3.2	7.0	8.9	15.5	15.7
Korean FDI overseas	6.3	5.8	5.1	4.6	3.4

Source: Ministry of Finance and Economy.

Table 8.10 Trends in foreign portfolio investment in Korea, 1996–2000 (trillion won)

	1996	1997	1998	1999	2000
Market value of stocks acquired by foreigners (per cent)	15.2 (13.0)	10.4 (14.6)	25.6 (18.6)	76.6 (21.9)	56.6 (30.1)
Foreign investment in bonds	–	–	1.0	1.2	0.7
Securities holdings by foreign banks in Korea	1.9	5.9	5.4	7.6	11.2

Source: Financial Supervisory Service.

investor, FDI from the European Union totalled $4.6 billion, from the USA $2.9 billion and from Japan $2.4 billion in 2000. Meanwhile Korean direct investment abroad, which surged from the late 1980s to 1996, fell dramatically after the crisis. In 2000 it amounted to $3.4 billion, only a little over half of the amount recorded in 1996. The USA was the top recipient, with $1.1 billion, and China came second with $0.6 billion.

Foreign portfolio investment also surged, with the net inflow rising to $11.6 billion in 2000, more than twice the amount recorded the previous year. Investment from the USA amounted to $8.6 billion, equivalent to 74 per cent of the total inflow. As shown in Table 8.10, the value of foreign-owned stock holdings rose dramatically from 15.2 trillion won in 1996 to 76.6 trillion won in 1999. The fall to 56.6 trillion won in 2000 reflected a plunge in share prices. The share of foreign investors in listed stock holdings also increased dramatically, rising from 13.0 per cent in 1996 to 30.1 per cent in 2000. Foreign investment in bonds and securities likewise increased, but less dramatically.

8.5 Recent trends and future prospects

8.4.1 Recent trends

As discussed in Chapters 4 and 5 the Korean economy made a strong and rapid recovery from the unprecedented financial crisis of 1997–98. The real GDP growth rates in 1999 and 2000 were 10.9 per cent and 8.8 per cent respectively – very high by OECD standards (see Table 5.15). As discussed in some detail in Chapter 5, the implementation of wide-ranging reforms, to create a market based economy laid the foundations for the recovery of investor confidence, encouraged large capital inflows and contributed to the normalisation of the financial market. The reforms included measures to boost competition, strengthen corporate governance and address the problems of non-performing loans and the recapitalisation of financial institutions. With this new framework in place the economy experienced a strong recovery, boosted by a mixture of positive external and domestic factors.

On the external side, the economy benefited from buoyant world demand, particularly from the USA; a strong world demand for Korean exports, particularly from the ICT sector; and the depreciation of the won, which strengthened Korea's competitive position. In December 2000 foreign debt amounted to $131.7 billion, while Korea's foreign credit amounted $164.7 billion. Thus Korea enjoyed a positive net foreign credit of $33.1 billion. Its usable foreign exchange reserves, a key factor in the crisis in November 1997, reached a healthy $96.2 billion. The exchange rate strengthened, which enabled interest rates to be reduced significantly from their levels during the peak of the crisis, and indeed to fall below where they had stood before the crisis erupted.

On the domestic side, the government's determination to implement necessary structural reforms in the wake of the crisis deserves considerable praise as it helped Korea to regain its creditworthiness in international capital markets. As discussed in Chapter 6 the Internet boom and massive investment in the ICT sector also played a principal role in Korea's recovery from the crisis. These developments were backed up by macroeconomic policies designed to stabilise and strengthen the economy.

During most of 2000 it seemed as though the Korean economy had overcome the worst of the crisis, but the strong recovery came to an end in the fourth quarter of 2000 through a combination of external and domestic factors. On the external side, the sharp rise in oil prices in mid 1999 eventually hit Korea, there was a deceleration of world economic growth, particularly in the USA, and there was a sharp decline in exports, mainly from the ICT sector. On the domestic side there was a noticeable deterioration in the confidence of the household and business sectors, which led to stagnation in consumption expenditure and a sharp decline in investment and stock-building. This contributed to a 50 per cent fall in the Korea Stock Exchange, and the resultant negative wealth effect, in conjunction with declining household income and business profits, contributed to the overall decline in spending.

In the first half of 2001 there were some signs that the economic downturn might be short-lived, but in the second half of the year the domestic and global environment deteriorated considerably. The global situation became even more uncertain after the terrorist attack on the World Trade Centre on 11 September 2001. The real GDP growth rate was only 3.0 per cent in 2001.

The short-term future of the Korean economy depends on a number of external and domestic factors. On the external side, recovery depends on an upturn in the global economy, and especially in the USA. However recent indicators suggest that the global economic downturn is likely to be prolonged. On the domestic side, there continues to be considerable uncertainty about the credit worthiness of some of the large *chaebols* as the financial difficulties of firms with interest coverage ratios of below one (a quarter of all enterprises in 2000) were exacerbated by the crisis. The challenge is to restructure the corporate and financial sectors in a way that will reduce market uncertainty, although this may have negative short-term effects on employment and growth. But considering a presidential election is due in December 2002, tangible restructuring progress is not to be expected. Thus the economic downturn is unlikely to be a short one. However the possibility of a repetition of the 1997 external liquidity crisis seems remote, particularly in light of Korea's large foreign exchange reserves relative to its short-term overseas debt and its net creditor status. As an increasingly open economy, however, Korea is likely to become more vulnerable to shocks from abroad. This will be accentuated by the fact that semiconductors and other cyclical ICT products make up a large share of Korean exports.

8.4.2 Medium and long-term prospects: will the Korean economic miracle revive or fade?

Effective restructuring of the economy is vital not only to the country's short-term economic welfare but also to its growth in the medium to long term. From the 1980s the country's sources of growth were split about equally between factor accumulation, inputs of labour and capital, and productivity growth (Table 8.11). During the 1980s, factor inputs contributed 4.5 points of growth per year, slowing to 3.4 points during the 1990s – a further slowdown is likely during the coming years as labour inputs are expected to fall sharply for demographic reasons (OECD, 2001). In addition, capital accumulation may make a smaller contribution than in previous years as firms are scaling back investment because of their greater awareness of the risks of borrowing, and the contribution of productivity growth will tend to fall as the technology gap between Korea and the leading industrial nations narrows. The maintenance of a stable macroeconomic environment,

Table 8.11 Projected GDP growth rate, annual percentage change, 1991–2010

	1991–2000	2001–10
Actual GDP	5.8	–
Projected GDP	6.7	5.1
Factor inputs	3.4	2.4
Labour	1.5	0.3
Capital	1.9	2.1
Total factor productivity growth	3.4	2.7
Economies of scale	1.5	0.9
Resource allocation	0.7	0.6
Technical progress	1.2	1.2

Source: Korea Development Institute.

based on sound monetary and fiscal policies, would, however, be conducive to supporting the growth of total factor productivity.

Therefore the question of whether Korea will be able to revive and sustain its economic miracle will depend on how it tackles these diminishing sources of economic growth. In the previous chapters three areas were identified that needed to be dealt with successfully in the interest of future development. First, as stated at the start of this section, successful restructuring is essential to the country's long-term growth. Market principles and free competition can increase the efficiency of the overall economy, including the factor markets for labour and land, and particularly the constituents of the 'old' economy (this includes the privatisation of state-owned enterprises). This means increasing the capacity for total factor productivity growth which will help boost investment from domestic and external sources and result in greater capital accumulation.

Second, the adoption of ICT innovations and the transformation of the old economy into a 'new' economy will be crucial as knowledge is becoming the most important production input. Although the worldwide downturn in the ICT sector in 2000 and 2001 had a severe adverse impact on Korea, this does not mean that the virtues of ICT are no longer valid. Instead the current hardship will curb overinvestment and strengthen the growth potential of the ICT sector. There is no doubt that the this sector will play a leading part in Korea's recovery from the economic slowdown, and perhaps even the revival of its economic miracle.

Thirdly, expanding Korea's economic territory by accomplishing economic integration with North Korea is another key to the revival of the economic miracle as it would provide a new market for South Korean goods, a new investment opportunity for South Korean firms and an additional source of labour.

In addition to the above, this chapter has discussed three other key areas that have to be addressed in order to revive the economic miracle and improve the quality of life of the Korean people: reform of the education system, welfare reform, and the promotion of competition by further opening up the economy to trade and investment.

In conclusion, the Korean economy is standing at a crossroads. There are many tasks still to be accomplished, but if the key areas discussed above are addressed adequately and necessary preconditions are met, the crisis could turn out to be a blessing in disguise and will clear the way for another economic miracle and sustainable growth in the twenty-first century.

Notes

2 Korea's Economic Miracle

1. The year 1989 is seen as a watershed year for Korea in terms of rapid economic growth and development for three main reasons. First, per capita GDP exceeded $5000 for the first time in history. Second, four consecutive years of current account surpluses ended in 1989. Third, Korea officially graduated from its status of developing country.
2. The domestic savings rate, starting from a low base of 11.0 per cent in 1962, grew rapidly to 17.1 per cent in 1972, 25.4 per cent in 1982 and 37.6 per cent in 1989 (Table 2.1).
3. During the period 1945–60 Korea received a total of $3 billion of foreign aid. Although this contributed greatly to the reconstruction of the economy after the war and enabled consumer demand to be met, it did not provide a strong foundation upon which to build a self-supporting economy, which was the ultimate goal of the country (Tae, 1972, pp. 12–13).
4. Korean people placed a high value on education. In the 1960s the illiteracy rate was well below 10 per cent, and educational expenditure reached a level that seemed almost excessive. This strong emphasis on education resulted in a high-quality labour force with the modern management ability required for industrialisation (see for example Tae, 1972 p. 56).
5. A policy stance compatible with a strong sense of nationalism.
6. During the initial stages of development, markets were almost non-existent. In particular the lack of entrepreneurs required the government to play a crucial role in investment decisions and in the allocation of resources more generally. The government emphasised the growth of *chaebols* and the development of publicly owned banks for the economic development of the economy.

3 The Fading Miracle

1. A major factor in this was the construction of two million new houses over the period 1988–91. This ultimately contributed to excess demand in the economy, and a bubble in both land and stock prices from 1992–94.
2. Korea is the world's largest manufacturer of such chips.
3. Estimated at that time to be $130 billion.
4. This slow increase in the unemployment rate reflected the fact that labour laws made worker lay-offs extremely difficult. However with the introduction of labour market reforms and the establishment of the Tripartite Commission in January 1998 (a body composed of representatives of workers, management and the government) lay-offs were made easier. This is discussed in more detail in Chapter 5.
5. However the financial crisis of 1997 and the subsequent agreement on legalising lay-offs, in conjunction with the structural change from labour-intensive to technology-intensive industries, caused unemployment to rise to 6.8 per cent in 1998.
6. Of all the other OECD economies only Norway had a negative government net debt (larger than Korea's) and a government financial surplus (again larger than Korea's). Korea's position, however, deteriorated considerably from 1998, with

the onset of the economic crisis and the fiscal commitments required by the government to recapitalise the banking sector.

7. Industries in which the *chaebols* concentrated their activities.
8. For example the top 10 export items accounted for 53 per cent of the total value of shipments in 1995, up from 50 per cent in 1994. These and other manufactured goods accounted for 85 per cent of exports.
9. During the depth of the economic crisis in 1998 imports collapsed dramatically.
10. This is discussed in more detail in Chapter 4.
11. Mergers and acquisitions became the main vehicle of FDI in 1998.
12. This corresponded with developments in the international capital markets. After 1994, following the Latin American financial crisis, capital inflows into the emerging market economies of East Asia increased markedly.
13. This move reflected the government's strategy of beginning capital account liberalisation with trade-related financial flows, which were not considered to pose a threat to the conduct of monetary policy based on quantity controls. Direct overseas borrowing was limited to four categories of borrower: SMEs, companies investing in public infrastructural projects, subsidiaries of foreign companies in technology-based business areas, and companies paying foreign debt prematurely. In the case of indirect borrowing through Korean banks, SMEs could borrow 100 per cent of the value of their capital good imports. For large firms, borrowing was limited to 90 per cent in manufacturing and 80 per cent in services until May 1995, when the ceiling was lowered to 70 per cent.
14. Those wishing to obtain long-term foreign loans had to provide detailed information to, and obtain the approval of, the Ministry of Finance and Economy, while short-term borrowers faced no such requirement.
15. These merchant banks had previously operated as finance companies, and had not been allowed to deal in foreign currency. Upon becoming so-called merchant banks they continued to operate as short-term finance companies. In addition commercial banks opened 28 foreign branches between 1994 and 1996.
16. The liquidity risk reflected a maturity mismatch – a high ratio of short-term liabilities to assets. Sixty-four per cent of the merchant banks' borrowings were short term while 85 per cent of their loans were long term (Chang *et al.* 1998). The foreign exchange risk was due to the failure of most corporations to hedge their foreign currency loans. Consequently the depreciation of the won resulted in a deterioration of the banks' balance sheets.
17. The *chaebols* dominated the economy. The top five groups accounted for about 10 per cent of GDP and the top four accounted for about 14 per cent of manufacturing output. Worldwide sales by the top four *chaebols* was equivalent to 47 per cent of Korea's total output, the combined revenue of the top 49 *chaebols* was equivalent to 97 per cent of the country's GDP, and they also accounted for nearly half of its exports. The 30 largest *chaebols* more or less controlled the entire economy if downstream suppliers and all the small businesses and employees that depended on them are included. There was considerable replication amongst the *chaebols*, resulting in low profit margins for all. Each of the top three *chaebols*, for example, had well over 100 businesses, but 80 per cent of their revenues came from 20 per cent of these businesses, and virtually all the profits from just one or two. Combined profits amounted to a paltry $65 million in 1996, according to Goldman Sachs (1998), giving the *chaebols* an average return on equity of only 3 per cent, while 13 of the top 30 *chaebols* made losses in 1996. Hence their growth was profitless growth.

18. At least until the early 1980s strong government leadership was necessary and desirable because the domestic market was small, the structure of domestic industry was quite simple and Korea's participation in the world market was limited.
19. That is, intervention by the government in loan extensions to family-controlled *chaebols* and deciding major state-funded projects on the basis of political kick-backs.
20. For example, between 1986 and 1995 net income to total assets in manufacturing averaged only 2.3 per cent, about half the rate in the USA.
21. See for example OECD (1998), pp. 26–9.
22. On the basis of total assets in 1996 (see Table 3.10).
23. For a fixed period participating banks agreed to abstain from calling in their loans or exercising their claims against firms on the brink of insolvency because of temporary funding problems. During this period of grace the possibility of turning the firm around was assessed. If the assessment was positive the firm's rehabilitation programme was supported by a consortium of banks. In 1997 Jinro, Dainong, Kia Motors and TailJung Mil came under this agreement. In the event the standstill agreement proved futile as most of these firms eventually entered into a 'work-out' programme or went into receivership later in 1997.
24. In fact the commercial and merchant banks' capital adequacy ratios were barely one half of the officially declared rates, owing to regulatory forbearance about past investment losses.
25. While employment by banks in most countries remained steady or declined, it increased by about 25 per cent in Korea from 1990–96 (see Table 3.11).
26. For example at the end of June 1997 the official figures for Korean banks' bad loans was 6.1 per cent of total loans outstanding, but if international provisioning norms are applied the figure rises to more than 15 per cent. For the nine largest banks bad loans ranged from 94 per cent to 376 per cent of their capital, hence most of them were technically insolvent. In short Korea's financial system was probably twice as highly geared as portrayed by official data.
27. It is also worth stressing that not all banks were the same. Those banks that had avoided loan concentration to the *chaebols* and had developed skills in credit analysis tended to perform better. For example, the Kookmin Bank had a strong deposit base and specialised in the consumer and medium-sized company market sectors. As a result its credit evaluation skills were better, its loan losses lower and its margins higher. The strongest banks were those which had deviated from the predominant pattern of policy-directed loans and high exposure to the *chaebols*.
28. By December 1997 these two banks were effectively insolvent and had to be nationalised. A majority stake in Korea First Bank was later sold to Newbridge Capital, a foreign company. A similar effort to sell a majority stake in Seoul Bank had not yet borne fruit at the time of writing.
29. The merchant banks acted as major intermediaries in raising finance for the *chaebols*, including finance from overseas. Many of them had considerable *chaebol* involvement in their ownership. They found themselves in an increasingly weak financial position because of their overexposure to the *chaebols* and to overseas borrowing. These institutions were ultimately revealed to be very weak and lacking in information transparency
30. Of particular concern were the trust accounts held by the banks.

31. This is a common problem in developing countries, and indeed can be found in some developed countries, such as Germany and Japan.
32. Trade unions had been allowed to operate since 1953, although the authoritarian governments in the 1960s, 1970s and 1980s severely restricted their right to engage in collective bargaining and take industrial action. Nonetheless it was very difficult to lay off workers and this remained the case until the reforms of 1998.
33. Park (1996) and Kim (1997) provide summaries of the liberalisation process.
34. However this liberalisation was imbalanced in terms of internal versus external liberalisation. There was rapid external liberalisation but regulation of the domestic financial sector remained.
35. For example *The Economist* (1997), UBS (1996) and Sarel (1996).

4 Financial Crisis and the IMF Bailout

1. There have been numerous works on the causes of the financial crisis in Asia, most of which are available at the following website: http://www.stern.nyu.edu/globalmacro/. Research papers on the causes of Korea's 1997 crisis include Bank of Korea (1998), Park and Rhee (1998), Min (1998), Kwon (1998), Jwa and Huh (1998), Smith (1998), OECD (1998), Borensztein and Lee (1999), Australian Department of Foreign Affairs and Trade (1999) and Park and Song (2000).
2. Many non-economists, mainly politicians and journalists, put the blame on policy failures in the afflicted countries before the crisis occurred, and external factors such as abrupt changes in international market conditions. For instance the Korean parliamentary hearing in early 1999 mainly focused on the policy mistakes made by the president and government officials. Some commentators even claimed that the Asian financial crisis was the result of hegemonic conflict between East and West.
3. Krugman later changed his position, arguing that the moral hazard position did not satisfactorily explain the crisis in East Asia.
4. In fact the premium on Korean sovereign debt in secondary markets initially rose relatively modestly to some 75 basis points after the Thai crisis.
5. By reactivating the resolution fund.
6. Specifically Malaysia, Indonesia and the Philippines.
7. Hong Kong, Korea, Singapore and Taiwan.
8. Indonesia, Malaysia, the Philippines and Thailand.
9. The desirability of liberalising long-term capital flows had been clearly stressed by the OECD (1996), p. 128.
10. These cooperative loans were often made at some 5 to 6 percentage points below those on corporate bonds.
11. Cooperative loans to distressed firms were reported to have risen by 2 trillion won after October 1997, reaching some 22 trillion won by mid May 1998. Of this, some 9 trillion won came from banks.
12. The exchange rate was allowed to fluctuate in a band of plus or minus 2.25 per cent a day. In theory the authorities intervened only to smooth erratic movements, but in practice, given continuing capital market restrictions, the system largely functioned as a fixed but adjustable peg.
13. Up to the end of October some 90 per cent of commercial bank credit lines were still being rolled over. However this dropped precipitously from 60 per cent to 20 per cent between November and December. In January 1998 the roll-over rate

recovered to some 80 per cent following an agreement to extend the maturity of Korea's foreign commercial bank debt.

14. The following discussion on strokes is based on a booklet entitled *Preventing Strokes: A Consumer's Reference Guide* (National Health and Medical Research Council, 1997). Consultations with medical doctors were also carried out. Readers, who wish to know more about strokes are referred to Barnett *et al.* (1992).
15. The total number of *chaebol* bankruptcies in 1997 was eight because one more *chaebol* went into bankruptcy after the IMF programme was agreed.
16. At the end of September 1997 the non-performing loans of commercial banks stood at 21.9 trillion won (6.4 per cent of total credit), nearly double the amount at the end of 1996. At the same time merchant banks recorded non-performing loans of 3.9 trillion won at the end of October 1997, three times the amount at the end of 1996.
17. This section draws heavily on Lee (2001).
18. The stand-by agreement projected GDP growth and inflation of some 2–3 per cent and 7 per cent respectively, and a small current account deficit.
19. Despite these sharp increases the exchange rate declined almost 40 per cent over the same period, from 1196 won to 1960 won to the dollar.
20. The IMF programme had numerous critics, the most notable being Radelet and Sachs (1998a, 1998b) and Feldstein (1998).
21. As mentioned previously, before the crisis Korea used the so-called market-average foreign exchange system that was adopted in 1990. Even though the daily fluctuation band had been gradually widened during the process of financial liberalisation, it was still only plus/minus 2.25 per cent just before the crisis. On the eve of turning to the IMF the government widened the band to plus/minus 10 per cent of the market average rate. On 16 December 1997 it shifted to a free-floating exchange rate system.
22. The sharp fall in per capita GDP was attributed more to the won's sharp depreciation than to the economic contraction.
23. The IMF made similar mistakes in its forecasts for other crisis-stricken economies. For example its projections for Thailand and Indonesia were revised four times in the first year of their programmes.
24. See Jack Boorman 'For the IMF and others, lessons from the Asian crisis', *International Herald Tribune*, 20 January 1999.
25. At their meetings in January 1998 the Korean government and the IMF agreed to allow for an increased fiscal deficit. In February the two sides also agreed to lower interest rates, and a downward adjustment was made during the following months.
26. Hubert Neiss, 'In defence of the IMF's emergency role in East Asia', *International Herald Tribune*, 9 October 1998.
27. The economy experienced negative growth in 1998 for the first time since 1980.
28. According to a private sector research institute, labour productivity in foreign-owned companies in Korea was over 40 per cent higher than in domestically owned firms (Samsung Economic Research Institute, 1998b). Moreover the ratio of financial expenses to sales was only half as much at foreign-owned firms.
29. The unemployment rate declined further to 4 per cent in April 2000.
30. It reached more than 4 per cent in the second half of 1999.
31. Those on permanent contracts.

32. This includes the impact of exports; almost half of imports were used in the production of exports.
33. ICT exports increased by more than 50 per cent in volume terms in 1999 and 2000. In 2000 they grew at an annual rate of 139 per cent in volume terms in the second quarter and slowed to under 40 per cent in the final quarter. This decline continued into the first quarter of 2001, when ICT exports fell by more than 50 per cent.
34. In 2000 Korea's semiconductor export prices fell by 12 per cent.
35. Korea recorded a 12.4 per cent fall in its terms of trade, its fifth consecutive annual decline.
36. For an overall evaluation of the IMF's current approach to financial crises and a proposal for an alternative approach, see Buira (1999).

5 The Post-Crisis Macroeconomic Framework and Structural Reform

1. Oh (2000b) and Cargill (2001) review the Korean inflation targeting system.
2. Oh (1999) estimates two underlying inflation rates using the adjustment by exclusion method and another using the trimmed mean method. He then examines their stability and usefulness to determine which would be the most suitable for inflation targeting in Korea. Of the two types of underlying inflation rates produced by adjustment by exclusion, one strips out the price of agricultural and marine products and energy from the components of the consumer price index and the other excludes all these plus the prices of public utilities. A trim of 15 per cent off both tails of the frequency distribution was adopted to estimate the trimmed mean inflation rate. Oh's results show that the first approach produces a relatively better performance in terms of stability and usefulness for monetary policy.
3. The mid-term inflation target was set at the same level as or lower than the short-term inflation target for the year in order to inspire confidence that inflation would be kept low and stable in the long term. The mid-term target was quoted as a point target without a toleration band because it was judged more important to demonstrate the strong commitment of the Bank to preventing the spread of inflationary expectations among the public than to take economic uncertainties into account.
4. First, the Bank set a price stability target for the following year in consultation with the government, and formulated and promulgated an operational plan for monetary and credit policies, including the price stability target. Second, every month it officially announced the monthly direction of monetary policy and the governor explained its details at a press briefing. Third, it published the minutes of Monetary Policy Committee meetings three months after each meeting. Fourth, it submitted a monetary and credit policy report to the National Assembly twice a year, normally in March and October, and the governor was required to answer questions by members of the National Assembly about the report.
5. See Chapter 4.
6. A unified body covering banking, insurance, non-banks and the capital market.
7. KAMCO's task was to purchase impaired assets and liquidate them as efficiently as possible. To this end, in November 1997 the Non Performing Loans Liquidation Fund was established to purchase and dispose of the bad loans of commercial and merchant banks. The funds initially made available to KAMCO

came from the Bank of Korea, the Korea Development Bank and other financial institutions, with the remainder coming from bond issuance.

8. The government and KDIC each invested 750 billion won in each institution.
9. For a discussion of the *chaebols* see Yoo (1995), Lee and Lee (1996) and Yoo and Lim (1997).
10. Sakong (2000) suggests that the debt to equity ratio of the top five *chaebols* fell to 150 per cent in 2000, although the absolute amount of their debt remained about the same as in 1997.
11. Initiating derivative suits: from 1.0 per cent to 0.01 per cent of the total shares issued. Requesting dismissal of directors for misconduct: from 3.0 per cent to 0.5 per cent of the total shares issued, reduced further to 0.05 per cent in 2000. Right to inspect the books and records: from 3.0 per cent to 1.0 per cent of the total shares issued, reduced further to 0.1 per cent in 2000. Shareholders right to make a proposal: from 3.0 per cent to 1.0 per cent of the total shares issued.
12. Such firms had to have at least two outside directors in 2001 and 2002, or one quarter of the total number of directors. Companies listed on KOSDAQ that have more than 2 trillion won of capital had to comply with the same corporate governance practices required of firms listed on the Korea Stock Exchange.
13. Allowing mutual funds to exercise their voting right, and monitor corporate performance.
14. Purchasers no longer had to report to the Financial Supervisory Commission prior to the announcement of a takeover bid, and they could acquire shares three days after the announcement rather than seven.
15. The ratio of operating profits to interest expenses.
16. The big five excluding Daewoo.
17. Specifically, the Government Reform Office at the PBC focuses on issues related to public sector reform. The PBC itself is currently under the Ministry of Planning and Budget and is a permanent government body.
18. The Agricultural and Fishery Marketing Corp., Korea Coal Corp., Korea Electric Power Corp., Korea Highway Corp., Korea Land Corp., Korea National Housing Corp., Korea National Tourist Organisation, Korea National Oil Corp. (formerly the Korea Petroleum Development Corp.), Korea Resources Corp., Korea Security Printing and Minting Corp., Korea Trade and Investment Promotion Agency, Korea Water Resources Corp. and Rural Development Corp.
19. The Daehan Oil Pipeline Corp., Korea District Heating Corp., Korea Gas Corp., Korea General Chemical Co., Korea Heavy Industries and Construction Co., Korea Telecom, Korea Tobacco and Ginseng Corp., Pohang Iron and Steel Co., Korea Housing Guarantee Co., Incheon International Airport Corp., Korea Appraisal Board, Korea Daily News and Korea Broadcasting System.
20. The PBC later merged with the Office of National Budget and became the Ministry of Planning and Budget (MPB) in 1999. The privatisation team in the MPB is in charge of the privatisation of non-financial corporations in which the central government has a stake. The privatisation of state-owned financial institutions is handled by the Ministry of Finance and Economy and the Financial Supervisory Commission. The privatisation of local public enterprises is handled by the Ministry of Government Administration and Home Affairs and the local governments.
21. However some countermeasures were introduced to avoid unnecessary instability on the foreign exchange market. First, cross-border capital movements would be closely monitored by a newly established foreign exchange monitoring

network, and individual foreign exchange transactions would be automatically recorded in the computer system of the Foreign Exchange Information Brokerage Centre. Information collected in the centre would be shared by the relevant supervisory authorities. Second, the Korea Centre for International Finance (KCIF) was established in April 1999 to collect and analyse information on foreign exchange and international financial market trends. Third, a legal framework was introduced to allow the government to impose emergency safeguard measures when necessary. However the terms and conditions for invoking the measures would be very stringent and would conform to international standards, such as the BOP safeguard provisions of the OECD and IMF. Examples of such measures are variable deposit requirements, concentration of foreign exchange and permission requirements for capital account transactions.

22. In order to deal with the possibility of capital flight in response to deteriorating internal and external economic environments and with illegal transactions such as money laundering and tax evasion, the government strengthened procedural aspects of its monitoring efforts by strengthening the requirement for some foreign exchange transactions to be reported to the National Tax Service and the National Customs Service; continuing to require capital account transactions to be processed through foreign exchange business institutions; introducing a system for reporting large external payments to the Bank of Korea; and requiring that overseas deposits and trust assets exceeding certain amounts be reported annually to the Bank of Korea.

6 The Boom in Information and Communication Technology

1. According to a survey concluded by the Korea Network Information Centre in March 2000, about 25 per cent of Netizens (a new word for people who use the Internet) use the Internet at Internet cafes (National Computerisation Agency and Ministry of Information and Communication, 2000).
2. See http://www.netvalue.com.
3. According to a prediction by Inews (http://www.inews24.com) the total amount of e-commerce will grow at an annual rate of 55 per cent, rising from 22.9 trillion won in 2000 to 204.1 trillion won in 2005.
4. This share is likely to become even greater in the coming years. The Korea Information Society Development Institute (2000), for example, predicts that output in the ICT industries will grow at an annual rate of 13.9 per cent during 2000–4, and hence the share of value added for the ICT sector in the gross domestic product will be 12.3 per cent in 2004, up from 9.9 per cent in 1999. Moon, *et al.* (2000), estimate that the ICT sector's share of value added will reach 18.1 per cent in 2004.
5. However, according to a survey by ZDNet (2001) Korea ranked third in terms of the number of domain names per country in January 2001.
6. SSL was developed by Netscape for encrypted transmission over TCP/IP networks. The most common application of SSL is 'https for ssl-encrypted http', which enables common forms of e-commerce to take place.
7. Purchasing power parity.
8. As discussed below the 'digital divide' refers to the social inequality between those who have access to ICT and those who do not.
9. The Internet infrastructure for Korea.
10. This issue will be addressed in more detail in Chapter 8.

7 Economic Integration with North Korea

1. On the other hand the Bank of Korea estimates that loans from international institutions to North Korea could amount to between $2.7 and $4.5 billion (Park, 1999).
2. It is reported that top officials at the IMF and the World Bank, in a meeting with President Kim Dae Jung in Washington DC in March 2001, expressed interest in assisting North Korea in its efforts to develop the economy, and in sending a fact-finding mission to North Korea to study its needs and how best to restructure its economy (*Korea Herald*, 10 July 2001).
3. With POC, South Korean firms send primary or unfinished goods to North Korea, where they are processed and shipped to Japan or Europe or returned to South Korea.
4. Russian President Vladimir Putin and North Korean leader Kim Jong Il have discussed the creation of a 'railroad transport corridor' linking Russia's Trans-Siberian Railway with the rail systems of the two Koreas. It has been reported that Russia is willing to provide about $2 billion for a railway modernisation project in North Korea in exchange for the linking of these systems (*Chosun Ilbo*, 2001d).
5. This would facilitate multilateral economic cooperation and exchanges throughout North-East Asia as it would also connect Japan with China and the Russian Far East.
6. Noland (2000b) has a similar view on this.
7. As shown by Noland *et al.* (1999, 2000), the formation of a customs union would have a big impact on North Korea. A customs union would represent major trade liberalisation on its part, while its economy would be too small to have much of an impact on that of the South.
8. The ASEAN countries are also politically and economically diverse and are at different stages of economic development, so a precedent has already been set.
9. This section draws heavily on Lee (1998).
10. At the same time, reconciliation and economic cooperation between the two Koreas is crucial to economic cooperation in North-East Asia as peace on the Korean peninsula would remove a major threat to the region's stability.

References

Adelman, I. (ed.) (1969) *Practical Approaches to Development Planning: Korea's Second Five Year Plan* (Baltimore, MD: Johns Hopkins University Press).

Ahn, B.J. (2000) 'Korean Peninsula after the Summit Meeting: From Economic to Security Cooperation', *The Economics of Korean Unification*, vol. 5, no. 1, pp. 16–23.

Australian Department of Foreign Affairs and Trade (1997) *Country Economic Brief – Korea* (Canberra, June).

Australian Department of Foreign Affairs and Trade (1998) *Country Economic Brief – Korea* (Canberra, December).

Australian Department of Foreign Affairs and Trade (1999), *Korea Rebuilds: From Crisis to Opportunity* (Canberra: East Asia Analytical Unit).

Bai, M. K. (1982) 'The turning point in the Korean economy', *Developing Economies*, vol. 20, no. 2.

Balassa, B. (1976) 'Korea's Development Strategy for the Fourth Five Year Plan Period (1977–81)', in Economic Planning Board (ed.), *Discussion Papers on the Draft of the Fourth Plan (1977–81)* (Seoul-EPB).

Balassa, B. (1985) 'The Role of Foreign Trade in the Economic Development of Korea', in Walter Galenson (ed.), *Foreign Trade and Investment: Economic Development in the Newly Industrialising Asian Countries* (University of Wisconsin Press).

Balassa, B. (1987) 'Korea during the Fifth Five Year Plan Period (1982–86)', in Il Sakong (ed.), *Macroeconomic Policy and Industrial Development Issues* (Seoul: Korea Development Institute Press).

Bank of Korea (various years) *Economic Statistics Yearbook* (Seoul: Bank of Korea).

Bank of Korea (1998) 'Financial Crisis in Korea – Why it Happened and How it Should be Overcome', SEACEN Centre seminar paper, July.

Bank of Korea (2000a) 'Effects of the Development of Information Technology Industry on the Productivity Growth', *Monthly Bulletin*, October (in Korean).

Bank of Korea (2000b) *Estimated Results of North Korean GDP, 1999* (Seoul: Bank of Korea).

Bank of Korea (2001a) *Estimated Results of North Korean GDP, 2000* (Seoul: Bank of Korea).

Bank of Korea (2001b) 'The Major Results of Financial Restructuring in 2000', *Josatonggye Wolbo* (Monthly Economic Bulletin), February (in Korean).

Barnett, H., J. P. Mohr, B. Stein and F. Yatsu (eds) (1992) *Stroke: Pathophysiology, Diagnosis, and Management*, 2nd edn (New York: Churchill Livingstone).

Basurto, G. and A. R. Ghosh (2000) 'The Interest Rate–Exchange Rate Nexus in the Asian Crisis Countries', IMF Working Paper, WP/00/19 (Washington, DC: IMF).

Bergstern, C. F. (2001) 'Brunei: A Turning Point for APEC', International Economic Policy Briefs, 01–1 (Washington DC: Institute for International Economics, February).

Bhagwati, J. (2001) 'Bilateral Agreements Threaten the Achievements of the WTO', *Financial Times*, 5 March.

Boorman, J. (1999) 'For the IMF and Others, Lessons from the Asian Crisis', *International Herald Tribune*, 20 January.

Booz Allen & Hamilton (1997) 'Revitalising the Korean economy towards the 21st century' (Seoul: Mael Economic Newspaper Co.).
Borensztein, E. and J. W. Lee (1999) 'Credit Allocation and Financial Crisis in Korea', IMF Working Paper, WP/99/20 (Washington, DC: IMF).
Bremmer, B. (2000) 'Korea is Leaving Japan in the Digital-Age Dust', *Business Week*, 8 August.
Brown, G. T. (1973) *Korean Policies and Economic Development in the 1960s* (Baltimore, MD: Johns Hopkins Press).
Buira, A. (1999) 'An Alternative Approach to Financial Crises', *Essays in International Finance*, no. 212 (Princeton University, February).
Calverley, J. (1982) *Korea: Exporting to Survive* (London: Euromoney).
Cargill, T.F. (2001) 'Central Bank Independence in Korea', *Journal of the Korean Economy*, vol. 2, no. 1, pp. 1–33.
Chang, H. J., H. J. Park and C. G. Yoo (1998) 'Interpreting the Korean Crisis: Financial Liberalisation, Industrial Policy and Corporate Governance', *Cambridge Journal of Economics*, vol. 22.
Chenery, H. B. and M. Syrquin (1975) *Patterns of Development 1950–1970* (New York: Oxford University Press).
Chenery, H. B. and L. Taylor (1968) 'Development Patterns among Countries and Over time', *Review of Economics and Statistics*, November.
Chinn, M. D. (1998) 'Before the Fall: Were East Asian Currencies Overvalued?' mimeo, University of California, Santa Cruz.
Cho, D. and K. D. West (1999) 'The Effect of Monetary Policy in Exchange Rate Stabilisation in Post-Crisis Korea', paper presented at the Conference of the Korean Econometric Society, November (in Korean).
Cho, M. C. and H. Zang (1999) 'The Present and Future Prospects of the North Korean Economy', Working Paper 99–07 (Seoul: Korea Institute for International Economic Policy).
Cho, S. (1994) *The Dynamics of Korean Economic Development* (Washington, DC: Institute for International Economics).
Chon, S. Y. (2000) 'East Asian Leaders Pledge Closer Economic Ties', *Korea Herald* (Seoul), 25 November.
Chosun Ilbo (2001a) 'Hyundai Mt. Kumgang Tour Project at a Crossroad', *Chosun Ilbo* (Seoul), 18 January.
Chosun Ilbo (2001b) 'North Korea to Introduce Farmers' Contract', *Chosun Ilbo* (Seoul), 5 March.
Chosun Ilbo (2001c) 'Small Firms Ready to Invest in N.K.', *Chosun Ilbo* (Seoul), 20 July.
Chosun Ilbo (2001d) 'Russia, N. Korea Leaders Sign Pact', *Chosun Ilbo* (Seoul), 6 August.
Corsetti, G., P. Pesenti and N. Roubini (1998a) 'Paper Tigers? A Preliminary Assessment of the Asian Crisis', mimeo, New York University.
Corsetti, G., P. Pesenti and N. Roubini (1998b) 'What Caused the Asian Currency and Financial Crisis?', mimeo, New York University.
Daniels, M. J. (1987) *Korea's Thirty Years of Growth and Change (1957–87)* (Seoul: Myung Hwa Press).
Denison, E. F. (1962) *The Sources of Economic Growth in the United States and the Alternative Before Us* (New York: Committee for Economic Development).
Denison, E. F. (1964) 'Sources of Postwar Growth in Nine Western Countries', *American Economic Review*, March.

Eberstadt, N. (2000) 'Our Own Style of Statistics: Availability and Reliability of Official Quantitative Data for the Democratic People's Republic of Korea', *The Economics of Korean Reunification* vol. 5, no. 1, pp. 68–93.

Economist (1997) 'The Asian Miracle – Is It Over', 17 March.

Economist (1998) 'A survey of East Asian Economies', 7 March.

Economist (2000a) 'The Other Side of North Korea', 15 June.

Economist (2000b) 'Hugs for Koreans', 17 August.

Economist (2000c) 'The Koreas Start a Slow March, not yet in Lockstep', 28 September.

Economist (2000d) 'The New Economy: Falling through the Net?', 26 December.

Feldstein, M. (1998) 'The IMF's Errors', *Foreign Affairs*, March/April.

Fischer, S. (1998) 'The Asian Crisis: a View from the IMF', address at the Midwinter Conference of the Bankers' Association for Foreign Trade, Washington, DC, 22 January.

Fitch IBCA (1999) *Rating Report: Republic of Korea*, New York: Fitch (http://www.fitchibc.com)

Goldfajn, I. and T. Baig (1998) 'Monetary Policy in the Aftermath of Currency Crisis: The Cases of Asia', IMF Working Paper WP/98/170 (Washington, DC: IMF).

Goldman Sachs Investment Research (1998) 'Korea *Chaebol* Restructuring II', mimeo (New York: Goldman Sachs).

Greenspan, A. (1998) 'Testimony before the Committee on Banking and Financial Services', US House of Representatives, 13 November.

Han, S. T. (2000) 'The Korean Perspective on the New Economy', paper presented at the Korea – OECD conference on 'Korea in the OECD Perspective: Shaping up for Globalisation', Seoul, December.

Hasan, P. and D. C. Rao (1979) *Korea: Policy Issues for Long-term Development* (Baltimore, MD: Johns Hopkins University Press).

Hill, H. (1998) 'Southeast Asia's Economic Crisis: Origins, Lessons, and the Way Forward', Paper presented at the Institute of Southeast Asian Studies' 30th Anniversary Conference on 'Southeast *Asia in the Twenty First Century: Challenges of Globalization', Singapore, August 1998.*

Hong, S. (2000) 'North Korea's Infrastructure Conditions and Strategies for Investment', *VIP Millennium Report* (Seoul: Hyundai Research Institute, July) pp. 14–18.

Hong, S. J. (2001) 'North Korea's Electric Power Conditions and Inter-Korean Cooperation', *VIP Millennium Report* (Seoul: Hyundai Research Institute, May), pp. 17–22.

ILO (2001) *World Employment Report 2001: Life at Work in the Information Economy* (Geneva: ILO).

IMF (1997) *World Economic Outlook – Interim Assessment* (Washington, DC: IMF).

IMF (1999a) *International Financial Statistics Yearbook* (Washington, DC: IMF)

IMF (1999b) *World Economic Outlook* (Washington, DC: IMF)

IMF (1999c) *The IMF's Response to the Asian Crisis* (Washington, DC: IMF).

IMF (1999d) *Direction of Trade Statistics* (Washington, DC: IMF).

International Telecommunications Union (2000) *ITU Telecommunication Indicators Update* (http://www.itu.int).

Joh, S. W. (1999) 'The Korean Corporate Sector: Crisis and Reform', KDI Working Paper no. 9912 (Seoul: Korea Development Institute).

Jorgensen, D. W. and F. Griliches (1967) 'The explanation of productivity change', *Review of Economic Studies*, July.

Jun, M. K. (2000) 'Has the "New Economy" Appeared in Korea?', *VIP Millennium Report* (Seoul: Hyundai Research Institute), (http://www.hri.co.kr).

Jung, Y. C. (2000) 'The Summit and Agreement on Unification Formula', *The Economics of Korean Unification*, vol. 5, no. 1, pp. 38–44.
Jwa, S. H. and C. K. Huh (1998) 'Korea's 1997 Currency Crisis: Causes and Implications', paper presented at the 8th International Conference of the Korean Economic Association, August.
Kendrick, J. W. and R. Sato (1963) 'Factor Prices, Productivity, and Growth', *American Economic Review*, December.
Kim, J. H. (1997) *Financial Liberalisation in Korea* (Seoul: Research Department, Bank of Korea).
Kim, K. S. and S. D. Hong (1997) *Accounting for Rapid Economic Growth in Korea, 1963–1995* (Seoul: Korea Development Institute).
Kim, K. S. and Park, J. K. (1985) *Sources of Economic Growth in Korea: 1963–1982* (Seoul: Korea Development Institute).
Kim, M. S. (2000) 'Financing Methods for North Korean Development', *The Economics of Korean Unification*, vol. 5, no. 1, pp. 138–147.
Kim, S. and J. H. Lee (1997) 'Industrial Relations and Human Resource Development', in D. S. Cha, K. S. Kim and D. H. Perkins (eds), *The Korean Economy 1945–1995* (Seoul: Korea Development Institute).
Kim, W. K. (1999) 'Total Factor Productivity and Competitiveness in Korea', *Productivity Journal* (APO), Summer.
Kim, W. S. (1995) 'The Korean Economy in Distress: Major Challenges in the 1990s', in T. Kawagoe and S. Sekiguchi (eds), *East Asian Economies – Transformation and Challenges*, Singapore: Institute of Southeast Asian Studies.
Korea Herald (2000) 'Universities Unsuitable Breeding Ground for Corporate Environment', 20 December.
Korea Herald (2001) 'IMF Ready to Provide Economic Aid to N. K.', 10 July.
Korea Information Society Development Institute (2000) 'Medium-term Projections for the Information and Communication Industries in Korea (2000–2004)' (Seoul: KISDI, http://www.kisdi.re.kr).
Kosai, Y. and Y. Ogino (1984) *The Contemporary Japanese Economy* (New York: M. E. Sharpe).
Krueger, A. (1979) *The Development Role of the Foreign Sector and Aid* (Cambridge, Mass.: Harvard University Press).
Krugman, P. (1995) 'The Myth of the Asian Miracle', *Foreign Affairs*, vol. 73, no. 6.
Krugman, P. (1998a) 'What Happened to Asia', mimeo, MIT, January (http://web.mit.edu/krugman/www/disinter.html).
Krugman, P. (1998b) 'Will Asia Bounce Back?', speech at Credit Suisse First Boston, Hong Kong, March.
Kuznets, S. (1955) 'Economic Growth and Income Inequality', *American Economic Review* vol. 45, pp. 1–25.
Kwon O. Y. (1998) 'An Analysis of the Causes of the Korean Financial Crisis: A Political Economy Approach', mimeo (Australia: Griffith University).
Lane, T., A. R. Ghosh, J. Hamann, S. Phillips, M. Schulze-Ghattas and T. Tsikata (1999) 'IMF-Supported Programs in Indonesia, Korea and Thailand: A Preliminary Assessment', (Washington, DC: IMF).
Lee, H. H. (1995) 'Prospects for South and North Korean Economic Cooperation and its Relation with the Development of the Russian Far East', in *Proceedings of the 2nd International Conference on The Economy of the Far East under Conditions of Reform* (Khabarovsk: Economic Research Institute), pp. 59–64.

Lee, H. H. (1998) 'Northeast Asian Economic Cooperation and Its Relation with Inter-Korean Economic Cooperation', in Sang-Oak Lee and Duk-Soo Park (eds), *Perspectives on Korea* (Sydney: Wild Pony), pp. 77–90.

Lee, H. H. (1999a) 'Korea's 1997 Financial Crisis: Causes, Consequences and Prospects', *Agenda* (Australian National University), vol. 6, pp. 353–65.

Lee, H. H. (1999b) 'A "Stroke" Hypothesis of Korea's 1997 Financial Crisis: Causes, Consequences and Prospects', University of Melbourne Research Paper no. 696 (available at http://www.ecom.unimelb.edu.au/ecowww/research/696.pdf).

Lee, H. H. (2001) 'The IMF Rescue Program: What Went Wrong?', *The Journal of the Korean Economy*, vol. 2, no. 1, pp. 69–86.

Lee, H. H. and Y. Cheong. (1997) 'Real Output and Inflation in a Small Open Economy: the Case of Korea', *Business & Economics for the 21st* Century, vol. I, pp. 273–83; also in *Proceedings of the Annual Meeting of the Econometrics Society of Korea* (Seoul: Econometrics Society of Korea).

Lee, J. (2001) 'College Educational System Fails to Meet Corporation Demands', *Korea Herald*, 4 January.

Lee, Jae Woong (2000) 'How We Got Wired', *Time*, 11 December.

Lee, Jong-Wha and C. Rhee (1999) 'Social Impacts of the Asian Crisis: Policy Challenges and Lessons', UNDP Working paper no. 33, New York: United Nations Development Programme.

Lee, Jong Won, H. H. Lee and D. Y. Yang (2001) 'Structural Reform in Korea: its Process and Consequences', in Tran Van Hoa (ed.), *The Asia Recovery: Issues and Aspects of Growth, Development, Trade, and Investment* (Cheltenham: Edward Elgar).

Lee, K. U. (1987) 'Concentration of Economic Power in Korea', mimeo, (Seoul: Korea Development Institute).

Lee, K. U. and S. S. Lee (1985) 'Business Integration and Concentration of Economic Power', research report 85-02 (Seoul: Korea Development Institute).

Lee, K. U. and J. H. Lee. (1996) 'Business Groups (*Chaebols*) in Korea Characteristics and Government Policy', Occasional paper no. 23 (Seoul: Korea Institute for Industrial Economics and Trade).

Lee, Y. Y. and H. H. Lee. (2000) 'Financial Crisis, Structural Reform and Social Consequences in Korea', in Tran Van Hoa (ed.), *Social Impact of the Asian Financial Crisis* (London: Macmillan).

Min, B. S. (1998) 'Causes of Korea's Economic Turmoil in 1997 and Implications for Industrial Policy', paper presented at the conference on 'The Asian Crisis: Economic Analysis and Market Intelligence', University of Melbourne, May.

Ministry of Information and Communication (MIC) (1999), *Cyber Korea 21* (http://www.mic.go.kr/ck21/eng/index.html).

Moon, S. W., Y. Kim and D. P. Hong (2000) 'The Economic Importance of the Information and Communications Technology (ICT) Industry in Korea: A CGE Approach', paper presented at the Third Conference on Global Economic Analysis, Melbourne, June.

Nam, I. C. *et al.* (1999) 'Corporate Governance in Korea', paper prepared for an OECD conference, Seoul, March.

National Computerisation Agency and Ministry of Information and Communication, (2000), *2000 Korea Internet White Paper*, October (http://www.nca.or.kr).

National Computerisation Agency and Ministry of Information and Communication (2001) *2001 Korea Internet White Paper* (http://www.nca.or.kr).

National Health and Medical Research Council (1997) *Preventing Stroke: A Consumer's Reference Guide* (Canbera: Australian Government Publishing Service).
Neiss, H. (1998) 'In Defence of the IMF's Emergency Role in East Asia', *International Herald Tribune*, 9 October.
New York Times (2001) 'North Korean Placed Focus on Business on China Visit', 21 January.
Noland, M. (2000a) *Avoiding the Apocalypse: the Future of the Two Koreas*, (Washington, DC: Institute for International Economics).
Noland, M. (2000b) 'Economic Integration and Cooperation on the Korean Peninsula', paper presented at the conference on 'New Challenges in Inter-Korean Economic Cooperation and Integration', Stanford University, October.
Noland, M. (2000c) 'The Summit and the Economic Future of the Peninsula', *The Economics of Korean Reunification*, vol. 5, no. 1, pp. 30–6.
Noland, M., S. Robinson and L. G. Liu (1999) 'The Economics of Korean Economic Unification', *Journal of Policy Reform*, vol. 3, pp. 255–99.
Noland, M., S. Robinson and T. Wang. (2000) 'Modelling Korean Unification', *Journal of Comparative Economics*. vol 28, no 2, pp. 400–25.
OECD (1996) *Economic surveys – Korea* (Paris: OECD).
OECD (1998) *Economic surveys – Korea* (Paris: OECD).
OECD (1999a) *Economic Surveys – Korea* (Paris: OECD).
OECD (1999b) *Measuring the ICT Sector* (Paris: OECD).
OECD (2000a) *Economic Surveys – Korea* (Paris: OECD).
OECD (2000b) *A New Economy? The Changing Role of Innovation and Information Technology in Growth* (Paris: OECD).
OECD (2000c) *Local Access Pricing and E-Commerce* (Paris: OECD).
OECD (2000d) *Pushing Ahead with Reform in Korea: Labour Market and Social Safety-Net Policies* (Paris: OECD).
OECD (2000e) *Education at a Glance 2000* (Paris: OECD).
OECD (2001) *Economic Surveys – Korea* (Paris: OECD).
OECD and World Bank (2000) *Korea and the Knowledge-based Economy: Making the Transition* (Paris: OECD).
Oh, J. (1999) 'How Useful is an Underlying Inflation Rate for Inflation Targeting?', *Economic Papers*, vol. 2, no. 2 (Bank of Korea).
Oh, J. (2000a) *The Financial Crisis and Financial and Monetary Policies* (Seoul: Dasanbooks) (in Korean).
Oh, J. (2000b) 'Inflation Targeting: A New Monetary Policy Framework in Korea', paper presented at the International Symposium on Inflation Targeting, Bank of Thailand, Bangkok, October.
Oh, J. (2000c) 'Dynamic Correlations between Interest Rates, Stock Prices, the Exchange Rate and the Current Account in an Open Economy in which the Stock Market is More Active Than the Bond Market', Working Paper no. 104 (Seoul: Economic Research Office, Bank of Korea) (in Korean).
Oh, J. (2001) 'Governance Reinvented: The Progress, Constraints and Remaining Agenda in Bank and Corporate Restructuring in Korea', paper presented at the ESCAP/Korea University International Conference, Korea University, Seoul, May.
Oh, J., J. Kim and B. Bae (2001) *The Effectiveness of Economic Policies* (Seoul: Bank of Korea) (in Korean).
Oh, K. and R. C. Hassig (2000) *North Korea: Through the Looking Glass* (Washington, DC: Brookings Institution Press).
Park, C. and M. Kim (1998) *Current Poverty Issues and Counter Policies in Korea* (Seoul: Korea Institute for Health and Social Affairs).

Park, D and I. Choi (1999) 'Was the High Interest Rate Policy Effective in Stabilising the Exchange Rate?', paper presented at a Seminar at the Bank of Korea, November (in Korean).
Park, D. and C. Rhee (1998) 'Currency Crisis in Korea: Could It Have Been Avoided?', mimeo (Seoul: Seoul National University)
Park, W. A. (1996) 'Financial Liberalisation: the Korean Experience' in Ito Takatoshi and A. O. Krueger (eds), *Financial Deregulation and Integration in East Asia* (Chicago, Ill.: University of Chicago Press).
Park, Y. C. (1998) 'The Financial Crisis in Korea: From Miracle to Meltdown', mimeo (Seoul: Korea Institute of Finance).
Park, S. (1999) *Estimated Scale of Possible Loans from International Financial Institutions to North Korea* (Seoul: Bank of Korea) (in Korean).
Park, Y. C. and C. H. Song (2000) 'Financial Contagion in the East Asian crisis – with Special Reference to the Republic of Korea, mimeo (Cambridge, Mass.: NBER).
Perry, W. J. (1999) 'Review of United States Toward North Korea: Findings and Recommendations', (available at http://www.state.gov/www/regions/eap/991012_northkorea_rpt.html).
Pilat, D. (2000) 'The New Economy: Prospects and Challenges', paper presented at the conference on 'Korea in the OECD Perspective: Shaping up for Globalisation', Seoul, December.
Radelet, S. and J. Sachs (1998a) 'The Onset of the East Asian Financial Crisis', mimeo (Cambridge: Harvard Institute For International Development).
Radelet, S. and J. Sachs (1998b) 'The East Asian Financial Crisis: Diagnosis, Remedies, Prospects', *Brookings Papers on Economic Activity*, vol. I (April) pp. 1–74.
Ranis, G. (1971) 'The Role of the Industrial Sector in Korea's Transition to Economic Maturity', paper presented at the ILCORK conference, Seoul, 22–29 August.
Ranis, G. (1989) 'The Political Economy of Development Policy Change: a Comparative Study of Taiwan and Korea', Working Paper no. 8916 (Seoul: Korea Development Institute).
Roubini, N., Asia Crisis Homepage (http://www.stern.nyu.edu/globalmacro/).
Sakong, I. (2000) 'Korean Economic Restructuring: Current Status and Prospects', keynote address at the conference entitled 'Has Economic Reform in Korea Stalled? Assessing Progress in Restructuring the Korean Economy', Korean Society, New York, 11 December.
Samsung Economic Research Institute (1998a) 'Korean Economic Trends', mimeo (Seoul: SERI).
Samsung Economic Research Institute (1998b) 'One year after the IMF bailout', (Seoul: SERI).
Samsung Economic Research Institute (2000) 'Two Years after the IMF Bailout: A Review of the Korean Economy's Transformation', mimeo (Seoul: SERI).
Sarel, M. (1996) 'Growth and Productivity in ASEAN Economies', paper presented at the IMF conference, Jakarta, November.
Smith, H. (1998) 'Korea', in R. McLeod and R. Garnaut (eds), *East Asia in Crisis: From Being a Miracle to Needing One?* (London: Routledge).
Sohn, C. H., J. Yang and H. S. Yim (1998) 'Korea's Trade and Industrial Policies: 1948–1998. Why the Era of Active Policy is Over', KIEP Working Paper, 98–05 (Seoul: Korea Institute for International Economic Policy).
Solow, R. M. (1957) 'Technical Change and the Aggregate Production Function', *Review of Economics and Statistics*, August.
Song, B. N. (1990) *The Rise of the Korean Economy* (Hong Kong: Oxford University Press).

Stiglitz, J. (1999) 'Reforming the Global Financial Architecture: Lessons from Recent Crises', *Journal of Finance*, vol. 54 no. 4, pp 1508–22.

Suh, D. M. (2000) 'Normalisation of Pyongyang-Tokyo Relations: Its Prospects and Seoul's Role', *The Economics of Korean Unification*, vol. 5, no. 1, pp. 104–19.

Tae, W. S. (1972) *Development of the Korean Economy – Past, Present and Future* (Seoul: Samhwa).

Time (2000) 'Korea Gets Wired: Life on the Cutting Edge of Internet Culture', 11 December.

UBS (1996) 'The Asian Economic Miracle', *International Finance*, issue 29 (Autumn).

Veale, J. (2000) 'It's Tough to Be a Working Woman. But the Web is a Bright Spot', *Business Week*, 24 July.

Wall Street Journal (2001) 'North Korea Approves Law to Draw Foreign Investment', 25 April.

Westphal, L. E. (1990) 'Industrial Policy in an Export Propelled Economy: Lessons from South Korea's Experience', *Journal of Economic Perspectives*, vol. 4, no. 3, pp. 41–59.

World Bank (1987a), *World Development Report* (Oxford University Press, New York, USA: World Bank).

World Bank (1987b) *Korea – Managing the Industrial Transition, World Bank Country Study, Volume II, Selected Topics and Case Studies* (Washington, DC: World Bank).

World Bank (1988), *World Development Report*, (Oxford University Press, New York, USA: World Bank).

World Bank (1993) *The East Asian Miracle* (New York: Oxford University Press).

World Bank (1999a) 'Republic of Korea: Establishing a New Foundation for Sustained Growth', report no. 19595 KO (Washington, DC: World Bank).

World Bank (1999b) *World Development Report 1998/9*, (Oxford University Press, New York: World Bank).

Wyplosz, C. (1998) 'Globalised Financial Markets and Financial Crises', paper presented at the conference on 'Coping with Financial Crises in Developing and Transition Countries: Regulatory and Supervisory Challenges in a New Era of Global Financial Finance', organised by the Forum on Debt and Development, Amsterdam, March.

Yoo, S. M. (1995) '*Chaebol* in Korea: Misconceptions, Realities and Policies', Korea Development Institute Working Paper no. 9507 (Seoul: Korea Development Institute).

Yoo, S. M. (1997) 'Evolution of Government–Business Interface in Korea: Progress to Date and Reform Agenda Ahead, mimeo (Seoul: Korea Development Institute).

Yoo, S. M. and Y. J. Lim (1997) 'Big Business in Korea: New Learnings and Policy Issues', mimeo (Seoul: Korea Development Institute).

ZDNet (2001) 'Seoul is the Capital City for Domain Names', 15 January (http://www.nua.ie/surveys).

Index